The Ten
Most Influential
Churches
of the Past Century

ELMER L. TOWNS

Bestselling Author of *Fasting for Spiritual Breakthrough*

DESTINY IMAGE® PUBLISHERS, INC.

P.O. Box 310, Shippensburg, PA 17257-0310

"Promoting Inspired Lives."

This book and all other Destiny Image and Destiny Image Fiction books are available at Christian bookstores and distributors worldwide.

Cover design by: Robert Williams

For more information on foreign distributors, call 717-532-3040.

Or reach us on the Internet: www.destinyimage.com

ISBN 13 TP: 978-0-7684-0541-5

ISBN 13 EBook: 978-0-7684-0542-2

For Worldwide Distribution, Printed in the U.S.A.

1 2 3 4 5 6 7 8 9 10 11 /17 16 15 14

Contents

Part One:
The 10 Most Influential Churches

Part Two:
Other Churches and Trends

Appendix

Ed Stetzer

Warren Bird

Foreword

By Ed Stetzer and Warren Bird

At some level, all Christians want their churches to be influential in carrying out the work of God. One pathway to increased influence is a road we often overlook—the one behind us.

Looking back can be good. It can give us wisdom and perspective. It can also help us look forward to what God is doing next in your churches and ours.

This helpful book looks back at ten historic spiritual shifts of the last century and identifies a church closest to the center of each one. You may not have heard of these pioneering churches and their leaders, but we suspect you have been influenced by them far more than you realize. And we strongly suspect that after reading each of their stories, you'll be glad you did—and you'll have a better perspective on your own church and how God is at work in and around it.

It is hard to imagine anyone more qualified to identify and describe these trends and the personalities behind them than our friend, mentor, co-author and fellow researcher Elmer Towns. Starting in the 1960s he became the nation's leading figure in creating "top 10" lists and narratives about influential churches. Both of us have a shelf full of his books and magazine articles that we've underlined and dog-eared, gaining important insights about where we've come from and therefore where we're headed.

His motive in this book is to help expand *your* impact. As he was formulating the idea for this book, emailing us with his thoughts, it was very clear that he believes the most influential churches in the last 100 years can motivate every church to become a church of greater influence. Even his title, *The Ten Most Influential Churches of the Past Century,* is designed to capture people's attention and help them become more influential.

Overview of the Top Ten

The first chapter is about the Pentecostal/Charismatic movement. Even if you don't identify with that approach to Christianity, you need to know that roughly one in four people globally who claim to follow Jesus Christ identify with it.

That explosive growth has occurred in just over 100 years. The Pentecostal movement began with a few churches (usually on the other side of the tracks) that appealed to a marginal population. Mainstream Christianity labeled them as fanatical or excessive. Some called them weird or heretical—or much worse.

It all went viral when a 1906 revival broke out in an Azusa Street mission church located among the poor in Los Angeles, California. Visitors came from all over the world to be touched by the Holy Spirit, and then went back launching Pentecostal/Charismatic denominations/movements that in turn touched the world. Today, some of the largest congregations in the world are Pentecostal driven (see Warren's list at www.leadnet.org/world).

A second phenomenon in the last 100 years has been the explosive growth of house churches in Communist China. When the bamboo curtain slammed down in 1958, many Westerners thought the light of Christianity would be extinguished and all the missionary work for hundreds of years would be lost.

However, we've learned in recent decades that one of the greatest church movements in the world has been the underground church in China, multiplying exponentially without foreign mission supervision, Western missionaries, seminaries, denominational structure, or even buildings. They have none of the physical assets we find in American Christianity, yet the world marvels at what God has done.

A third trend in the Christian church has been the growing interactions of people, leading to multicultural and multiethnic churches around the world. After World War II, the restrictive borders in most nations came down, and the church entered the era of the *Interstate* and the *Internet* (i.e., the *Interstate* stands for an explosion in transportation, while the *Internet* stands for explosion of communications). People from various cultures that make up the many nations of the world have traveled extensively, and most of the churches have thrown their doors open to win any and all to Jesus Christ. While America has struggled to overcome its background of slavery and segregation, many churches have led the way in modeling worship that welcomes every tribe, nation, people and language (see Rev. 5:9) so that what the children sing in Sunday school is true: "Red and yellow, black and white, all are precious in His sight, Jesus loves the little children of the world."[1]

A fourth phenomenon is the largest church in history, the Yoido Full Gospel Church in Seoul, Korea, which reached 760,000 members at its peak. In 2007, when pastor David Yonggi Cho retired, he turned the reins over to a second-generation pastor, Yong-hoon Lee. This church was not built on massive evangelism in large meetings; or through radio, television, or the media; or even through evangelism experienced in the church services of its home on Yoido Island. Rather, 35,000 small groups located in living rooms, laundry rooms, restaurants and apartment building exercise rooms have produced unparalleled growth and influence around the world. Yonggi Cho has said, "Just as the physical body grows by the division of its biological cells, so the spiritual body of Jesus Christ grows by the division of its spiritual cells."[2]

The fifth chapter describes the exponential growth of the Southern Baptist Convention, which grew from a small denomination located primarily in the southeast United States in 1900 to become the largest Protestant denomination in America. While many contributing personalities and policies are responsible for the growth of Southern Baptist, the most illustrative example is the First Baptist Church in Dallas, Texas, where Dr. W.A. Criswell motivated and organized lay workers of a large, wealthy downtown church to build the biggest church in America through Sunday school visitation. They expanded their Sunday school classes, and as a result the church grew.

A sixth trend among churches is reflective of the ever-expanding educational growth in the United States as well as throughout the world. A history of preaching reveals that most sermons were devotional, motivational, and/or topical three-point messages followed by a poem. But C.I. Scofield might have been the man who changed the focus of sermons.

When Scofield edited the footnotes of the *Scofield Reference Bible*, it became one of the biggest sellers in America and across the English-speaking world, selling more than 2 million copies in 30 years. The *Scofield Reference Bible* became one of the most influential books of evangelical Christianity in the last 100 years. It gave international fame to Scofield as a Bible teacher who visited the great Bible conferences of the late 1800s and early 1900s to teach the Word of God. He then brought an educational methodology to his pulpit in Dallas, Texas. His Bible expositional teaching became a standard at Dallas Theological Seminary, and it influenced a large section of the evangelical world to use the Sunday morning sermon not as a motivational pulpit, but to teach the Word of God.

A seventh church to influence evangelicalism was not designed for Christians but for the unchurched. Bill Hybels designed a church service where those who did not have a church background would be comfortable and have the gospel presented to them with contemporary music, drama, and messages all found within a contemporary environment. This church coined the phrase "seeker services," where an unsaved person could seek God in the integrity of his or her pursuit. Many thousands of pastors visited the Willow Creek pastors' conferences and went home to duplicate the influence of the church.

An eighth trend traces the growth and worldwide influence of what some call praise-worship music. Church historian Kenneth Scott Latourette said that whenever there was a true revival among God's people, inevitably there was also a new hymnody—the revived church praised the Lord with music expressing its own genre. In each revival, believers sang to God with the music they sang in their normal lives. No one can doubt the explosive influence of praise-worship music across the churches of the world, and no church better reflects that movement than a church in Sydney, Australia, that changed its name to Hillsong—since its music label was so widely known. Darlene Zschech, worship leader for the church, brought tears to the eyes of many as they sang, "My Jesus. . . my Savior. . . shout to the Lord."[3]

A ninth trend is the church embracing advertisement, marketing, and media to carry out its strategy of evangelism and communicate its message to the masses. Beginning in approximately 1900, many churches embraced a radio ministry. Continuing into the 1950s, many other churches embraced television ministry. Perhaps none was more effective than Jerry Falwell and the *Old Time Gospel Hour*. During the late 1970s, his church service was televised into every MIA (media impact area) across America. But Falwell did more than preaching; he also used his mailing ministry to rally his viewing audience to the church's causes, and he created teaching programs (the Liberty Home Bible Institute, with more than 100,000 graduates). Eventually, the church's ministry was expanded through what would later become Liberty University Online, where more than 90,000 students enroll in accredited courses, learning through their computer from a uniquely Christian university.

A tenth trend is noted for its transforming influence on church culture as much as its influence on new methods and new programs. After World War II, the parents who were responsible for winning World War II gave birth to the generation known as the Baby Boomers. These children were influenced by television, wealth, and changing expectations of cultures. The churches struggled to incorporate the growing numbers of Baby Boomers into their traditional church culture. The young didn't think like their parents, did not dress like their parents, did not sing like them, did not eat like them, nor did they dream like them. Some Baby Boomers were initially focused on "California Dreaming," and they were representative of the multiple thousands of young people who rebelled against what they called the recessive middle class and became hippies in California.

It was there that the tenth church in this study, Calvary Chapel, and its pastor, Chuck Smith, presented the historic message of Jesus Christ in a new package. Many youth were converted and were called "Jesus People." Smith let them sing their new music and dress their comfortable way, and a new counterculture church began to spread across America. No more suits and ties; rather, young people dressed leisurely. A new culture took over from the old traditional church culture. It impacted many.

Types of Influence

Looking through these ten historical windows that Elmer Towns has opened for us, we note the various ways that the influence of each church was effective. We broke the categories into four realms: (1) inward for spiritual growth, (2) upward to God, (3) relational to other believers, and (4) outward to the non-Christian.

First, we see the inward influence of Azusa Street Revival, where believers experienced the Holy Spirit in renewal and revival. Then, the Scofield Church taught members the Word of God, and biblical knowledge became foundational to their lives and service.

Second, we see the upward influences of Hillsong Church and praise-worship music that focused on praising God and glorifying Him.

A third area was relational to each another. The most obvious was Ebenezer Baptist Church and Martin Luther King, Jr.'s emphasis on racial reconciliation and integration so that all ethnic groups would be one in Christ. Another is the powerful *koinonia* of the Chinese underground church, where they clung to one another when there was no outward reinforcement of their faith. Then there is the intimacy of the cell groups in Yonggi Cho's Full Gospel Church, which preached spiritual strength. Finally, we observe that Calvary Chapel refashioned its music, dress, programming, and outward expressions of faith so the young people worshiped differently from what they perceived as dead Christianity.

A final area is outward influence of evangelism. Obviously, First Baptist Church of Dallas was Great Commission-oriented in its evangelistic Sunday school-class outreach. So was Thomas Road Baptist Church in its media and advertising outreach to communicate the gospel to every available person, with every available method, at every available time.

Types of Methods

From these ten churches and corresponding movements, we note the various methods used by each church that made it influential. *A church method is the application of biblical principles to the culture where a church is located.* Some churches became influential just by "being," while others employed distinct methods that they copied and followed.

The Azusa Street Revival clearly sought the filling of the Holy Spirit and His coming on individuals. The Chinese underground church gathered in house churches, just as the Early Church did in the book of Acts. Yonggi Cho also applied biblical patterns of small groups when he divided his church into cells to do the work of ministry. Then Hillsong influenced the evangelical world by worshiping God through praise music.

Martin Luther King, Jr. used *nonviolent civil disobedience* as a method to bring racial harmony, and W.A. Criswell used *Sunday school visitation* to influence his church. Scofield applied a *teaching pulpit,* and Bill Hybels used a *seeker-sensitive* methodology. Jerry Falwell used *saturation evangelism*, and Calvary Chapel used a tool that later was described as *contemporary and casual church.*

Types of Leadership

Finally, we can't help but observe the role of leadership in the ten chapters. Two of the trends seemed to grow indigenously from inside the church. The first was the Chinese house church movement, where no one individual leader seemed to be the dominant force behind the influential trend. The second was the Calvary Chapel movement, where the Baby Boomers that founded the movement basically remapped how people would do church.

The other eight churches were led by people who conceived of a new idea of serving God and began to implement it in their churches. These leaders were revolutionary. . . cataclysmic. . . change agents. Their leadership was measured by the obstacles they had to overcome—so much so that their names became symbolic of the influence they spawned.

These were often leaders who prevailed against insurmountable odds, with limited resources, in difficult circumstances, all to glorify God. And, might we add, to the influence of other churches. They were leaders who believed God wanted them to do what they did and then influences others to do the same.

Ask God for Boldness and Courage

Every church leader should read the stories of these 10 churches and compare their own experiences to these trends. This certainly doesn't mean that every church has to become like one of the churches in these pages, but pastors and leaders can learn this: they can gain discernment in what to change (culture) and what not to change (the gospel). Also, as those reading this book will see how one church can influence the world, they might pray to do the same.

What's going to happen one hundred years from now? What 10 churches will be the most influential for the years AD 2000–2100? We have no idea. But if Jesus does not come in the next one hundred years, we do have an idea that great churches will be led by great innovators who take a great idea, and with great courage implement the method that God has placed on their hearts. May that happen for you.

Enjoy reading *The Ten Most Influential Churches of the Past Century*. We certainly have.

Sincerely yours,

Ed Stetzer
Executive Director, LifeWay Research
Missiologist in Residence

Warren Bird
Director of Research
Leadership Network

Introduction

Finding the Most Influential Churches

This book is about finding the 10 most influential churches in the world in the past 100 years. What a task. First, I had to determine the 10 major influences on Christianity in the past 100 years.[1] Second, I had to discover the churches that best reflected these 10 influences, and then link their influence to worldwide Christianity.[2] Third, I had to research the small details and the larger scope that explains the greatness of each church. Fourth, I had to write the facts of each church in a compelling story that would accurately tell why each is an influencer-church. Then, finally, I had to write each story to actually convince you to go be an *influencer-pastor*.

I want this book to motivate both scholar and fellow researcher to continue studying churches. But mostly, I want pastors and church workers to get a greater desire to build their church. I want them to be influential in their churches, just as the 10 pastors I highlight in this book were influential in their churches.

Many churches have a great influence on a few people in their congregation, and some have great influence on most in their congregation. But few have great influence on their immediate culture, and even fewer have great influence on their entire city and nation. But who are the 10 churches that had the greatest influence on Christianity worldwide in the past 100 years?

Let's describe what we're *not* looking for before we explain the criteria that determine the 10 greatest church influencers in the world. First, just because a church is large does not mean it is an *influencer-church*. Large is commendable, but influence is eternal. So, we are not just looking for large churches.

Also, just because a church is famous does not mean it is an *influencer-church*. In the 1930s and 1940s there was a nationwide radio program about the famous "Little Brown Church in the Vale." Almost no one remembers that church today. There have been many extremely well-known preachers in the past, but their churches didn't influence their surrounding world or the larger Christian community, much less become one of the 10 *influencer-churches* in the past 100 years. So, we're not just looking for the best-known churches.

There have been many innovative churches that did things differently and were effective in their innovations; and, yes, they probably influenced churches around them. But to be one of the 10 *church influencers* in the world, a congregation had to be influential both cross-culturally and span across a century of time.

In 1991, I wrote a book called *Ten of Today's Innovated Churches* (Regal Books, Ventura, California), which described innovative churches. These 10 churches were successful, but not all of them could be considered worldwide *influencer-churches*. In 1969, I wrote the bestseller *The 10 Largest Sunday Schools and What Makes Them Grow* (Baker Book House, Grand Rapids, Michigan). Again, some of these churches were innovative and influential, but they were not worldwide influencers, and they definitely did not have a 100-year church influence.

What Churches Are Measured?

This book is about Protestant churches, because the nature of a local New Testament church is different from Roman Catholic churches. I chose not to write about Roman Catholic churches because they are different in *message* and *methods* from Protestant churches. Some Roman Catholic churches are extremely large and have had a significant influence on other churches, their community, and the world.

In addition, this book is not about those churches that most sociologists have defined as a cult.[3] So, this book does not include the Mormon Tabernacle or the Mormon Temple in Salt Lake City, Utah. The Mormon Church has had a significant impact on people's moral values in other places than Salt Lake City, and their churches have had great moral and social influences on individuals, families, and communities. The same could be said about the Christian Scientists, Jehovah Witnesses, and other groups who identify themselves by the title "Christian" but are not recognized in the historic Christian Protestant tradition. These types of churches are not included because they do not fit the New Testament model of a church by practice or doctrine.

Why This Book?

I did not write this book to satisfy people's curiosity or to create a novelty list. I want pastors to know that the great things God has done in the past can be done today. I want them to realize they can influence the future. The past church influencers should challenge us to be more influential in the future. Some of these church leaders in *influencer-churches* were average people whom God used in above-average ways. Some of these church leaders had little or no theological education, yet they overcame obstacles and built some of the greatest *church influencers* in history.

Why not you?

After reading this book, plan to do the impossible (to you), and then yield yourself to God and give yourself to sacrificial prayer. You may find that when you touch God, He in turn will touch you, and you can touch the world.

Sincerely yours in Christ,
Elmer L. Towns

Written from my home
on top of Liberty Mountain,
Lynchburg, Virginia

Elmer L. Towns

Part One

The Ten Most
Influential Churches

The Apostolic Faith Mission
Azusa Street, Los Angeles, California*

William Seymour*

The Spread and Growth of Pentecostalism Worldwide

The Apostolic Faith Mission

Los Angeles, California (The Azusa Street Revival)

The Apostolic Faith Mission in Los Angeles, California, known as being the site of the Azusa Street Revival in 1906, captured the explosive movement of the Holy Spirit and spread its influence around the world. Azusa Street gave birth to approximately 19 denominations and/or organizations, each dwarfing the original manifestations of the Azusa Street Mission. The Holy Spirit was poured out on Azusa Street in abundant measure, and delegates came from around the world to taste of Him and be changed by the experience. They then returned home to duplicate in their lives and transformational ministry that which they drank in this tiny two-story building that seated less than 300 worshipers.

This little Apostolic Faith Mission on Azusa Street became the most powerful *church influence* of all other churches in the past 100 years, and did it in approximately 7 years. While the church lasted longer than 7 years, the power of the Holy Spirit was so great that within a few years it shook the world—and Christianity has never been the same. Billy Wilson, executive officer of the Azusa Street Centennial, said, "A handful of people in Los Angeles, led by a one-eyed black man who was the son of former slaves, has turned into a movement of over 600 million people around the world who claimed to be filled with the Holy Spirit."[1]

The Apostolic Faith Mission
Azusa Street, Los Angeles, California

William Seymour

*E*ach *of the 10 churches in this book either began a new movement for God or grew out of a new trend that gave it strength and breath. The Apostolic Faith Mission on Azusa Street in Los Angeles, California, captured the explosive movement of the Holy Spirit and spread its influence around the world. Azusa Street gave birth to approximately 19 denominations and/or organizations, each dwarfing the original manifestations of the Azusa Street Mission. The Holy Spirit was poured out on Azusa Street in abundant measure, and delegates came from around the world to taste of Him and be changed by the experience. They then returned home to duplicate in their lives and ministry the transformation they received from this tiny two-story building that seated less than 300 worshipers.*

On April 14 and 18, 1906, two events in California shook the world. On the first day, April 14, the baptism of the Holy Ghost fell on a small group of worshipers and erupted into tongues speaking, making this small church the fountainhead of the Pentecostal church movement that spread around the world. William Seymour preached that tongues was a sign that the end of the world was coming and that California would be rocked with an earthquake. Four days later, it happened.

The stillness of the morning of April 18 was unusual for San Francisco, California. Suddenly, at 5:12 AM, this giant city was shaken and destroyed. First the silence was seductive, and then the roar of the ground buckling was deafening. Buildings crumbled. Bricks hurled menacingly to the streets. Power poles snapped like toothpicks. San Francisco bore the brunt of a 40-second earthquake that was the most destructive force the inhabitants had ever seen.

Businessman Jerome B. Clark of Berkeley described what he saw when stepping off the ferry that morning:

> The streetcar tracks were bent and twisted out of shape. Electric wires lay in every direction. Streets on all sides were filled with brick and mortar, buildings either completely collapsed or brick fronts had just dropped completely off. Wagons with horses hitched to them, drivers and all, lying on the streets, all dead, struck and killed by the falling bricks, these mostly the wagons of the produce dealers, who do the greater part of their work at that hour of the morning.[2]

Immediately, fire broke out everywhere. The network of underground gas pipes snapped, and sparks set buildings ablaze. Water—normally available for firefighters—gushed useless from broken fire hydrants.

In minutes the entire 410,000 inhabitants of San Francisco were held bondage to the threat of death.

Fire wreaked havoc on the city for three days before a large thunderstorm intervened. When it was over, the devastation included the destruction of 490 city blocks and 25,000 buildings. Two hundred fifty thousand people were left homeless.[3] Some estimate that almost 3,000 were killed in and around the city.

In his book *The Barbary Coast*, Herbert Asbury called San Francisco the "wickedest city on the continent."[4] Was the earthquake God's retribution for the city's flagrant sin? If God was going to manifest His power in this destructive way, it seems He told the preacher on Azusa Street what was coming. Four days before the 1906 San Francisco earthquake, on April 14, God began to display His power at 321 Azusa Street in Los Angeles. A preacher predicted coming judgment to California in an earthquake. Who would believe such a wild prediction—especially coming from a ramshackle old building that could barely seat 300 worshipers?

Perhaps the *Los Angeles Times* printed the prediction so people would laugh at the fanatical happenings on Azusa Street. But doesn't God always get the last laugh? The *Los Angeles Times* article documented a work of God with its sarcastic description, hoping for people to laugh at the frenzied emotionalism. But their article documented the credibility of God's moving on Azusa Street:

> Meetings are held in a tumble-down shack on Azusa Street, and the devotees of the weird doctrine practice the most fanatical rites, preach the wildest theories and work themselves into a state of mad excitement in their peculiar zeal. Colored people and a sprinkling of whites compose the congregation, and night is made hideous in the neighborhood by the howling of the worshipers, who spend hours swaying forth and back in a nerve-racking attitude of prayer and supplication. They claim to have the "gift of tongues" and be able to understand the babel.[5]

Again, God had the last laugh. The reporter only saw what he wanted to see. He didn't see the Holy Spirit working in hearts. He didn't see lives being transformed. He didn't see an influence that would change the world.

Why Azusa Street Was Chosen

The manifestations of the Holy Spirit at Azusa Street were not the first "Pentecostal" experiences in church history, nor the first in the United

States. Church historian Curtis Ward suggests there is an unbroken Pentecostal lineage from the early church to the present, with tongues speaking and other "gifts."[6] Many individuals throughout church history practiced the gifts, but they were schismatic—attacking the church—or in some occasions, heretical in doctrine (such as Montanus during the second century).[7] None of these outcroppings became a formidable movement until Azusa Street at the beginning of the twentieth century.

There were reports in the Second Great Awakening in Cane Ridge, Kentucky, 1801–1803, of speaking in tongues, howling, running in the spirit, and slaying in the Spirit. Several circuit riders for the early Methodist church reported "gifts" of the Spirit, not apparently as a holiness way of life but as a manifestation of power in ministry. Before the Azusa Street Revival, Agnes Ozman spoke in tongues at Bethel Bible College in Topeka, Kansas, in the 1890s.

At the same time, groups drifting toward Pentecostalism were being formulated in North Carolina out of the Wesleyan holiness tradition. Abner Crumpler was tried in an ecclesiastical court for preaching a holiness doctrine. He eventually saw two groups come together in Falcone, North Carolina, in 1911 to form the Pentecostal Holiness Church. One of the leaders, Gaston B. Cashwell, traveled to Azusa Street and came back teaching that the evidence of the baptism of the Holy Ghost was speaking in tongues.

The Apostolic Faith Mission was chosen to be included in this book because of its influence that gave birth to approximately 19 Pentecostal denominations and/or organizations. Beginning on April 14, 1906, the Azusa Street Revival forever changed the landscape of Christianity around the globe. In fact, when the Associated Press noted the 100 most important events in the twentieth century, it included only one religious event: the Azusa Street Revival.

The Azusa Street Revival marked the beginning of a new "brand" of Christianity. The textbook *Worship Through the Ages* summarizes the international influence of the Azusa Street Revival.[8]

William Durham, a prominent Chicago pastor, was deeply impressed by Seymour and the events at Azusa Street. Durham maintained a close friendship with the Azusa Street organization for years. He influenced *Eudorous Bell*, who was instrumental in establishing the *Assemblies of God*, Springfield, Missouri.[9] The Pentecostal Assemblies of Canada recognized their spiritual indebtedness to Seymour and the Azusa Street vision as well, especially the early manifestations of charismatic phenomena in Winnipeg and Toronto.

Bell encouraged *Howard Goss*, who helped establish the *United Pentecostal Church. Aimee Semple [McPherson]* supported and was encouraged by Azusa Street participants; then she established the *International Church of the Foursquare Gospel. Charles Harrison Mason* considered Seymour his "father in the faith." Mason established the predominately black *Church of God in Christ.*

Another Church of God denomination, this one white, became Pentecostal when *G.B. Cashwell*, an Azusa Street convert, described the revival at a national convention. During the meeting, the denomination's general overseer, *A.J. Thomlinson,* listened attentively. Then suddenly he fell out of his chair and began speaking in tongues at Cashwell's feet. While a few churches left the movement, most of them embraced the Pentecostal message. Soon, the *Church of God of Prophecy* was another fast-growing denomination.[10]

John G. Lake visited the Azusa Street meetings, and then took the Pentecostal message to South Africa in 1908.[11] Within five years, he established 500 black and 125 white Pentecostal churches in that nation.

Others took the Pentecostal message to Europe and Asia. The *Apostolic Faith* reported: "Pentecost has crossed the water on both sides to the Hawaiian Islands on the west, and England, Norway, Sweden and India on the east. . . . We rejoice to hear that Pentecost has fallen in Calcutta, India. . . . We have letters from China, Germany, Switzerland, Norway, Sweden, England, Ireland, Australia and other countries from hungry souls that want their Pentecost. . . . In Stockholm, Sweden. . . the first soul came through tonight, receiving the baptism with the Holy Ghost with Bible evidence. . . . In Christiana, Norway—God is wonderfully demonstrating His power."[12]

The Azusa Revival influenced international organizations, mission initiatives, Bible colleges, and parachurch organizations.[13] Within 50 years, approximately 600 million people in almost all the nations of the earth called themselves Pentecostal or Charismatic—all descendants of Azusa Street.[14]

The Preacher God Used

The man God used in this movement was William Joseph Seymour, born in Centerville, Louisiana, on May 2, 1870 to parents who had been slaves.

He came under the ministry of "Evening Light Saints" in Cincinnati, Ohio, when he went there to work in a hotel dining room. That group predicted Christ was coming to establish His kingdom and that a sign of His coming would be a fresh outpouring of the Holy Spirit, called the "Latter Rain." The Evening Light Saints' mission was to prepare people for the return of Christ. This implanted in Seymour a sense of prophetic preaching and anticipation of the Lord's return.

Seymour contracted smallpox. In those days many people died from the dreaded disease, because there was no known cure for it. Then one night in a dream, God told Seymour he would be healed if he would preach the gospel. It was then that Seymour surrendered to God's call to preach. Seymour was healed, and the only result of the smallpox was that he lost sight in his left eye. Later in life, some ridiculed him as the "one-eyed preacher."

Next, Seymour went to Houston and attended an African American church. There he heard a woman speaking in another language, which was something he had never heard before. The Evening Light congregation had taught him that such an outpouring would usher in the return of Christ.

Lucy Farrow, the woman speaking in tongues, told Seymour that Charles Parham had taught it to her in Topeka, Kansas. Parham was in charge of Bethel College, a holiness Bible college that taught "the baptism of the Holy Ghost."

When Seymour arrived in Topeka, Parham recognized his zeal, but he was not ready to welcome a black student into the college. Parham allowed Seymour to listen to lectures from a chair outside an open window. Actually, a state law forbade white students from sitting in classrooms with blacks. Parham said that Seymour eagerly sought the baptism of the Holy Spirit, but without success.

Seymour went back home to Houston and began preaching in African American churches. A visitor from Los Angeles heard Seymour and returned to the California city to recommend him to her pastor.

Seymour borrowed money from Parham for a train trip to California and stayed in the home of Richard Asberry at 214 Bonnie Brae Street. He met Julia Hutchins, the California church's pastor, and preached his first sermon on a Sunday morning, saying that speaking in tongues and the baptism of the Holy Spirit were biblical. Hutchins recognized a big difference between her beliefs and Seymour's. Hutchins was an opinionated woman—she had led a split from Second Baptist Church over the baptism of the Holy Ghost—but she was not ready to add speaking in tongues. She considered Seymour "radical," and when he arrived back at the church to preach that evening, he was not allowed in. But Seymour would not be denied; he agreed to hold Bible studies in the home of Edward S. Lee on Bonnie Brae Street. (Hutchins eventually spoke in tongues, and her entire congregation was absorbed into Faith Apostolic Mission.)

Many came from Hutchins's church to hear Seymour preach. Most among the congregation were domestic servants who worked in menial tasks throughout the week. The congregation was also interracial, with both blacks and whites in attendance. There was no segregated seating, as in white churches of that day. The ironic thing was that the people came to hear a preacher tell them about speaking in tongues, but he himself had never spoken in tongues.

Seymour announced that they would be fasting for 10 days to receive the baptism of the Holy Ghost. On April 9, 1906, Edward Lee told Seymour that he received a vision that the 12 disciples came to him and taught him to speak in tongues. Lee predicted that they both would receive the gift of tongues. That night, God answered their prayer. During that evening's meeting, the Holy Spirit came on the little Bible study, and Seymour and seven members of that congregation began speaking in tongues. They testified that Jeannie Evans Moore (later Seymour's wife) played an upright piano and sang in Hebrew. They said she had never had a lesson, had never played before, and didn't know Hebrew.

News spread throughout the community, and the little home was overwhelmed. The next night the crowd got so large that the front porch collapsed and the people could not get into the small house. Seymour stood in front of the home and preached to more than a thousand people standing in the street. People began falling down, "slain in the spirit." The revival went three days, night and day, without stopping.

Seymour searched for a suitable building and found an old African Methodist Episcopal Church, a two-story building, on Azusa Street that had been used recently as a warehouse and livery stable. It was 60 feet by 40 feet, and the rent was $8 per month. The roof was off; it was a large square building in shambles. A few devoted followers cleaned it up, set up wooden boards for pews, and made a pulpit out of shipping crates. The ceiling was only 8 feet above the preaching hall on the first floor. The second floor had a sleeping room for Seymour and other workers, plus a large prayer room with chairs and a large prayer altar.

There were no musical instruments, no choir loft, and no collection was taken. A receptacle near the front door was available for free-will gifts. Looking at the substandard building demonstrated to everyone that God could use any type of structure to change the world. His presence was not in buildings or sanctuaries but in yielded people.

On April 14, 1906, Seymour's new Apostolic Faith Gospel Mission began holding services at 312 Azusa Street. The church had no organization, no advertisements, and no order of service. People were drawn by the power of God and wanted what the worshipers of Azusa Street had. Seymour warned his listeners that Jesus was coming soon to judge the world and to establish His kingdom. He preached that there would be "latter rain," which was the outpouring of the Holy Spirit that included speaking in tongues. In response many people repented, confessed their sins, and began waiting for the appearance of Jesus Christ. People were healed, and each evening the church attracted people from a wider area around Los Angeles. Eventually, people came from around the world to experience what God was doing at Azusa Street.

Every night more than a thousand people gathered around the Azusa Street mission, listening to every word and searching for the experience that had transformed the lives of those on the inside. At times Seymour would go out to preach to those who had overflowed to the dirt street in front of the mission. At the same time, the revival continued inside.

Four days after Seymour's prediction that a great earthquake was coming, the earth shook under San Francisco. Because the prediction was documented in newspapers, there was a tremendous spike in attendance at the Azusa Street mission.

Within a few months, Seymour began publishing a four-page tabloid called *The Apostolic Faith,* in which he described and explained the manifestation of tongues in his meetings. There were 1,800 copies of the first edition printed, and eventually they reached 50,000 readers. The paper was filled with incredible testimonies from people who had spoken in tongues, were healed, or experienced demonic deliverance and other miraculous occurrences.

Clare Lum, a white gifted editor, worked closely with Seymour from 1906 to 1908 to help publish *Apostolic Faith*. At one point, she wrote the following about the singing at the Azusa Street meetings:

> There is singing in the Spirit. . . the music is not learned. No one can join in unless it is given to them [by the Spirit]. They sing in different tongues at the same time, and the different parts are songs. Sometimes, one is singing in English, thus interpreting while the others are singing [in tongues].[15]

Another pastor who spread the good news of Azusa Street was Frank Bartleman. He was a former Baptist itinerate evangelist who drifted from one church group to another, and he went to Azusa Street in search of the baptism of the Holy Spirit. Bartleman published a tract about the connection between the San Francisco earthquake and Seymour's end-time prophecies. The tract went around the world, thus spreading knowledge about the Azusa Street Revival in Los Angeles.

Bartleman constantly wrote "Letters to the Editor" in newspapers to tell the story of the revival. He traveled extensively, telling the story of Azusa Street everywhere he went. Technically, he would be called a "carrier of revival"; that is, one who plants the same initial fire at other places.

> The centrality of Azusa Street in the story of Pentecostalism is due in large part to the work of the revival's tireless promoter Frank Bartleman. A restless maverick driven from place to place by his determination to be part of whatever God was doing in the world, Bartleman singlehandedly turned the Azusa Street Revival into a literary event of global magnitude by chronicling his impressions and assigning them meaning in a widely circulated book, *How Pentecost Came to Los Angeles*.[16]

Frank Bartleman also reported that the racial harmony was evidence of God's work on Azusa Street:

> The color line was washed away in the blood [of Jesus]. . . it was something very extraordinary. . . white pastors from the south were early prepared to go to Los Angeles to Negroes [*sic*], to fellowship with them and to receive through their prayers and intercessions the blessings of the Spirit. And it was still more wonderful that these white pastors went back to the south and reported that they had been together with Negroes [*sic*], that they had prayed in one Spirit and received the same blessing.[17]

Of interest is the fact that there was no platform or stage to elevate the preacher; everyone stood on equal ground.[18] It was a multiracial and multiethnic congregation in which people from different backgrounds and cultures worshiped side by side. There were well-dressed white upper-class women who sat beside African-American women dressed in the clothes they wore to work. There were Hispanics, Asians and those from other ethnic neighborhoods in Los Angeles.

Seymour began adding new evidence besides tongues to the baptism of the Holy Spirit. He maintained that the dissolution of racial barriers was positive proof that the New Jerusalem was coming and that the baptism of the Holy Spirit was real in the lives of those who came. Historian Estrelda Y. Alexander described the phenomena in this way:

Men and women, adults and children, black, white, yellow, and red freely worshiped God and admonished each other to holiness of life through speaking in tongues and interpretation, prophecy, testimony, song, prayer, miraculous signs and preaching. Each one, in order, as they felt directed by the Holy Spirit, gave vent to the fire that was shut deep within their bones and glorified God for their newfound freedom and empowerment. Women and men freely participated as they felt God leading them. Even children who felt inspired by God had a voice in the worship and received Pentecostal Holy Spirit baptism.[19]

Meetings were held daily at 10:00 AM, 12 noon and evenings, but usually one meeting flowed into the next. The camp-meeting-style gatherings went on for more than three years. Often services would run from 10:00 AM until midnight or later.[20]

Seymour did most of the preaching. He was a man of discipline who did not speak with a loud or boisterous tone. He simply encouraged worshipers to seek a Savior that could meet their every need—emotional, physical, spiritual and intellectual. Constant shouts punctuated his sermons.

Though many gave impromptu sermons as prompted by the Spirit, Seymour was the main preacher. He apparently did not fit the Bible thumping caricature often ascribed to Pentecostal preachers, but his messages were powerful enough that the altars of the mission were regularly filled with those seeking repentance, sanctification, Holy Spirit baptism or healing.[21]

Seymour advised his listeners to speak to outsiders about their need for Jesus Christ as Savior and not about the mystery of glossolalia (speaking in tongues).[22] The people went everywhere and spoke about their experiences at Azusa Street. Everything was spontaneous. Sermons were unannounced, and rivers of revival poured out from Faith Apostolic Church. Changed lives were its compelling attraction, and experiencing God was its foundation.[23]

The newspaper *Apostolic Faith* brought in letters testifying from other places where the baptism of the Holy Spirit had fallen. These testimonies were read publicly to the crowds. At the end of each reading, there followed loud shouts of "Hallelujah, Amen, and glory to God."

Not everyone was enthusiastic about an interracial church. Parham, who visited Azusa Street church six months after the initial baptism of the Holy Spirit, came with great anticipation but was disappointed when he saw blacks and whites praying at the same altar. He was especially horrified to see a white woman who was "slain in the spirit" being caught in the arms of a black man. During his message, Parham rebuked the congregation for their disregard of racial differences. Seymour and the elders of the church—both black and white—asked him to leave and told him he could not come back.

However, Parham was not alone in his perspective. Within a decade, some segregated Pentecostal denominations appeared on the scene. The Church of God in Christ was African American, while the Assembly of God was white. These denominations were not segregated by design but by natural relationships. They embraced the experience of tongues learned from Azusa Street but didn't fulfill Seymour's vision of racial integration.

Innovations in Worship

There were many innovations in worship at the Azusa Street meetings. First, clergy and laypeople alike gave impromptu sermons, and there were several sermons in each service. Second, the congregation sang both in English and in tongues. When people sang songs on the spot, it was said that the English was an interpretation of the unknown tongue used in the same song. Third, prophesying, divine healings and exorcisms were common. Fourth, the people freely shared their testimonies as the Spirit led them. Fifth, meetings included anointing with oil, laying on of hands, and praying over things such as prayer cloths (which were used when praying for those in pain, sorrowing, suffering and grieving). Sixth, women were active in leading worship, preaching, teaching, and exhorting. They prayed, gave prophetic witness, spoke in tounges and interpreted. [24]

There were also other manifestations of the Spirit.

> While many were saved in this move of God, the main force was the re-discovered gift of the baptism of the Holy Spirit. Other manifestations were present as well, such as. . . running [they would arise from their seats and run all over the building, hugging as many people as possible because of the joy they were

experiencing]; healing and falling under the power of the Spirit.[25] Men would fall all over the house like slain in battle, or they would rush to the altar en masse to seek God. The scene often resembled a forest of fallen trees.[26]

The role of women in the revival is especially noteworthy. Years before women had paraded in the streets of America, demanding the right to vote. Ten years earlier, lawmakers had approved the Nineteenth Amendment to the U.S. Constitution, giving women the right to vote. At Azusa Street, women were given full access to ministry as they prayed, but they also preached, led meetings, taught, healed, gave prophetic utterances, spoke in tongues and interpreted tongues, just like the male leaders.[27] This was not a politically correct move, nor did it come about as a result of pressure from the congregation or even the women themselves. The women led because they had received the baptism of the Holy Ghost and because God had anointed their ministry.[28]

Relationship Between the Azusa Street Revival and the Welsh Revival

In 1904, two years before the Azusa Street Revival broke out, a revival began in Wales.[29] More than 100,000 people all across the region were converted to Christ. The primary source of the revival was the preaching of Evan Roberts, a former coal miner in his twenties, though there were many others who also spread the revival.

As this Welsh revival moved around the world, it spread to Los Angeles, California, through the leadership of Joseph Smale, pastor of First Baptist Church. He traveled to Wales to witness personally the revival, and when he returned he tried to initiate the same type of revival meetings in his own congregation. However, he was ousted, so he left and founded the New Testament Church of Los Angeles. There an ongoing revival broke out based on the confession of sin, the search for holiness, and a new experience with God. It did not include the baptism of the Spirit and speaking in tongues, but it did create an expectancy of revival in the greater Los Angeles area.

This revival, and other works of God that grew out of the Welsh Revival, were like "mercy drops of sprinkling rain." However, when Seymour established the Apostolic Faith Mission, there was a torrential downpour that Seymour described as "latter rain." While the Welsh Revival emphasized the "deeper life" experience, Seymour initiated the sign of speaking in tongues and other phenomena that demonstrated the baptism of the Holy Ghost.

The newspaper industry spread the word about both revivals. Positive reporting in *The Western Mail* and the *South Wales Daily News* spread the news of the Welsh Revival, while negative reporting by the *Los Angeles Times* spread the news of the Azusa Street Revival. The power of both revivals touched the world, but they were different in manifestations. The Azusa Street meetings were clearly a Pentecostal manifestation, while the Welsh Revival had great spiritual energy and was not centered on a second work of the Holy Spirit as manifested by tongues. The one great difference in the Welsh Revival was the emphasis on evangelism and souls being saved. According to Baptist minister and author J. Edwin Orr, "The awakening swept the rest of Britain, Scandinavia, ports of Europe, North American, the mission fields of India, the Orient, Africa and Latin America."[30]

What God began through Evan Roberts in the Welsh Revival influenced the Azusa Street Revival. Both Evan Roberts and Seymour had long meetings, unplanned worship, spontaneous testimonies, and singing and more singing. Several traits in the Welsh Revival were also found in the Azusa Street Revival, including (1) focus on personal worship rather than group liturgy; (2) focus on repenting from sin so one can know Jesus Christ personally; (3) focus on holiness and sanctification; (4) singing songs to God; (5) focus on impromptu preaching by both laymen and clergy; (6) camp-meeting style services—sometimes lasting 10 to 12 hours, including extended time for singing, confession of sins, the Lord's Table, foot washing, prayer, healing and usually more than one sermon; (7) prophesying the future with public pronouncements; and (8) growing emotional expressions during worship.

Other Early Pentecostal Churches

As previously mentioned, Azusa Street was not the first appearance of the phenomena of the baptism of the Holy Spirit and speaking in tongues. There had been a continuous manifestation of tongues since the Day of Pentecost in Acts 2, but recorded examples by the formal church authority were few before the Azusa Street Revival.[31] Pastor and evangelist Dale A. Robbins describes the history of tongues speaking:

Some have sought to discredit the modern-day validity of speaking in tongues, claiming that it vanished with the other Charismatic gifts at the close of the apostolic era. However, any good student of church history realizes this theory is baseless, as numerous references to tongues and other gifts are consistently seen in the writings of church leaders for twenty centuries. *The History of the Christian Church*, by Philip Schaff, records that speaking in tongues occurred among the Camisards, the Cevennes in France, among the early Quakers and Methodists in the Irish revival of 1859, and among the Irvingites in 1831. *The Encyclopedia Britannica* states that glossolalia (speaking in tongues) has recurred in Christian revivals of every age—among the mendicant friars of the thirteenth century, among the Jasenists and early Quakers, the persecuted Protestants of the Cevennes, and the Irvingites.[32]

Pentecostal church historians suggest a continuous unbroken Pentecostal stream from the New Testament to the present. However, they consider the Azusa Street movement a latter-day restoration of the church's apostolic power, and most historians of modern Pentecostalism write that the movement emerged from the late nineteenth century as a radical revival in America and Great Britain.[33] Many historical evidences of tongues did not result in a continuous movement, as did the influence of William Seymour's meetings at Azusa Street. What happened in Los Angeles was identifiable, transferrable and repeatable—the criteria scientists use to verify credibility. What Seymour experienced was "bottled" and shipped around the world. His was not the first, nor will it be the last, outbreak of a charismatic experience.

Those who reject the Pentecostal experience of the Spirit's baptism as evidenced by speaking in tongues might recognize the presence of actual experiences, but they deny they are biblical expressions generated by the Holy Spirit. However, no one can deny the explosive influence of Azusa Street and its impact on the Christian world. Many Pentecostal churches grew out of Seymour's Apostolic Faith Mission. They were greater in size, and in some cases they attracted more attention from the general public than did Seymour. Seymour's popularity was within church circles, not with the unsaved masses.

Aimee Semple McPherson visited Azusa Street and was greatly influenced by its message. She went on to found the historic Angelus Temple in 1923 and build a new denomination based on the baptism of the Holy Spirit and speaking in tongues. She first preached in 1922 that in Ezekiel's inaugural vision was a heavenly being with four different faces: a man, a lion, an ox and an eagle (see Ezekiel 1). She compared these images to the four phases of the gospel of Jesus Christ. The man was Jesus the Savior; the lion was Jesus the Mighty Baptizer, with the Holy Spirit and fire; the ox was Jesus the Healer, our Burden-Bearer who took on our sins and sickness on the cross; and the eagle was Jesus the

Coming King, who will return to give victory. These four principles in the movement became known as the "Foursquare Gospel," and the church developed four symbols: the cross, the cup, the dove and the crown. Today, the movement is known as the International Church of the Foursquare.

Immediately after building a 5,300-seat auditorium in Los Angeles, McPherson commissioned Vincente and Teodora De Fante as missionaries to the Philippines.[34] From the beginning the Foursquare Church became a mission-sending organization, and today it has reached more than 8 million people worldwide. The denomination has 78,000 congregations and meeting places throughout the world.[35] The church's weekly newspaper, the *Foursquare Crusader*, and monthly magazine, *The Bridal Call*, spread McPherson's influence. She built a radio station to reach larger audiences.

Some think McPherson's church should be listed as one of the most influential churches in the past 100 years. However, the Angelus Temple and the Foursquare Church should be seen as two streams that emanated from the fountain on Azusa Street. Other great Pentecostal churches could also be considered among the 10 most influential churches, but though they were great and powerful, the original influence came from Seymour.[36]

Revival Fire Burns Low on Azusa Street

The Azusa Street Revival continued for a few years, but every time God works, Satan is sure to counterattack. Many denominational churches attacked the emotionalism of the baptism of the Holy Spirit, and the negative reports by the *Los Angeles Times* spread its condemning poison. When Seymour married Jeanne Evans Moore on May 13, 1908, it caused many who disagreed with the marriage to leave the church. Charles Parham and others who believed that white and black races should not mix caused another split.

> Seymour eventually encountered some negative experiences with white women in the Revival who did not share his perspective on racial unity. . . . Clare Lum and another [who] helped him to publish the periodical Apostolic Faith, with an international circulation of 50,000 subscribers, effectively destroyed Seymour's publication outreach ministry by taking both the periodical and mailing list to Portland, Oregon, where one of them founded another evangelistic organization.[37]

Harvey Cox, in his book *Fire from Heaven*, states that when Seymour saw the rise of racism in the revival, his "disillusionment with white women affected his understanding of the gift of tongues. . . . Finding that some people could speak in tongues and continue to abhor their fellow Christians convinced him that it was not tongues speaking, but the dissolution of the racial barriers, that was the surest sign of the Spirit's Pentecostal presence and the approaching New Jerusalem."[38]

Seymour began traveling extensively to spread the flame of the Azusa Revival, but an unintended consequence was that he allowed the home fires to die. Yet he helped establish new churches that had the same fire of the old Azusa Street. He even wrote and published a book, *The Doctrines and Discipline of the Apostolic Faith Mission*, which was the standard by which the newly established churches were governed.[39]

As the length of the daily meetings shortened, and then the revival shortened to fewer days each week, ethnic groups began to spin off. The Spanish Apostolic Faith Mission began holding meetings in Spanish. The Italian Pentecostal Mission was begun, and the 51st Street Apostolic Faith Mission was also started. Several other strong personalities siphoned off other groups to begin Pentecostal missions. Beyond the ethnic divide was the doctrinal divide. Some groups remained Pentecostal but differed with the perspective of Seymour's Apostolic Faith Mission.

A few years after the revival subsided, only a skeleton congregation remained at the Azusa Street Mission, and these were mostly from the early Bonnie Brae congregation. Crowds began to dwindle. The whites began to leave, and soon the congregation at Azusa Street was almost entirely black.[40] Just as every tree reaches its height, so Seymour reached his height of influence; and just as every tree grows through its cycle of life before it dies, attendance at the Apostolic Faith Mission dwindled down to fit inside the walls of its original building.

On September 28, 1922, Seymour experienced chest pains and shortness of breath and passed into eternity. Some said that he died of a broken heart. He was buried in Los Angeles Evergreen Cemetery, where his gravestone simply reads, "Our Pastor." After Seymour died, his wife, Jeanne, took over pastoring the mission. In 1931 the congregation lost the property, and the building was torn down by the city of Los Angeles.

Wrap Up

The Azusa Street Revival was one of the brightest stars to illuminate the dark night of the twentieth century. Just as every tree explodes in the brilliance of autumn before it dies under the onslaught of winter, so the Apostolic Faith Mission died. But the life of the little Apostolic

Faith Mission did not die an ignominious death; it lives today in dozens of massive denominations that expanded the message of the baptism of the Holy Ghost as reflected in speaking in tongues.

Azusa Street lives in interchurch organizations such as the Full Gospel Business Men's Fellowship, *Charisma Magazine*, and thousands of other organizations that have the same ministry. It lives in educational institutions such as Evangel University in Springfield, Missouri; Oral Roberts University in Tulsa, Oklahoma; Regent University in Virginia Beach, Virginia; and scores of other schools in almost every nation of the world. Azusa Street continued in the television ministry of Jan and Paul Crouch, who carried on the message of William Seymour on TBN, the world's largest television network. There are also thousands of other radio, television and Internet organizations that keep the message going.

This little Apostolic Faith Mission on Azusa Street became the most powerful church influence of all other churches in the past 100 years. Billy Wilson, executive officer of the *Azusa Street Centennial*, said, "A handful of people in Los Angeles, led by a one-eyed black man who was the son of former slaves, has turned into a movement of over 600 million people around the world who claimed to be filled with the Holy Spirit."[41]

House Church*

Unknown Leader*

2

The Unseen but Ever-Present Influence of House Churches

Chinese Organic House Churches
Mainland China

The house church movement in China is located almost everywhere in the country, but almost no one knows how to find one. Without advertisements, sanctuaries or any type of publicity, the Chinese house church (also known as the underground church) has become one of the most powerful Christian movements in the world.

Unofficially, there are more than 130 million believers in China. While there is an official Three-Self Church in China, with a registration of approximately 23.5 million members, almost 100 million people meet in house churches in homes, apartments, restaurants and other places. Observers suggest there were no underground churches in 1949 when the Communists took over China, yet today Christianity has exploded in this country of 1.5 billion people. China represents one-fifth of the world's population, and its government is considered unfriendly to Christianity, if not hostile. The house church movement has grown without buildings, organized structure, programs, denominational support, or influence from outside nations.

When the Bamboo Curtain was slammed shut with the fall of Nationalist China and the formation of Communist China, many thought the Christian church in China would collapse. Why is that? Many put their trust in buildings, programs, organizational networks and the outward things that hold Christian churches together.

Yet it seems that the more the Communists persecuted the church in China, the more it exploded in growth and power—again, without Western missionaries, Western money, Western technology, or Western guidance. These house churches continue to grow without seminary-trained pastors, denominational programs, and Sunday school resources. Many of the churches didn't even have a Bible, and in some places Bibles were loaned from church to church.[1]

The amazing report is that there are now more than 130 million believers, many in underground churches, who meet in homes. Humans can't explain this strength; the house church movement is a phenomenon that can only be explained by God.

China underwent a huge political revolution after World War II. Nationalist China, led by Chiang Kai-shek, had been given recognition and membership in the United Nations. But the Communists organized a rebellious army led by Mao Zedong to take over the country. In 1949, Chiang Kai-shek and the Nationalist army retreated across the Sea of Japan to the island of Taiwan and established it as Nationalist China. Thus began two Chinas: one a republic and the other a Communist dictatorship.

Mao Zedong was able to solidify the anger of the Chinese against Western imperialism and colonialism because of its perceived control of China by outsiders. He was able to convince most Chinese that Chiang Kai-shek was a puppet of the United States. Also, Mao pledged to return China to its historic past and said that Chinese people should rule China.

When the Communists took over the nation, there were approximately one million Christians of all denominations. But Mao wanted to destroy Christianity in China, and this meant eliminating all traces of religion—or the "opiate of the masses," as Marx called it back in 1844.[2] This set up a threat to the Christian church in China.

Just as the Iron Curtain had slammed down in Europe, cutting off the Communist nations from the West, so the Bamboo Curtain in China slammed just as decisively, cutting off almost all Western influence in China. Many wondered what would happen to the one million Christians and what would happen to Christianity in China.

When the new Communist government was established, they chased out all foreign missionaries. By 1958, the last Western missionary left. The government instigated an attack against the church and those who followed Jesus Christ. Many Christians went to jail, including pastors, leaders and educators. Some were martyred. Those Christians who only outwardly professed Christianity denied the Lord and turned away from the church. Some betrayed their friends and relatives, resulting in further imprisonment of Christians.

Just as in the second century AD when Satan thought he could destroy the church through persecution and martyrdom, the true light of the gospel shines brightest when evil tries hardest to extinguish it. And just as the church overcame Rome and became one of the largest forces in the Roman Empire, so the church of Jesus Christ has become one of the largest forces in China today. Many estimate the house church in China has approximately 130 million believers, perhaps 10 percent of China's population.

What Is a House Church?

A "house church" is a term used to describe an independent assembly of Christians who gather to carry out the functions of the Bible that are described in the New Testament and attributed to a church. Some describe a house church as smaller than a usual institutional church. Others describe a house church as the most appropriate place to gather because the church family should gather in the same way that a physical family gathers. Some call it a house church because it supports their view that the Christian church met in homes during the book of Acts. There are those who believe that the home is the most effective way to establish Christian community because each believer shares his or her faith in Christ with all other believers in the house church. Also, it makes outreach more natural; i.e., family to family. Many believe that Jesus intended that the churches should be in houses.

In China, the house church is also identified as a persecuted and/or an underground Christian movement of churches that meets primarily in homes. They usually do not meet in community buildings and/or public facilities because of opposition and because the government has made their activities illegal. The word "cell groups" and/or "cell churches" are not the same as a house church. A cell of people is an extension of a larger church, and there may be many cells connected with one church. However, a house church is usually independent from association with other groups and organizations.

In 2010, I talked to 22 directors of house churches in Shanghai. Each leader supervised approximately 20 to 100 churches.[3] The meeting was set up by Dr. Christian Wei of UCON International College, Saipan, an island off the coast of China where a Christian college trains leaders for China. I learned three things after spending more than three hours with these house church leaders.

First, the only ones who had been arrested and/or jailed were women, because they taught classes for young people. In China, it's not against the law to teach your children, but it's against the law to indoctrinate and/or proselyte children who are not your own. That group of leaders told me that because women teach the children under 18 years of age, five of their Sunday school teachers had been jailed. One of the 22 leaders was a woman, and she told me she had been jailed five times for teaching children the Word of God. (Even though there were many of the women had been arrested and in the group of 22 directors, there are still many men who are persecuted and have been arrested as well. They may not attend the meetings of these 22 directors but we knew many men, leaders of the house churches and even laymen who have been arrested because of faith.)

Second, the directors explained that persecution caused the church in China to grow. Every time a man is converted, he is told to come to the house church meeting prepared to speak and/or teach the Word of God. Therefore, from the very beginning, everyone is being trained to be a leader in the house church. The directors explained that when the authorities found too many bicycles in front of an apartment in the evening, they knew it was a house church. Authorities would then cancel the lease on the apartment. Christians, realizing that they had gotten too big, split into three or four house churches. The new leaders came from those who were being prepared on a weekly basis.

Third, there was no such thing as voting on church membership or being put on a church roll. Every person who received Christ became part of the community, and everyone was expected to be responsible for one another, pray for one another, and minister to one another. Therefore, the growth of new house churches came easily, as they were based on relationships and community.

Foundation for House Churches

In the providence of God, Chairman Mao did two things that laid the foundation for one of the greatest explosions of Christianity ever. Yes, Mao did throw the Western church out of China, but he also laid the foundation for the enormously powerful underground church of China. First, he organized the people into small training classes that met all across China, and these became the outward prototype of the house church movement. Second, Mao mandated a new simplification of the Chinese language and ordered that everyone use this language in these small classes. Therefore, all Chinese speak and read the same language, allowing all to attend a house church and learn the Word of God.

Mao organized the people into small training groups with the view of studying his *Little Red Book,* which were his slogans based on his idealistic Communist way of life. Whether the Chinese wanted to or not, they were forced to attend these indoctrination classes and, hence, small classes became entrenched in their individual and corporate psyche. It was felt that these classes were a method to bring in change and social revolution to the masses. Little did Mao realize that he was laying the foundation for small underground churches and classes that would introduce Christianity to the entire nation. While the Chinese generally rejected Communist doctrines, they adopted the trans-cultured nature of pure Christianity. Today, at least 10 percent of the Chinese have accepted Christianity.

> For a short period in the late sixties the "Little Red Book" containing the thoughts of Chinese Communist Party Chairman Mao Zedong (or, as his name was spelled in English at the time, "Mao Tse-Tung") was one of the most intensively studied books in the world. Assembled by party editors from old speeches and writings of Mao, it was intended as a guide for those involved in the Cultural Revolution of 1966–1969. Mao argued that the Chinese Revolution had become rigid and betrayed its basic principles. To reinvigorate it, he invited young people to join the Red Guards and attack "bourgeois" elements in society. Everyone in China was forced to gather in study groups to spend hours discussing every line of the Quotations and applying them to their lives.[4]

Mao also brought about the introduction of the new international Chinese language, hence consolidating the way the Chinese would learn and think. Historically, Cantonese and Mandarin were the two primary languages in China, both spoken and written. But the new international language put all Chinese on the same page and made it possible for every Chinese person to study and learn the Word of God in small underground churches.

> Chairman's Mao's reform of the Chinese language is one of his less well-known achievements. The changes served to simplify and rationalize a language that by its nature accumulates poor usage over the millennia. It also introduced *pinyin* as an alternative written form of the language. By instituting these changes Mao proclaimed full-scale revolution that touched all parts of China, including the language itself.[5]

The new expression of the language transformed Chinese from pictorial symbols to phonetic letters. By making the script phonetic, the Chinese began to think in terms of cause and effect relationships.

It is well known and documented that the Chinese Communists were firmly committed to language reform after their 1949 takeover. They initially concentrated on simplifying the traditional writing system and on a massive literacy program (about 80 percent of the population was largely illiterate at the time of the proclamation of the People's Republic). Their less successful endeavors were the unification and dissemination of *putonghua*, or "common language" (actually, the speech of Beijing), and the popularization of the phonetic transcription system, known as *pinyin*, in order to phoneticise the script and thus abolish the traditional writing system. Most forcefully propagated and enforced, however, was the successful program of linguistic engineering during the Great Proletarian Cultural Revolution (1966–1976). It was used as an instrument of ideological persuasion to create new, revolutionary human beings.[6]

Development of Christianity in China

Since the Bamboo Curtain of 1949, two forces have influenced the Christian church in China. First, there was the obvious dogma of atheistic Marxism, which is theoretically and actively opposed to Christianity. The second was the Chinese reaction against colonialism. The Christian church not only brought the message of Jesus Christ, but it also attempted to reform the ancient Chinese empire into a government like the one in Europe or the United States. Therefore, in 1949 the Chinese government ordered all Christian missionaries out of the country, not just because of their beliefs but also because of the politics represented in the countries that sent them.

Historically, China had welcomed Christianity. The Tang rulers (AD 618–907) had welcomed Christians. In the seventeenth century, the government welcomed Jesuit missionaries. It was Mateo Ricci, a Jesuit, who did much to make early maps of China, thus helping the Chinese know their vast geography. Also, Jesuit missionaries translated many books on science and technology into Chinese.

As Christian missionaries worked more and more into the interior of China during the twentieth century, many Chinese felt it was just a "pretense" for Westerners to penetrate the rural communities of China for future economic or military actions against them. This led to future suspicion and intolerance of the Western colonial empires until the Boxer Rebellion in 1900.

Also, buildings and property became an issue. In past strategies, missionary organizations purchased church properties and constructed buildings under an agreement with the Qing court. As a result, the local governments did not tax churches, nor were those churches registered with local governments. After the Communist Revolution, many local governments began confiscating churches on the basis of unpaid taxes. Part of the Communist thinking was that if Christians did not have buildings, land or facilities in which to minister, they would eventually go out of existence. In the face of this problem, the Pope withdrew all Roman Catholic seminaries from China and moved them to neutral countries.

The Communist government and leaders of the existing churches discussed how churches could remain in China yet be loyal to the government. They issued a public statement that was "anti-imperialistic." They decided the churches in China would become independent of foreign connections in three areas: administration, finances and propagation of faith. This was known in Chinese as *sanzi yundong*, which means self-governing, self-financing and self-teaching.

As a result, China has two major organized Christian movements that are recognized by the government. The first is the Three-Self Patriotic Movement (TSPM), which represents Protestant denominations. The second is the Chinese Catholic Bishop Council (CCBC), which represents Roman Catholics. These are called "Three-Self" because of the historic missiological designation for indigenous churches; i.e., (1) self-governing, (2) self-supporting and (3) self-propagating. The word "indigenous" means that a church should not be controlled by outside influences (i.e., Western Christianity), but a church should control itself under God in its beliefs and practices (i.e., its finances and outreach).

The Chinese Communist government recognizes Three-Self churches because they are government-controlled, Chinese-supported and Chinese-propagated. All the Three-Self churches are registered with the government. Today, there are approximately 23 million Chinese associated with the Three-Self Movement.[7]

One of the issues the government had with the Roman Catholic Church in China was its allegiance to the Pope and the Vatican. So an agreement was made between Catholic leaders and the government for a separation between religious doctrinal matters and politics. That way, the Catholic Church could maintain its integrity of doctrine so that faithful

Communist Catholics could be attached to the Pope. The Catholic Church made the appropriate concession to have government control in the practice of religion yet under ecclesiastical authority of Pope. The Chinese government requires all churches to become a part of the TSPM/CCBC, and the Communist party of China's United Front Work Department must approve churches and/or their leaders.

During the Cultural Revolution—a socio-political movement within China from 1966–1976 (the year of Mao's death)—Christian worship in the Three-Self churches was prohibited, and even those official or recognized churches were closed for a while. It was Mao's purpose to enforce Communism on the country by removing capitalism and the traditional values of the historic Chinese culture. He alleged that the bourgeois was infiltrating his Communist government. To impose his Marxist legalism, he mandated everyone meet in small classes, where they were taught from the little red book *The Sayings of Mao*. He tried to replace the traditional Cantonese language with a modernized simple Chinese or International Chinese language.

The Chinese youth responded by organizing the Red Guard, which went throughout the country producing "class struggles" or violence. There was a mass purge of senior officials in politics, military and governmental offices by accusing them of having "capitalist" interests. There was a wide range of attacks on leaders, including public denunciation, arbitrary imprisonment, torture, seizure of property and forced work details. A great number of city youth were sent to rural areas. Priceless artifacts and historic relics were destroyed. The arrest of the "Gang of Four" (Mao's wife and her three close associates) is usually viewed as the terminal date of the Cultural Revolution.

It seems the Holy Spirit let the forces of evil spin its web as far as possible, and then the abuses of evil opened the door for people to seek God and find Him in His church; i.e., the house church. It was during the Cultural Revolution that the house church movement received its greatest impetus, and it has continued growing ever since. The Chinese Communist government moved away from the Cultural Revolution, perhaps because it simply didn't work. The authorities still tightly controlled religious practices, but the meetings of the Three-Self churches were again permitted. Also, the government allowed officially sanctioned Christian meetings through their China Christian Council.

The Communist government still does not approve of the house church, and as a result local government officials have continued some levels of persecution against the churches. They do this by breaking up meetings, forcing Christians to stay home on Sunday, making arrests, imprisoning Christians and, at times, forcing them to undergo "re-education" through heavy labor. Sometimes the government fines local churches, and when that does not work, local officials watch for gatherings of people and then cancel the lease on the apartment or house where the church meets. Their thinking is that the church will dissolve if it doesn't have a place to meet.

From the end of the Cultural Revolution in 1976 to the end of the Beijing Olympics in 2008, there seemed to be less persecution of churches and more tolerance on the part of the government. The government was not that concerned about the churches' opposition to their position on atheism; rather, they were concerned about potential disturbances caused by a mass of society, such as a local church, mobilizing itself. Perhaps their fear grew out of the Tiananmen Square protests in 1989 or the Falun Gong problem in Beijing in 1999.

The government may fear house churches because they believe outside influence (Western) could make them a tool of imperialism. Another thing the Chinese government fears is how American evangelists show their zeal of going after people. Therefore, it's against the law to proselyte or indoctrinate anyone under the age of 18. However, the American concept of evangelism is contrary to historic Chinese culture. So don't think of the house church as those doing evangelism by going door to door as Sunday school evangelists did during the early part of the 1900s, especially among the Southern Baptists. No, think of an energetic young church attracting new members by believers sharing with others their love of Christ, love of worship, and a display of supernatural gifts.

A New Persecution

According to *Christianity Today*, a new wave of persecution began in January 2012 when the State Administration of Religious Affairs secretly began investigating house churches and creating files on them. This led to a crackdown on house churches, especially those who broke the law by proselyting and/or indoctrinating those under 18 years of age. The government then began calling them "house gatherings" and banned the term "house churches." Some thought that unregistered churches would go away if their identifications as churches were not used.[8]

Why House Churches?

Neil Cole observes in his book *Organic Church* that "the world is interested in Jesus; it is His wife [the church is the bride of Christ] that they do not want to spend time with."[9] He feels that many churches have lost their way because they invest their finances in buildings, programs or salaries of the clergy. He says that too many established facility-based churches have "lost the plot."[10] He states, "Attendance on Sundays does not transform lives; Jesus within their heart is what changes people."[11]

In his personal life, Cole left the world of institutional churches in an era when American churches were better organized than ever before, had some of the best facilities in history, had some of the best programs and best educational resources, and had some of the best preachers ever. He did this to identify with the organic house church movement, which has none of those advantages. He calls it "reversion from excessive success."[12]

Why do people attend a house church? Because they feel welcomed, feel loved and, in turn, they get to love others. They feel warm, and they participate in community. Isn't that what is supposed to happen in the body of Christ? We are all one in Jesus Christ, and are we not joined to one another? We are family, like living together in a "house" or in a "church." The Communist party used the slogan "harmonious society" to proselytize their public policy, but it has not happened. Yet in the churches, the people experience the "harmonious society" that the government promised.

Today, premier Wen Jiao Bao says that people are talking about a "spiritual crisis" in China. He does not mean that in a Christian way—he is referring to a crisis against the traditional Chinese ways. The old dogma of Marxist-Leninism has not controlled the thinking of the people. People are rushing toward capitalism, and the government is trying to control it in a unique and different way. The young are paying a steep price to get rich, and money is becoming the new god of the Chinese people. Becoming successful in life has become many people's purpose in life. Professor He Guanghu, a philosopher of religion at Renmin University in Beijing, said, "The worship of mammon [money]... has become many people's life purpose."[13]

Only time will tell what will happen to China and its powerful house church. While many pray for relief from persecution, perhaps it might be best for China and its Christians if the government kept its pressure on the church. That might make it healthy and survivable.

Strengths and Weaknesses of the House Church

The house church has many strengths, and among them is community. The house church is a community of convictions. People who attend the house church do so because they identify with those who have the same convictions as they have; i.e., like attracts like. But house churches are also communities where the people can come together to learn. They learn not just from the pastoral leader but also from one another because they share, pray together, and live together. The oneness of the house church's membership leads to a oneness of learning experiences. In contrast, the isolated nature of individualistic Christianity is why so many individuals can walk away from the church or not grow in Christ.

Another strength of the house church is that it is a faith-formation community. Faith is not just a noun; it's a verb to be lived out. House churches live together, pray together and, many times, are persecuted together. As a result, they trust God individually, but also they trust God corporately.

Then, as members talk with one another, their inner faith (verb) molds the outer faith (noun) of each another. This leads to another strength—house churches are value-forming communities. In many house churches practical application is just as big, if not bigger, than doctrinal exposure. As a result, they share life with one another, and in so doing they acquire the values and attitudes of one another. It's in this community that people form their "self-identity" and become like others in their house church and become more like Jesus Christ. Christianity is much more personal in a house church than in a traditional church.

Another strength is that house churches are not joined. Just as one belongs to a family, people are accepted into a house church for who they are, not necessarily what they know or their status in life. Therefore, house churches become a powerful force that influences lives with a new purpose as people are accepted.

No one seems to know how many house churches there are in America. Some people guess a few, while others have made outrageous estimations. A *Los Angeles Times* article on house churches states that George Barna of the Barna Group predicts that "within the next 20 to 25 years, there is going to be a significant decrease in the number and influence of the congregational churches and a substantial rise of and influence of the new model churches."[14] The article featured Spencer Burke and his website, *THEOOZE,* as a proponent of the emergence of the house church in America.[15] I interviewed Burke, and he told me there are more than 10,000 house churches in the United States—"thousands upon thousands." Therefore, one of the problems with house churches is finding them, counting them and reporting them.

The average American expectation is that a church should have a building, it should meet on Sunday morning, and that people should be able to see it as they drive to work or should know about its existence. That's because churches are everywhere around us—all sizes, all denominations, effective and tradition-bound.

A second weakness of the house church is its implied lack of organization. It may or may not have a leader/pastor. It may or may not have a representative group who helps in organization, outreach and ministry. It may or may not have a doctrinal statement to which people are required to adhere before they become a part of the house church. And it may or may not have a structured curriculum for preaching and teaching, so that it is giving a complete, comprehensive and healthy coverage of all Scripture, doctrinal truth and life expectations.

When a house church is criticized, it probably reflects the weakness of those who criticize them. In a house church believers are a community, while believers in a traditional church enjoy greater freedom to express their faith as they please. That may mean freedom from a doctrinal creed, attendance, financial obligation and support of the church's programs. That freedom involves freedom to wander into heresy, the freedom for antinomianism or legalism, and/or the freedom to disassociate and dissolve.

Wrap Up

In the book of Acts, Christians met primarily in house churches. "So continuing daily with one another in the temple, and breaking bread from house to house, they ate their food with gladness and simplicity of heart" (Acts 2:46). Within a brief period of time, they probably had up to 25,000 Christians in Jerusalem. "Those who heard the Word believed; and the number of the men came to be about 5,000" (Acts 4:4) The Greek word for "men" is *males*. The early church was influenced by the Old Testament way of numbering people—in the book of Numbers, they counted just men or heads of households. Thus, the early church counted 5,000 "households," but including women and children, it probably had around 25,000, obviously the first megachurch in history.

When the early church was primarily Jewish, it met in a Jewish synagogue located in each city. However, with time and Jewish persecution, Paul left the synagogue and "departed from there and entered the house of a certain man named Justus, one who worshiped God, whose house was next door to the synagogue" (Acts 18:7). While this seems acceptable to us in our society, it was a radical move for Paul. As a result, "the Lord spoke to Paul in the night by a vision, 'Do not be afraid. . . for I am with you'" (Acts 18:9-10). When Paul went to Ephesus, he did the same thing; "he went into the synagogue and spoke boldly for three months" (Acts 19:8). But after the Jews rejected him, "he departed from them and withdrew the disciples, reasoning daily in the school of Tyrannus" (Acts 19:9). Thus, the early church met in houses.

Over time Christianity built churches, organized meetings, trained its ministers in seminaries, and instituted programs. When missionaries originally went to China, they ministered the way it was done back home. But when the Communists took over, everything changed. The new government threw out Western imperialism along with the vestigial remains of organized Western Christianity.

Then a new pure form of Christianity was born in house churches. It was authentic Christianity without Western acculturated forms. As much as Communism is atheistic, anti-materialistic and anti-free enterprise, Communism was fostering a return to pure Christianity by the Chinese. And what has come of that? The house church of China is one of the strongest and most robust forms of Christianity on the globe. We can all learn from what has happened in China.

Ebenezer Baptist Church
Atlanta, Georgia*

Martin Luther King, Jr.*

3

A Non-Violent Revolution that Led to Racial Integration in Churches

Ebenezer Baptist Church

Atlanta, Georgia

Perhaps the best-known advocate of the Civil Rights Movement was Martin Luther King, Jr., and his platform was Ebenezer Baptist Church in Atlanta, Georgia. He advanced the cause of racial integration for not just blacks in America but also for all races around the world. He aggressively attacked racial segregation using passive non-violent civil disobedience to the laws he considered were unrighteous. Hence, he built a movement of social justice.

Another exemplary church that successfully broke through cultural barriers was the Brooklyn Tabernacle and its well-known Grammy-award winning multiracial choir. Whereas King was reactive against the negatives of culture, Pastor Jim Cymbala was proactive in worship that blended the races—not into one another, but all were lifted into a higher oneness in Jesus Christ. Cymbala reflected this in worship when he wrote his well-known books *Fresh Wind, Fresh Fire; Fresh Faith;* and *Fresh Power.*[1]

While many African-American churches followed King's role of civil disobedience, there were many Anglo-Saxon churches that followed the Brooklyn Tabernacle's example of creating an integrated congregation around worship, revival and seeking the presence of God in their midst.

*Photo from historical sources found on the Internet.
*Wikipedia, The Free Encyclopedia http://creativecommons.org/licenses/by-sa/3.0/

From the platform of Ebenezer Baptist Church in Atlanta, Georgia, Martin Luther King, Jr. led the civil rights movement that influenced the United States to give equal rights to African Americans and other minorities. His "non-violent" revolution led to the 1964 Civil Rights Act, which was passed and signed into law by President Lyndon Johnson. The influence of this church and Martin Luther King, Jr. has influenced every area of American life from wheelchair ramps, to equal rights of employment, to Title IX for women's sports in colleges. This church has perhaps affected the social integration of minorities more than any other American church.

Martin Luther King, Jr. was an African-American clergyman who became the leader of the Civil Rights Movement. He is best known for his role in advancing the cause of blacks in America through nonviolent civil disobedience. King's rise to national leadership began in March 1955 when a 15-year-old schoolgirl named Claudette Colvin from Montgomery refused to give up her seat to a white man. Martin Luther King, Jr. was a member of the Birmingham African-American committee that looked into the case, and eventually he became the spokesman for it. However, because Colvin was pregnant and unmarried, the committee decided to wait for a better case to pursue.

A nation-changing event occurred on December 1, 1955, when Rosa Parks was arrested for refusing to give up her seat on a bus to a white person. Under the direction of King, the Montgomery Bus Boycott was planned and launched. It lasted 385 days, and at one point the situation became so tense that King's house was bombed. During the campaign, King was even arrested. A United States district court ruling in Browder vs. Gayle ended racial segregation on all Montgomery public buses.[2] It was King's role in the successful bus boycott that made him a national leader in integration causes, and he became the national spokesman for the Civil Rights Movement.

In 1962, King led nonviolent protests in Birmingham, Alabama, that attracted the attention of the American media when the police gave the blacks savage beatings in response to their demands for equal rights. With this martyr image, the movement gained additional national notoriety.

King led a 1963 march of more than one million African-Americans on Washington, DC, where he delivered his famous "I Have a Dream" sermon. Many have said this sermon was one of the greatest orations in the history of America and one of the greatest sermons in Christianity because of its beauty, eloquence and, most of all, its powerful influence on culture. It was probably the public relations wedge that drove the Civil Rights Law through Congress, which was signed by President Lyndon Johnson in 1964.[3]

In 1965, King and the Southern Christian Leadership Conference (SCLC) organized a march from Selma, Alabama, to Montgomery that was met with police resistance. When the police dogs attacked King's followers, they didn't turn back. When the fire hoses were turned on them, they didn't give up. When the police blocked their march, they continued. The great suffering of King's followers gave stature to his growing influence among African-Americans and the rest of America as well.

In the final years of his life, King expanded his agenda to include Vietnam and poverty, but he was assassinated on April 4, 1968, in Memphis, Tennessee. His death was followed by racial riots throughout many of the largest cities of the United States. The riots were motivated in part by rumors that James Earl Ray, the man later convicted of killing King, had acted in accordance with the government. That rumor persisted for many years after King's death.

King received the Nobel Peace Prize in 1964 for his nonviolent approach to racial integration. Posthumously, King was awarded the Presidential Merit of Freedom and the Congressional Gold Medal. Martin Luther King, Jr. Day was also established as a federal holiday in 1986. There is a memorial statue of King in the National Mall, which opened in 2011.

The Early Life of Martin Luther King, Jr.

Both Martin Luther King, Jr. and his father were born Michael King, but King, Sr. changed both names in 1934 when he attended the fifth meeting of the Baptist World Alliance in Berlin, Germany. It was there that King, Sr. saw the greatness of Martin Luther and the Protestant Reformation that had begun in 1519. In honor of the reformer, King, Sr. took his name and also gave it to his son.

Early on, King, Jr. denied the bodily resurrection of Jesus at a Sunday school meeting. Later, he said, "Doubts began to spring forth unrelentingly." He went into ministry regardless because he concluded that there are many profound truths that one cannot escape. He skipped both the ninth and twelfth grades and entered Morehouse College at age 15, where he graduated with a Bachelor of Art's degree in sociology in 1948. He then enrolled in Crozer Technological Seminary in Chester, Pennsylvania, where he received his Bachelor of Divinity degree in 1951.

King married Coretta Scott on June 18, 1963, on the front lawn of her parent's home in Heiberger, Alabama. The couple had four children. King pastored Dexter Avenue Baptist Church in Montgomery, Alabama, and began doctoral studies in systematic theology at Boston University, where he received his Ph.D. on June 5, 1955. Attacks were made questioning the integrity of his dissertation, "A Comparison of the Conceptions of God in the Thinking of Paul Tillich and Henry Nelson Wieman." An academic inquiry concluded in 1991 that portions of the dissertation had been plagiarized and that King had acted improperly, but the committee concluded that the intelligent contribution to scholarship of the dissertation was worthy of the degree.[4]

Because of King's perceived antiestablishment approach, the FBI investigated him for possible Communist ties, and in the process recorded his extramarital affairs. There were various government officials who tried to discredit him. While no one approved of his fallacies, King's universal message and unique accomplishments have arisen to overshadow his weaknesses.

King represents all reformers and ministers, none of whom are perfect. "If we say that we have no sin, we deceive ourselves" (1 John 1:8). We must recognize the moral imperfections of all and testify, "We have this treasure in earthen vessels" (2 Cor. 4:7).

Learning Non-Violence

King's nonviolent theology came from his study of the gospel and the person of Jesus Christ. King said his faith was based on loving God above all, and then loving your enemies, loving your neighbor as yourself, and praying for others. Quite often he said his nonviolent view came from Jesus' admonition to "turn the other cheek" (see Matt. 5:39). He often quoted Jesus' admonition to Peter, "Put your sword in its place" (Matt. 26:52).

In his *Letter from a Birmingham Jail*, written when King was jailed in 1963, he represented himself as a "Jesus Extremist" and quoted numerous other Christian pacifist authors.[5] In his famous speech "I've Been to the Mountaintop," he stated that nonviolence was doing God's will.[6]

In 1959, King visited the birthplace of Mahatma Gandhi in India. This influenced King's nonviolent approach to America's struggles and problems. He stated, "Since being in India, I am more convinced than ever before that the method of nonviolent resistance is the most potent weapon available to oppressed people in their struggle for justice and human dignity."[7] King was also influenced by Henry David Thoreau's "On Civil Disobedience," which he read as a student.[8] The writing led him to the idea of not cooperating with the system that he called evil. After reading the liberal theologians Reinhold Niebuhr and Paul Tillich,

King said his nonviolent methods were more influenced by Niebuhr and Tillich than by Gandhi.[9]

The Cradle of the Civil Rights Movement

When the Reverend John A. Parker founded Ebenezer Baptist Church in 1886 among former slaves in the poor section of African-Americans of Atlanta, Georgia, no one could have guessed it would become one of the most influential churches for racial integration in the United States—if not the entire world. Parker was an African-American with a ministry to those who had been slaves but had been freed by the Emancipation Proclamation during the Civil War.

Eight years later, Alfred Daniel Williams became Ebenezer's second pastor and grew the church from 13 members to more than 750 by 1913. The church moved twice under Williams's leadership, finally to a lot on the corner of Auburn Avenue and Jackson Street, and announced plans to raise $25,000 for an auditorium that would seat 1,250. The new building was dedicated in March 1914.

Williams died in 1931, and Martin Luther King, Sr., who had married Williams's daughter Alberta, became pastor. At that time, King's wife began serving as the music director. The father and mother raised their four children, including Martin Luther King, Jr., in this one church. In the fall of 1947, King, Jr. was ordained and delivered his first sermon at Ebenezer.

In 1954, Martin Luther King, Jr. accepted the pastorate at Dexter Avenue Baptist Church in Montgomery, Alabama. Many of the members from Ebenezer traveled to the Alabama city to express their support of the young King. At that time, King said, "I want you to know, Ebenezer, that I feel greatly indebted to you, and that whatever success I might achieve in my life's work you will have helped to make it possible."[10]

In 1959, King accepted Ebenezer's call to be co-pastor with his father, a move that brought him to the geographical center of the South.

African-American Church History

Early Baptist evangelists in Georgia preached a message that called for repentance, conversion and a challenge to follow Jesus Christ as the hallmark of pure Christianity. The *New Georgia Encyclopedia* has described the early black Baptist leaders as willing to "embrace existing societal conventions. . . . Baptist churches came to resemble more traditional, hierarchical churches, with galleries in the back for slaves—and a religious message teaching social deference."[11]

During the Reconstruction Era (1865–1877), many black Baptists left white churches and began to openly organize their once-underground meetings. Before the Civil War, many blacks had refused to attend services in white churches where they were forced to sit in the balcony, so they met in their slave quarters and other places. It was there that they sang their indigenous songs, later called "spirituals." These congregations enjoyed freedom of worship, but not freedom in open culture. What had been a culture of slavery before the Civil War became a culture of segregation in the South after the war. To many blacks, church represented freedom.

In an organizational sense, black Baptist churches were a reflection of white Baptist churches because the sermon was the centerpiece of the worship service. As such, sermons called for a distinctive, inward personal response to the gospel. These churches received an individual member only when he or she made a repentant belief in Christ and made his or her own commitment of faith. One was not born into a Baptist church; rather, each had to be born again into God's family (see John 3:1-8) and then, through immersion into water, he or she became a member of the black congregation.

Many black Baptist churches came together in 1895 to form the National Baptist Convention of the USA. Twenty years later, a debate over the way the denomination was managed caused it to split into two groups: the original National Baptist Convention of the USA, and a new group called the National Baptist Convention of America. Later, in 1961, there were debates over tenure and civil rights, and as a result the Progressive National Baptist Convention was formed. These three groups represent the largest African-American Baptist denominations in America.

National Baptist Association of the USA	5 million
National Baptist of America	3.5 million
Progressive Baptists	2.5 million

Certain themes developed within the black worship experience. The first was freedom. The black worshiper wanted not only to act free but also to feel free. It was an existential experience that white America did not understand and could never feel because they had never been slaves. The music in black churches contains cadence and rhythm that has distinctive African origin. It is singing from the soul—a free expression of the peoples' feelings and hopes.

A third theme is "survival," which was an experience of slaves attempting to survive the system into which they were born and the persecution they endured as slaves. In this way, the engagement of black churches in matters of politics and social justice can be seen as a matter of survival for African-American life.

In contrast to white Baptists, who insisted on separation of church and state, black Baptists joined with the government and worked with it, even teaching citizenship classes in their churches. They gave social activism a high meaning in their lifestyle, and social justice was one of their implied values. This is all seen in Martin Luther King's sermon "I've Been to the Mountaintop."[12]

Integration of Local Churches and Worship

There is a great difference between interracial and multiracial churches. When a church is *multiracial*, it simply means it has members of different races that are attending the services. For instance, you may say that a church is made up of 20 percent Hispanic, 30 percent African-American, and 50 percent Anglo-Saxon. However, just because different races attend a service does not mean it is an integrated or interracial church.

In multiracial churches, there may be a white minister preaching and a white music director leading worship. The worship service is probably traditional Anglo-Saxon in structure. Thus, in that church, the African-Americans and the Hispanics are led to worship the way Anglo-Saxons worship, not the way they would worship in their ethnic integrity.

Yancey defines "multiracial" as "a church in which no one racial group makes up more than 80% of attendees of at least one of the major worship services."[13] That suggests only eight percent of all American churches are multiracial.

An integrated church may be represented by a bag of marbles. In the bag, you have 20 percent brown marbles, 30 percent black marbles, and 50 percent white marbles. Just because the marbles are all in one bag does not mean they are integrated—it just means that they are in the bag together. To have a *multiracial* church, the worship service must reflect the worship experiences of each race. There will be representatives from the various races on the platform, leading worship in a way that reflects their attitudes, values and orientations.

Intercultural worship (another term for multiracial) is when elements from each culture become part of the worship experience for all. As an illustration, when African-Americans come to worship, they bring their past slavery orientation and desires to demonstrate their freedom from

- *Multiracial:* more than one race makes up a church family, and all members are equally recognized.
- *Multicultural:* church leadership is representative of each race within the congregation and worship, learning and fellowship are expressive of each representative race within the church.
- *Integration:* races are merged and there is full-group acceptance of individuals into government, church, education and school culture.
- *Civil Rights:* the rights of life, liberty and the pursuit of happiness are guaranteed to every citizen of the United States under the Thirteenth and Fourteenth Amendments to the Constitution and by a 1964 Act of Congress.

slavery in their expression of worship. In contrast, Hispanics express the element of joy and triumphantalism in their worship. Also, the element of rational Christianity expresses an element of Anglo-Saxon worship.

A multiracial church "emphasizes contrasting racial groups bringing distinct cultures into the congregation, such as through multiple choirs with different styles, rotated preachers, intentional multicultural staff, classes in cross-cultural ministry, bilingual worship, and multi-congregational facility usage."[14]

A better illustration for an interracial church might be a "stew pot," a term I first heard from C. Peter Wagner in the 1980s. The stew sauce is a combination of all the elements in the pot, but each element retains its integrity and taste; i.e., the carrot is still a carrot, the onion is still an onion, and meat still has the taste and texture of meat. Yet they are cooked together so that the taste of each is present in all vegetables and meat. So, in intercultural worship, elements from each segment of the worshiping body will be found in the worship. All cultures in a worshiping body respect the other groups, and all groups blend together for a great "stew."

Christians have the best possibility to bring integration into the American culture. Christians have the ability to think in a missional, multicultural and transcultural manner. This means they can think beyond their present situation. Christians have the ability to understand how cross-cultural relationships can bring people together as "one in Christ." Both the black culture and the white, Oriental, or Hispanic culture are accepted equally and expressed equally. The cultures influence each other as they become one in Jesus Christ.

In the past, the church has done a poor job of integration because most members have thought of their own race and/or their own culture. They have not thought transculturally. But today the church—primarily the megachurch movement—is becoming more integrated than in the past.

African-Americans find it difficult to identify with white culture churches because the white church does not reinforce their racial identity and their religious involvement does not move them toward a transcending racial identity. Their blackness is not reinforced in a white church, and they do not find themselves moving toward an experience that transcends black or white. Therefore, for an African-American to worship in a white culture, they have to follow a white role model and worship as a white person, which suggests they eventually assume the values of a white person.

However, African-Americans love their worship in their own church. They bring the residual memory of slavery and place it on the altar. Here they become free to move, shout and preach—in essence, they want freedom now.

While many people are asking for total race integration, we must ask the question, "Is total race integration possible?" In heaven, yes! But on earth, is it possible? It should be our goal.

While African-Americans are asked to participate in a culture that is different from their own, they also have the right to demand multiracial worship. Interracial means more than acceptance to sit in a white culture church. Multiracial means worship that expresses their race in prayer, music and preaching.

Have white-dominated churches accepted the black congregation as a "haven" where blacks are affirmed, protected and even participate in a way that acknowledges their shared African-American heritage? This is difficult in a single-cell church where "everyone knows everyone, everyone relates to everyone, and everyone waits on everyone."[15]

We have to remember that the Christian congregation is a voluntary organization. Those who worship have voluntarily taken on the worship experiences that appeal to their inner social selves. This involves the interests, beliefs, values and life experiences that connect them to others with the same ancestral nature.

Integration and Denominations

It is one thing for a local church to integrate more than one race so it can share the same worship experience. It's another thing for a denomination to add churches that reflect different races and cultures.

Southern Baptists are becoming integrated at a rapid rate. The number of non-white congregations in the Southern Baptist Convention (SBC) has grown by 66 percent since 1988. A survey done by the North American Mission Board's Center for Missional Research in 2011 found 10,049 of 50,768 SBC congregations identified themselves with ethnicity other than white. In 1998, the non-white congregations totaled 6,044.[16] So, it is clear that Southern Baptists are becoming more multiethnic and integrated. The diversity of the SBC is happening at the same time as the United States becomes more racially diverse.

The largest growth in the SBC has been in the number of African-American congregations. Between 1988 and 2011, African-American congregations grew by 82.7 percent in the SBC.[17] During that time, Fred Luter, pastor of Franklin Avenue Baptist Church in New Orleans, Louisiana, became the first-ever African-American president of the SBC, reflecting this diverse integration. Luter is quoted as saying, "I remember at one time I was the only African-American pastor in my city who was Southern Baptist."[18]

There have also been a great number of Hispanic congregations that have been added or planted by the SBC. The number of Hispanic congregations grew nearly 63 percent from 1998 to 2011, and Asian congregations affiliated with the SBC have grown by 55 percent.[19]

Charter for the Current Percentages of Ethnic vs. Anglo-Saxon Churches[20]

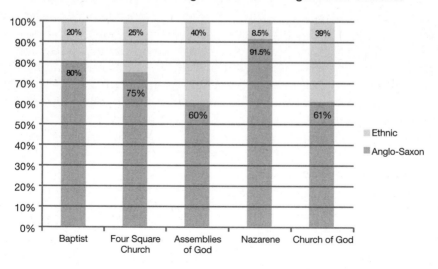

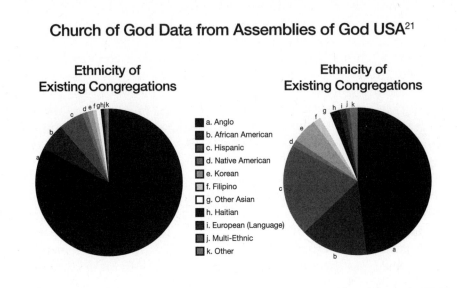

Church of God Data from Assemblies of God USA[21]

Ethnicity of Existing Congregations

Ethnicity of Existing Congregations

- a. Anglo
- b. African American
- c. Hispanic
- d. Native American
- e. Korean
- f. Filipino
- g. Other Asian
- h. Haitian
- i. European (Language)
- j. Multi-Ethnic
- k. Other

Data for Integration Within Churches

The racial reconciliation movement of the 1990s, which sought to heal racial divides in the church, inspired religious institutions in America to make diversity a priority. The popularity of the so-called megachurches, with membership in the thousands, has greatly contributed to diversifying U.S. churches. According to Michael Emerson, a specialist on race and faith at Rice University, the proportion of American churches with 20 percent or more minority participation has languished at about 7.5 percent for nearly a decade. Megachurches, on the other hand, have quadrupled their minority membership—from 6 percent in 1998 to 25 percent in 2007.[22]

Spiritual Integration

One of the more integrated churches in America is Brooklyn Tabernacle in New York. As Ruth Dailey stated in the *Pittsburg Post-Gazette*, "Integration is not a cosmetic Sunday Morning-only gesture. . . the mighty Brooklyn Tabernacle, a veritable United Nations of the gospel, draws 10,000 members from the New York's areas diverse millions."[23] Dennis Farro, a licensed counselor and ordained minister, describes it this way: "For those of you unfamiliar with Brooklyn Tabernacle, it is a large multiracial, multiethnic church in Brooklyn, New York, known for its choir, explosion in intercessory prayer, and oft-expressed desire to serve others."[24]

The Tabernacle has more than 16,000 members and serves the many ethnic groups of New York City. It achieved integration not by attacking racial segregation, nor by its members being included in marches or pickets. It doesn't have a negative program against the social injustices found in any metropolitan area where there is a mixture of races. Rather, Christ is the center of its message, proclaiming that He is the Savior of the world. Those who believe in Jesus Christ become part of a new spiritual union that the Bible describes as "in Christ," and they become members of the body of Christ that is called Brooklyn Tabernacle.

Those in Christ are given new perspectives of themselves, others and the world. They leave Sunday services as ambassadors for Christ. Their aim is not to correct social injustices in the world but to present Jesus Christ to *everyone*—not just those of their own race or ethnic background. They proclaim what Christ has done for them and what He can do for all. The church presents the transformation by Christ through soul-stirring worship. When the Brooklyn Tabernacle choir sings, the worshipers join them in praise to God. When all worship God, the Lord comes to receive their worship and all are lifted to new heavenly experiences.

In Christ each finds a new identity. Rather than feel discriminated against, or different from others, they feel oneness in Christ. They see how much they are alike in the heavenly family. They are sisters and brothers, and God is their father.

Strengths and Weaknesses

There are many strengths and/or arguments for integration within churches. First, the integrated church represents the American dream, as reflected in the quotation on the Statue of Liberty: "Give me your tired, your poor, your huddled masses yearning to breathe free, the wretched refuse of your teeming shore. Send these, the homeless, tempest-tost to me, I lift my lamp beside the golden door!"[25] Also, the Declaration of Independence demands an integrated church where every American citizen has the "right to life, liberty, and the pursuit of happiness." This right is reinforced by the Declaration of Independence and the Fifth and Fourteenth Amendments to the Constitution of the United States. Any anti-integration attitude and/or action would be condemned by the general American population and is contrary to American laws.

Second, a more compelling reason is the biblical mandate of spiritual union. Paul told the Galatians that in Christ "there is neither Jew nor Greek, there is neither slave nor free, there is neither male nor female; for you are all one in Christ Jesus" (Gal. 3:28). He repeated the exhortation to the Colossians but included racial or cultural unity, as seen in *The Living Bible* translation: "In this new life one's neutrality or race, or education, or social position is unimportant; such things mean nothing" (Col. 3:11).

Third, an integrated church with multiracial worship will carry out the Great Commission. Jesus commanded, "Go and make disciples of all ethnic groups [*ethne*]" (Matt. 28:19, *author's translation*). This broad, sweeping command means the disciples of Christ should target all ethnic groups. This inclusive evangelism will attract all races of people from all types of cultures. It will tell prospective believers that the church accepts them as God accepts them. This is a positive way of building an integrated church without any natural barriers to conversion and/or worship. Didn't the Good Samaritan accept the Jewish man who had been mugged?

Fourth, the integrated church strengthens the believers within the church. As they learn about others and accept people from different cultures, they learn something about themselves and become stronger in the faith and stronger in the cross-cultural outreach to those of other races.

Fifth, a multiracial/multicultural church is a reflection of heaven. When we get to heaven, Christians will all be one community, each worshiping Jesus Christ without regard to race, color or nationality. What will the worship scene in heaven look like?

> You are worthy to take the scroll,
> And to open its seals;
> For You were slain,
> And have redeemed us to God by Your blood
> Out of every tribe and tongue and people and nation,
> And have made us kings and priests to our God;
> And we shall reign on the earth (Rev. 5:9-11).

Since we will be singing praises for all eternity alongside a multicultural host of people, then perhaps we should get used to that experience in the church on earth.

A sixth strength is that the multiracial/multicultural church is a testimony to the unsaved people of this world that Jesus Christ has overcome the sin of racism individually and corporately. A multiethnic and multiracial church living together in harmony demonstrates to the world the power of Jesus Christ to transform people. David Anderson, in his book *Multicultural Ministry: Finding Your Church's Unique Rhythm*, has said:

> Evidence of this country's rich racial mix is all around us in our schools, our stores, our neighborhoods, our recreational facilities—everywhere except our churches. Heaven may include every culture, tongue, and tribe, but in the United States, Sunday morning remains one of the bastions of ethnic separationism. It's time to stop merely talking about multicultural worship, and start living it.[26]

A seventh strength is that a multiracial/multicultural church is a powerful apologetic message to the community that it has love one for another (see John 13:34-35; 1 John 4:7-8). The best demonstration that a church can give of true Christianity is when outsiders see it loving people across cultural barriers, accepting each person for the individual he or she is, and esteeming others better than themselves (see Phil. 2:3).

Yes, we should crawl over our barriers, and we should experience worship with one another. But in the final analysis, our worship should come from the bottom of our hearts, not necessarily from the experiences we learn from other people's culture.

At the same time, there are some weaknesses in integrated worship. First, the nature of worship demands whole-hearted responses to God where worshipers give to God the worth-ship that is due to Him.[27] When a worshiper has to adapt to the praise-style of another culture that is not indigenous to himself or herself, can he or she give a wholehearted response to God? Can the reserved Korean give the exuberant emotional worship of a Brazilian and still be true to himself or herself? If one ethnic worshiper assumes a different expression from a different group, is it authentic worship?

While some criticize the 11:00 AM worship hours in America as being the most segregated hour of the week, perhaps there is some integrity in segregated worship. However, when a neighborhood is integrated, shouldn't the neighborhood church reflect the racial mix on Sunday that is evident in the public schools and businesses on Monday?

A second argument is that integration for the sake of integration forces people or churches to do something that it is not natural for them to do. Should a quiet reserved woman be forced to shout in explosive worship? Some would integrate a church to fulfill a civil rights expectation or to be politically correct, but is that biblically correct? Should anyone force one race to worship like another race? Should any believer respond in worship like another believer just to cooperate? The purpose for being a multiracial church must be bigger than integration; it must be as big as the heart of God, as inclusive as the Great Commission, and it must reflect heaven itself.

If a neighborhood is totally black, must these people go out and find whites to be a true New Testament church? No! Must a white church congregation in a totally white community go out and find blacks to be an integrated church? No! But if any believer in either congregation was opposed to bringing in someone from another race—that's being racist. That's sin!

Therefore, let's ask two questions. First, why shouldn't a church go outside its "Jerusalem" to integrate its congregation so its members can grow and learn Christianity from the expression of other races? Second, can a church go outside of its "Jerusalem" to bring in "outsiders" and become authentically multicultural? Concluding question: When do these churches reflect the weakness of their movement, not its strength?

Shouldn't the various voices that join together in worship lift one another into God's presence? They become a new worshiping body unconcerned with the racial words, values or taboos of another culture—they become one in Jesus Christ. The term "atmospheric worship" means God came to manifest His presence in a worshiping body. Didn't Jesus tell us "the Father seeks worship" (John 4:23, *author's translation*)? Because the Father is looking for worship, He comes to receive it when offered rightly.

Wrap Up

When Christianity is acculturated into a new society, it should treat all persons equally in Christ Jesus, but that hasn't happened. To paraphrase the explanation of Paul, "The things that I should do—break down racial barriers—I do not, and the evil which I should not—looking at people through segregated eyes—I do" (Rom. 7:19, *author's paraphrase*). As a result, Sunday morning at 11:00 AM in the United States has been labeled "the most segregated hour of the week."

Some have attacked the evils of segregation and unrighteous laws with peaceful means to demonstrate the love of God. Martin Luther King, Jr. and Ebenezer Baptist Church did that. Some have attacked the evils of segregation with violence, which probably reflect the evil of their hearts. Others have manifested the positive force of worship that lifts all people of all races into a new identity in Christ and a new oneness of fellowship. God has used both means.

Yoido Full Gospel Church
Seoul, South Korea*

David Yonggi Cho*

4

Home Cells Used for Church Ministry and Outreach

The Yoido Full Gospel Church
Seoul, South Korea

The Yoido Full Gospel Church used lay ministry in home cells throughout the city of Seoul, South Korea, and became the largest church in history. David Yonggi Cho founded the church in 1958, and it rapidly grew to more than 3,000 in attendance. Cho had a heart attack while baptizing one Sunday morning after the church started holding three Sunday morning services in its 2,400-seat auditorium. Cho then realized he could not pastor or build the church on his own strength.

During his recuperation, Cho came up with a plan to use small cells, placed strategically in every part of the city, to reach and nurture people for Jesus Christ. Each cell would be an extension of his church where the Word of God was taught and people prayed, worshiped God and spoke in tongues as evidence of the baptism of the Holy Spirit. By 1978,

Cho reached 100,000 people, and the church continued to grow. By 2008, when Cho retired, the church had reached 760,000 in attendance, with 32,000 small groups and 50 satellite locations throughout the city and in other areas.

Just as the physical body grows by the division of cells, so the local church body grows by the division of small cells.[1]

The largest local church in Christian history is the Yoido Full Gospel Church in Seoul, South Korea. Begun in 1958 by David Yonggi Cho, it reached approximately 3,000 in attendance through traditional church ministry that featured the energetic and gifted pastor. When Cho had a heart attack, God gave him a vision of a cell-church where thousands of lay people would do the work of ministry in small groups located throughout the city. Cho's philosophy of the home cell church was similar to how the physical body grows by the division of cells; in the same way, the church body grows by the division of cells.

Many thought the biggest local church in history would be built in the United States. After all, everything is big in the U.S. The Americans were the driving force to win the two greatest wars in history—World War I and World War II. America was the first to have the biggest atomic explosion in history. America had the biggest budget and was the wealthiest nation in history. But Americans didn't build the biggest church in history. The biggest church was built in a war-ravaged country, suggesting there is a spiritual power from God alone that builds big churches.

As a matter of fact, the biggest church was founded in one of the weakest financial nations in the 1950s. At the time, Communistic North Korea had invaded South Korea and destroyed more than 2,000 churches and murdered more than 500 pastors. Town after town was leveled by the war. There was not a building left standing in Seoul, Korea, that was taller than 3 stories, and they were constructed of wood. Most of the citizens were peasants.

But when God builds a church, He doesn't construct it with the treasure of this earth. He doesn't use the wisest leaders of the academy, nor does He use the powerful from the legislators, nor the glamorous from the entertainment industry. God uses humble leaders who rely on His wisdom. God uses the economically poor who rely on His treasures. God uses people who work with their hands—common people—to build the greatest church on earth.

God found Yonggi Cho, a young Korean man with only a Bible college education, and filled him with the Holy Spirit. Cho rallied common day laborers to attend his church and believed his God could do supernatural miracles. Cho's followers knew the power of God could fall on others as it had fallen on him. So they sought the filling of the Spirit and ministered in small home cells to lead others in prayer, Bible study, worship and evangelism. These little cells met in living rooms, laundry rooms and in the back of restaurants where God's power filled these meetings of 10 to 12 people. These little cells grew, then divided, and then grew again. They multiplied and exponentially expanded until almost 40,000 cells were embedded all over greater Seoul.

Some cells became churches but remained part of Yonggi Cho's church network. Some of these churches averaged 5,000 to 10,000 worshipers each Sunday morning. The number of churches stretched out over Seoul and then began popping up in Japan, China and in the United States. Today, there are as many as 50 churches in Los Angeles.

Yonggi Cho's church had more people than some could accurately count. Some estimated one million worshipers gathered under the covering of Yonggi Cho. Pessimists guessed smaller crowds. I received a letter from Cho telling me the church probably had 760,000 in attendance when he retired at 72 years of age in 2008.

Founding and Growth

The church began in Taejo Dong, a poor section of Seoul. Today it sits on an island in the river filled with wealthy condos and is located next to the National Parliament Building. The Central Sanctuary is a remarkable edifice that almost any major city in the world would be proud to call its civic auditorium. Incredibly, it is not a national cultural center, fine arts building or museum. Rather it is a Christian church—designed, constructed and paid for by hundreds of thousands of humble Koreans. Even more incredibly, the vast structure is filled six to seven times each Sunday by these same vibrant, zealous Koreans who call this Yoido Island Full Gospel Central Church their spiritual home. Thirty years ago, I called this the "biggest little church in the world."[2]

"This building is only the hull," says Dr. Yonggi Cho, who has shepherded this flock since 1958, when it was just a tent and people sat on grass mats. "The real church is out there," Cho says with a sweep of his arm that includes the whole city of more than 20 million people.

By "out there," he probably had in mind a paper-walled house on a noisy street where 6 to 10 believers gather every Tuesday night—or any other night of their choice. The leader of this cell might be a busy housewife who has only a high school education and has never received a cent for her work. She leads a friendly and informal Bible study. Newcomers are introduced and welcomed. Singing is lively, and sharing is personal and welcomed. Someone may tell of a recent answer to prayer or report victory over a bad habit. Another will ask for prayer for a specific need, which might result in the whole group praying audibly and simultaneously. Before finishing with refreshments amid cheerful fellowship, this housewife leader leads her flock in a carefully prepared Bible study.

David Yonggi Cho

David Yonggi Cho was 17 years old when the Korean War came to a formal end in 1953. His ambition in life was to be a medical doctor. Cho was initially raised as a Buddhist but converted to Christianity at age 17. His conversion came as the result of a girl visiting him daily to tell him about Jesus Christ. One day she knelt by him to pray and began to cry. It was then that he told her, "Don't cry. . . I know about your Christian love." She gave him her Bible and said to read it carefully to find the words of eternal life. He was working as a tutor one day when his life was changed:

> One afternoon I was working as a tutor. Suddenly I felt something oozing up from deep inside my chest. My mouth felt full. I thought I would choke. As I opened my mouth, blood began to gush out. I tried to stop the bleeding, but blood continued to flow from my nostrils and mouth. My stomach and chest soon filled with blood. Severely weakened, I fainted. . . I was 19 years old, and I was dying.[3]

The doctors said that Cho was going to die and gave him three or four months to live. He had tuberculosis, a problem among many of the poor in Korea. Out of this depth, Cho invited Jesus Christ to do what his prayers to Buddha had not done—heal him and let him live. Shortly thereafter, Cho experienced a Pentecostal baptism of the Holy Spirit and experienced glossolalia, or speaking in tongues. He also saw Jesus in a vision and knew that God was calling him into full-time ministry.

In 1956, Cho received a scholarship to the Full Gospel Bible Institute in Seoul. There he met Ja-Shil Choi, who became his future mother-in-law and close ministerial associate. Following graduation, Cho planned to do further studies in the United States, but Choi needed help organizing a church in Taejo Dong. There was no money to buy bricks or wood, so they put together what cash they had to buy a U.S. Army tent that had been left over after the war. They had to frequently sew and patch the tent back together because of rain and wind. The people sat on straw mats on the ground.

Shortly after the tent was built, a typhoon ripped it apart. So, the young church met in Mrs. Choi's newly built house. The congregation began to grow, so they purchased a second tent and pitched it in front of the house. Soon word spread throughout the neighborhood that miracles were happening there, and people began to make their way to the tent where they were born again and filled with the Pentecostal baptism of the Holy Spirit. People began praying for healing.

To gather a crowd, Cho would go to a small hill nearby and yell to the neighborhood when it was time for a church service. Originally, his and Mrs. Choi's goal was to have 30 to 40 people in attendance, but crowds kept flooding into the tent because of the all-night prayer meetings where God manifested His presence. Cho thought soon he would be able to leave the young church in a stable position and go to America to study, but he never did. He and Choi were soon pastoring 300 members.

The church had a setback in January of 1961 when the South Korean Army conscripted Cho for military service. American missionary John Hurston from the Assembly of God denomination pastored the church while he was gone, but that did not last long.[4] Cho required surgery for serious intestinal illness and was shortly discharged from the army after seven months of service.

In 1962, Dr. Yonggi Cho was a dynamic 26-year-old pastor on the way up. He had an almost unbelievable amount of zeal and worked hard throughout the day, beginning with a 4:30 AM prayer service and finishing past midnight. Soon Cho saw his congregation swell to about 3,000 members. "I was young and puffed up and trying to do everything in my own strength," he said. "I carried the whole load of preaching, visiting, praying for the sick, counseling, writing books and articles, launching a radio ministry, and administering everything from the janitorial service to the Sunday school and youth groups."[5]

But one Sunday while preaching for the sixth time that day—and after personally baptizing 300 converts that afternoon—he collapsed in the pulpit and was carried out on a stretcher. "The doctor told me that I had the worst kind of nervous breakdown[6] and that if I wanted to live I would have to leave the ministry," he said.[7]

During his long convalescence, he struggled with the question of how he could change his approach so that he would not have to give up his growing ministry. As he studied the book of Acts and the Pauline epistles, the Holy Spirit repeatedly hammered into his mind the phrase, "church in the home." A new and daring plan began to form in his mind. He would turn the work of the ministry over to faithful "shepherds" who would establish home groups (cells) in their neighborhoods. They would do the teaching, administering, counseling, praying for the sick and visiting.

"But how can I get the ministers for this?" he questioned. The answer also came from the book of Acts. He read that such evangelists as Phillip were just deacons. This appeared to be against Korean tradition—as well as his theological training—but he thought he might as well try. He was dying, so what did he have to lose?

Calling his deacons together, he said, "I must choose one of two things: Either I leave this church or we reorganize and divide the church into districts and let the lay people minister in each section."[8] One deacon wanted Cho to resign, but the others did not. His mother-in-law—a gifted Christian leader in her own right—said the women would do it. She surveyed the congregation and divided the city up into districts. Then she gathered about 60 of the most suitable and trustworthy women to be leaders of church-in-the-home.

"Folks, you see that I am a sick man and you are the ministers now," Pastor Cho said to them. "As Christ is depending on me, I am now depending on you to win and train converts. I am a co-worker with the Lord, and in this new plan you also are co-workers with the Lord of the harvest. As the Lord called me and sent me to be a shepherd, so He is now sending you as shepherds into your neighborhoods."[9] Many of these humble folk wept at the words of their pastor. "No one has ever trusted us like this," they said. "We are just lay people."

They were not even the elite of the Central Church, which included a two-star general, a congressman and the vice-mayor of Seoul. Rather, they were housewives, schoolteachers, office workers, shop owners, small businessmen and laborers. Within time they became cell leaders, and two-thirds of them were women. None of them would ever be paid for their ministry.

As the leaders grew in the Lord, so their cells grew in spirituality and number. Then the whole church grew. Before that same year of 1964 was out, 85 cells were in full operation. A thousand more were added in each of the two following years, and 2,000 more in 1967.

It was then that Cho planned to move the church to Yoido Island next to the National Parliament Building in an undeveloped part of Seoul—an area slated to be the showplace of all Korea, with the strictest building code in the country. But it was a long way from where the people lived. "Cho, you are moving out in the sand dunes," warned a mission executive. "No one will come way out there. There isn't even good transportation to the island." Many people—including some in the Assemblies of God headquarters in Springfield, Missouri—predicted that the church would be a failure when the new site was selected.[10]

True to his New Testament vision, Cho replied, "I am not building a church to bring all the people out here. God told me one thing: the church is to be a training center. I will train all who come over here and send them out to saturate the whole city with cells."[11] Several years later, in 1973, Billy Graham preached on the mall on Yoido Island in front of the National Parliament Building to more than one million people. At that time it was the largest gathering in Christian history.

Yonggi Cho began building a 10,000-seat auditorium on Yoido Island at the cost of $2.5 million. However, during the Arab oil embargo, any optimistic plans for building in the city of Seoul, South Korea, were shut down, including the new sanctuary for the Full Gospel Church. Many members of the church lost their jobs, and church debt accumulated. Cho used his salary to pay the interest on the church loan, and many staff members went unpaid until the economy improved.

Hundreds of members gathered regularly in the church's basement to pray for a miracle. They felt that God would answer their prayer and that their church building would be completed. Some members sold their homes and moved into apartments. Others pledged a one-year salary and lived by faith alone. The building was dedicated on September 24, 1973. Cho and the others hung a large blue banner across the front of the auditorium proclaiming, "If thou canst believe, all things are possible to him that believeth" (Mark 9:23, *KJV*).

The Doctrine of Cells

I first met David Yonggi Cho on a Wednesday afternoon in June 1978. He had set aside an hour for me to interview him on the growth of his church.

Cho wanted to let me know that he didn't follow American church growth techniques. He explained, "I could not have built the largest church in the world if I followed the methods of Baptists in the United States."

I immediately wanted to debate him and talk about all the great churches that Baptists had built in the United States, but he continued. "Baptists build their churches through their Sunday school teachers and Sunday school classes." Cho understood better than most that the dynamics of Baptist church growth was dedicated laymen. He continued, "Baptists have to construct a small classroom for every class, and they only use it for one hour a week."

Then Cho made a startling statement: "If I were to grow my church the way Baptists grow, I would have to have a church campus as large as UCLA in Los Angeles, California. That university has 100,000 students, the same as my church." Then he asked me a question. "How large is UCLA's campus?"

I had been to the campus and said it was about 12 blocks by 15 blocks. I said it contained many three-story buildings, and some buildings were seven or eight stories high . . . there were hundreds of buildings.

"Yes . . . yes," Cho smiled as I gave my answer. "I have 100,000 people in my church today, and I would have to build a church campus 15 blocks by 12 blocks if I were to follow the Baptist model." Then Cho went on to explain that he didn't have the money to build a complex that vast, nor would the city of Seoul, South Korea, allow him to do so. So, he explained, "I use living rooms in homes, laundry rooms, and exercise rooms in apartment buildings to build my church. . . and I don't have to pay for them."

Cho said that he had 15,358 cell groups that met each week throughout the whole city of Seoul. "These cell groups produce spiritual energy that grows our church. In these small groups people worship together, study the Word of God, pray and fellowship, and from these groups they reach out to win other people to Jesus Christ."

Then Cho asked me a penetrating question: "What is the best picture or analogy of the church in the Bible?"

I answered, "The body. . . the body of Christ."

"Exactly," Cho replied. "The body is made up of cells—thousands and millions of cells. My church is one body, made up of thousands of cells, and one day I hope millions of cells."

Cho explained that a cell in a human body begins when the semen of a man joins to the egg of a woman. All the life of the man and the woman is found in that one cell. In the same way, he explained, all the life of his church was found in the people who made up his cell groups. Then he said, "The secret of the growth of the church is found in the cell; the body grows by the division of cells."

The Secret of the Largest Church in the World
"The body grows by the division of cells"

Cho explained that as you examine the cell through a microscope, the cell splits into two cells. An examination of either cell would not tell you which one was the original cell. They are the same, for all the life—the DNA—in the original cell is passed on to every cell. By this, he explained, the life of the Full Gospel Church is passed on to every member who meets in the cell. It is in the cell meetings that the strength and power of Christ is manifested.

Cho suppressed a grin as he told me, "If I could have looked through a microscope at your first cell, Dr. Towns, I would have seen a pale-faced, bald-headed man." We laughed together, and then Cho slyly said, "If you looked through a microscope at my first cell, you would have seen a brown-skinned, handsome man with a head full of black hair." We again laughed together. We became fast friends and laughed at his hair and my lack of it.

History of Small Groups

The very nature of the Greek word for church, *ekklesia,* means "to call out." The word comes from *ek,* "out," and *kaleo,* "to call." *Ekklesia* was a gathering of Christians who were "called out of the world" and "called together" to do the work of Christ.

In the early church, Christians went "from house to house" (Acts 2:46), which suggests small-group gatherings in homes for communion, Bible study, prayer and so forth. At the same time, Christians gathered "in the porch which is called Solomon's" (Acts 3:11), which seems to indicate a larger church meeting of Christians in Solomon's Temple. This suggests the church was made up of small groups in homes and a large group in the Temple.

Later in Acts, Christians met "daily in the temple, and in every house" (Acts 5:42), again suggesting large meetings in the Temple and small meetings in the house. This is supported by the fact that the church was described with a plural word, "multitudes" (Acts 5:14), which means more than one multitude or small group. In another place, the church is described as "a multitude" (Acts 5:16). This word is singular, suggesting it was one multitude—one body—in the city of Jerusalem made up of many multitudes—cells.

Around the third century AD, the church met in buildings for their Christian activity. About this time, monastic groups began meeting away from the church buildings. However, because of the length of time and experience in monastic groups, they were fundamentally different from the church and could not be what is called today "small groups."

During the Dark Ages, because of low literacy amongst Christians, lack of access to the Bible, and a clergy that discouraged small groups for fear of false teaching and/or sectarianism, there is not much evidence of small group meetings. During the Reformation, both Martin Luther and John Calvin strongly encouraged teaching in the home, but this was a family gathering and probably did not include people from outside of it. Calvin said, "Every family of the pious are to be a church."[12]

During the seventeenth century, the Brethren, Dissenters and Pietists began meeting in house churches rather than in institutional state churches (Lutheran, Anglican, Reformed, and so forth). Perhaps it was this influence that motivated John Wesley to advocate small groups meeting along with Methodist church worship.

In the 1780s, the Sunday school movement began in England when Robert Raikes, a newspaper publisher, paid Mrs. Meredith to teach children in her home. The church did not begin this movement, nor did it begin in a church building. But within a short period of time, the church took over the Sunday school movement as an arm for its teaching and evangelism.[13] The accelerated growth of the Southern Baptist Convention, beginning around 1900, is probably attributed to the strength of lay Sunday school teachers who reached children for their Sunday school classes. Also, the addition of adults in Sunday school helps explain the growth of Southern Baptists.[14]

Strengths and Weaknesses

There are obvious strengths in the small group as well as some hidden weaknesses.[15] Those who use small groups should understand the following assets.

First, the small groups give a doorway into local church membership because people come into a friendly, warm setting in a small group and feel acceptance. Small groups usually attract people like its members; i.e., "like attracts like." Therefore, in small groups the attraction factor eliminates the barriers that keep people out of churches; i.e., perceived negatives such as church buildings, ecclesiastical services, and so forth.

Second, small groups lead to conversion growth in churches. Because people identify with a small group, they also identify with individual Christians in a cell encounter. Barriers are taken down and someone who has an understanding of their need typically answers their questions. Because a small group usually does not meet in the church building, but rather out in the community, it reaches people where they are so they can believe in Jesus Christ.

Third, small groups assimilate new members into local churches. People take the first step toward church membership by becoming a part of a group. When they find their barriers removed, they become open to church membership, which may involve classes, baptism and other requirements.

Small groups usually lead to leadership multiplication. There are several studies dealing with group size, and when many people (more than one) lead Bible study or prayer in a small group, they are being prepared to become a leader of their own group. When groups are divided and/or new groups started, the people who have been mentored become leaders in the new group.

A fourth strength is communication of Christian attitudes, values and core values. In a larger congregational setting, people receive Bible content through teaching, exhortation and/or explanation; and while they may learn Bible content and/or doctrine through these methods, they sometimes miss the "inner" values of the Christian life. However, in small groups people assume those values as they pray and testify. They also prize those actions and attitudes, which is a first step toward living as a member of the group. Thus, small groups communicate the "spiritual" aspect of Christianity, not just the rational and/or conceptual concepts of the faith.

There are also some weaknesses in a small group. Because of the dynamics of individual interaction and the loose structure and/or agenda in small groups, they sometimes get sidetracked onto personal issues and/or private concerns. Whereas a teacher and curriculum drives a Sunday school class, small groups are need-driven and held together by relationships. Therefore, when members press their needs, they can sidetrack the whole group. Also, when members are either asking questions, answering or supporting one another, the contribution to other Christians in the group is marginalized.

Small groups can get sidetracked into Bible sectarianism, meaning people get hung up on side issues and/or issues that are inconsequential to doctrine and Christian living. Just as the strength of a small group is in relationship and meeting needs, so that strength also becomes its weakness. A group can lose its purpose and hence minimize the essentials of the faith.

A third negative is the introduction of false teaching. Pastor Yonggi Cho told me that as the leader of the church, he must be like Chancellor Bismarck, the iron-fisted dictator of Germany more than 100 years ago. He used the analogy of having "a velvet glove over an iron fist." By that he meant that he had to firmly control his small groups, but always with tender compassion.

A fourth weakness may be the lack of focus and/or direction of a small group. If a group is driven by its own dynamics, it can lose its vision and purpose. When everyone is in charge, no one is in charge. Without leadership, a small group will tend to wander from topic to topic and take the path of least resistance. Therefore, there must be a careful balance between the leader's direction and the individual involvement as they discuss their needs and problems.

Controversy and Unique Beliefs[16]

Yonggi Cho has some distinctive teachings that raise concerns for those in traditional Christianity. Cho believes that with salvation comes wellness of the soul, which is the basis for healing and wealth. He bases this view on 3 John 1:2: "Beloved, I wish above all things that thou mayest prosper and be in health, even as thy soul prospereth" (*KJV*). Cho calls these the "three-fold blessing":

1. *Salvation of the Soul:* "When a man accepts Christ as his savior and his spirit comes alive, that reborn spirit becomes the master of the soul, having command over it, and uses the body as a place of residence. A person who experiences a rebirth of the spirit also experiences a rebirth of the conscience, a longing for the will of God, a hope for the spiritual realm, begins to communicate with God through prayer and worship, praises the Lord, and comes to feel the existence of God through every fiber of the body."[17]
2. *Good Health:* "The physical curse of illness and death which were handed down through generations after the first sin of Adam . . . . Now we must base our lives on the redemption of Christ, and claim our right to health and divine healing. Also, Christians receive the seed of eternal life (1 Cor. 15:42-45)."[18]
3. *Prosperity:* "We must rethink our misguided thoughts considering material wealth as being equated with sin. We must drive out our subconsciously rooted thoughts of poverty, condemnation, and despair. God acts in accordance with our consciousness, if our thoughts are filled with. . . prosperity. . . God blesses us with material blessings."[19]

One of the negatives on Yonggi Cho was reported by *Christianity Today* on February 24, 2014.

The founding pastor of the world's largest Pentecostal congregation has been sentenced to three years in prison for embezzling 13 billion won (US$12 million) in church funds.

David Yonggi Cho, 78, founded Yoido Full Gospel Church, an Assemblies of God-affiliated denomination that has grown to more than 1 million members. Last year, *CT* noted how the pastor emeritus faced indictment for an alleged stock scheme with his son.

Last Thursday, the Seoul pastor was convicted of embezzlement as part of a scheme in which he arranged for the church to buy stock from his son Cho Hee-jun at more than three times the market price.

The Seoul Central District Court, which handed down its sentence Thursday, ordered Cho to pay a 5 billion won (US$4.7 million) fine. Cho's prison sentence was suspended five years.[20]

In fairness to Cho, many in the church appreciate his commitment to his son who was at the source of this indictment. The judge suspended prison sentence mentioning his appreciation to Cho's contribution to South Korea, his family and the church. Cho's commitment and family and Christian integrity is greatly appreciated by the church family and they have supported him through this ordeal. In no way does this episode take anything away from the greatness Cho has accomplished in building the world's largest church.

Wrap Up

The Yoido Full Gospel Church was reported to have one million people in 2007, which are the largest reported attendance figures to date.[21] Today, there are seven worship services each Sunday, and Cho preaches in two of those.

On June 26, 2011, I preached at the first service for Dr. Yonggi Cho, and we chatted briefly before he had to preach the next service. Also in that meeting was Reverend Yong-hoon Lee, the new pastor of the Yoido Full Gospel Church. Lee told me that on Cho's retirement in 2008 the 50 satellite churches were all "cut free" and given their autonomy. Some of those satellite churches had previously had a television hook-up to hear the sermons of Yonggi Cho (also called video venue or multisite). Other satellite churches were not connected by television link to the mother church, but their attendance was counted at the central church.

Lee told me that then the church had only 350,000 members at the mother church on Yoido Island. They had also cut loose the home cell groups associated with each of the satellite churches, and at the present time they only had 20,000 home cell groups. Yet it is still one of the largest Christian churches in history.

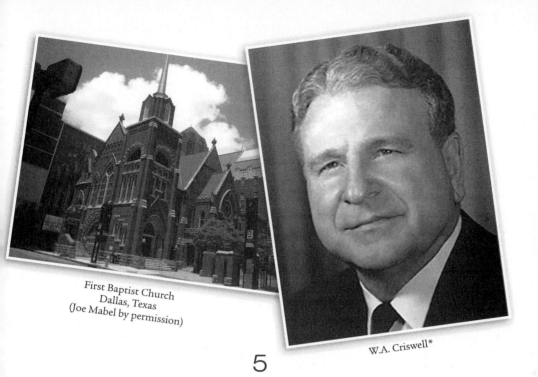

First Baptist Church
Dallas, Texas
(Joe Mabel by permission)

W.A. Criswell*

5

A Church Built on Sunday School Evangelism

First Baptist Church
Dallas, Texas

The Southern Baptist Convention (SBC) was a small Anglo conservative denomination located primarily in the southern United States at the beginning of the 1900s. Within 50 years it became the largest Protestant denomination in the world, characterized by strong evangelistic preaching in its pulpits. But preaching alone wouldn't have produced numerical growth if it were not for the aggressive outreach of its Sunday school teachers. Technically, the SBC grew through its employment of age-graded Sunday school classes built on the definition, "Sunday school is the reaching, teaching, soul-winning, and training arm of the local church."[1]

ELMER L. TOWNS

While First Baptist Church of Dallas, Texas, was not the fountainhead that began the Sunday school explosion in the SBC, it epitomizes Sunday school growth. W.A. Criswell, who pastored the church from 1944 to 1990, organized the church's Sunday school programs. By 1950, under his leadership First Baptist had become the largest Baptist church in the world, with the largest Sunday school in the world. Thus, the church is included as an example of influence through a Sunday school-driven church.

*F*irst Baptist Church of Dallas had two outstanding preachers in the twentieth century. The first was George Truett, who pastored from 1897 to 1949 and built the church up to 7,800 members based on strong pulpit preaching. W.A. Criswell pastored from 1944 to 2002 and built the church to more than 28,000 members by building a huge internal infrastructure; i.e., an organized evangelistic Sunday school. Sunday school attendance averaged more than 5,000 weekly at the main campus and 2,000 in Sunday school missions.

During Criswell's tenure, First Baptist Church of Dallas grew to be recognized as the largest Southern Baptist church in the world and the largest Sunday school in America. Criswell expanded the church to multiple buildings, covering five blocks of downtown Dallas. It spread out from building to building. Some were three stories tall, while others were up to eight stories tall.

The church became the talk of the nation when it built an eight-story gym that included a basketball court and track, weight room, bowling alley and roller-skating rink. Eventually, the church owned and operated a Christian school for grades kindergarten through twelfth, several radio stations,[2] and Dallas Life, a mission for the homeless. The church also began a number of mission Sunday schools (37 inner-city missions) surrounding the city of Dallas, a crisis pregnancy center, and an extensive television outreach that broadcast the gospel live throughout the city.[3] Its greatness today is seen in the Sunday school that involves more than 1,000 workers who reach, teach, win and mature people in the Word of God.[4]

W.A. Criswell was an early Sunday school innovator. He hired professionally trained Christian education directors for each age department and organized an aggressive visitation program to cover the city of Dallas. His goal was for them to visit every home until every person was reached.

The Influence of Arthur Flake

Arthur Flake was an early leader of the Sunday school department at the Baptist Sunday School Board (an organization now called LifeWay Christian Resources). Many credit Flake as the source of an evangelistic Sunday school strategy that propelled the Southern Baptist Convention into its great growth.

Flake was originally a traveling clothing salesman, but he settled down in Wynonna, Mississippi, in 1894 and entered the department store business. In 1895, he was the Sunday school superintendent of the Wynonna Baptist Church, where he organized a training union to prepare Sunday school teachers—the first in Mississippi to do so. Through

Sunday school outreach, his church became the largest in his association. He became the director of Sunday school in the association and led it to become the fastest-growing association in the state of Mississippi.

In 1909, he was employed by the Baptist Sunday School Board, where he traveled to Sunday schools to enrich and motivate them to grow. He had a five-step formula to growth called "Flake's Formula" that first appeared in 1919.

(1) *Know the Possibilities*. Flake taught Sunday school leaders to know the possibilities of growth and influence of Sunday school. Today, this would be called "vision." He felt leaders should know the potential of a Sunday school based on the size of the community and the church. That involved knowing prospects, knowing how to find them, and knowing how to enroll them.

(2) *Enlarge the Organization*. By this Flake meant divide classes, add classes and create new classes. He felt Sunday school attendance would grow when individual classes were added.

(3) *Enlist and Train the Workers*. By this Flake meant there should be one Sunday school teacher/worker for each 10 students. As an illustration, if a Sunday school had 200 in attendance, there needed to be 20 Sunday school teachers and/or classes.

(4) *Provide Space and Equipment*. By this Flake meant that leaders should use every available space in the local church for Sunday school classes. He was even known for suggesting the pastor and staff move out of their offices to create Sunday school classrooms. He also used portable spaces (i.e., trailers) and gave up their space for a new nursery for the Sunday school.

(5) *Go After the People*. Flake held Sunday school revivals in local churches. He did not preach a typical revival sermon to get people saved, as was done in most revivals. Instead, Flake used the revival to grow the Sunday schools through a scientific analysis and application of growth methods.

First, Flake examined Sunday school facilities to map out potential classrooms. If he could find 10 potential classrooms, he felt that church could add 10 classes and grow by 100 people.

Next, Flake preached on the need for Christians to surrender for Christian service in their church (specifically, he was looking for 10 workers to begin 10 new classes). Then he asked church members to make a decision to become Sunday school teachers. Because he had examined the church's Sunday school records, he knew what classes should be divided to create new classes. Flake asked his listeners to yield their lives to teach one of the new classes they were going to create. He gave a public invitation to walk forward and make their decision public.

Flake would then lead the new teachers to search the church rosters for families or members who were not enrolled in the Sunday school, and then he would instruct the teachers to enroll them in Sunday school. On Saturday, Flake would take the new teachers out into the neighborhood on a door-by-door canvassing to find people and enroll them in Sunday school.

Flake's formula was a contradiction to the traditional Sunday school methods found in most denominations at the beginning of the 1900s. In those days, most Sunday schools did not reach beyond 100 attendees, and most only had 10 classes. The average Sunday school consisted of these age groups: nursery, beginners, primaries, junior boys, junior girls, intermediates, young people (high school), young adults, middle-age adults, and senior adults. Flake's legacy impacted thousands of churches and denominations that were not Southern Baptist. They began adding new classes as well as age-graded classes (see material on Henrietta Mears).

Perhaps Arthur Flake was more influential in growing Southern Baptist churches than any other denomination because of his emphasis on small groups, lay involvement, evangelistic thrust and Bible teaching. These factors introduced into the world the Southern Baptist Convention Sunday school movement, which was the foundation that made Southern Baptists the fastest-growing Protestant denomination throughout the 1900s and eventually the largest Protestant denomination in the world.[5]

Growth of the Southern Baptist Convention Sunday School Movement

Year	Number of Churches	Number of Members	Money (Overall Income)
1900	19,464	1,610,753	$249,369.73[6]
1925	26,843	3,175,409	$31,945,687.00[7]
1950	27,285	6,761,265	$178,337,307.00[8]
1975	34,734	12,515,842	$624,251,867.00[9]
2000	41,099	15,851,756	$319,733,582.00[10]

Foundation for Growth

I began attending First Baptist Church in the fall of 1954, when I was a student at Dallas Theological Seminary, studying for the ministry. I sat under Dr. Criswell's ministry for one year. I was licensed for the ministry by the Savannah (Georgia) Presbytery of the Southern Presbyterian Church and had served as a student pastor at Westminster Presbyterian Church in Savannah, Georgia. But I became convinced of baptism by immersion under Dr. Criswell's preaching. He considered me a son in the ministry. I preached for him at First Baptist Church several times in prayer meetings and once on Sunday (Palm Sunday in 1971).[11]

Dr. Criswell and I had a long dinner together in October 1960 at the National Sunday School Convention, where he was the keynote speaker. I asked what was the foundation that made his church the largest Baptist church in the world. He answered:

> It wasn't my great preaching, although a church must have great preaching to grow the church. Also, it wasn't revival meetings and other programs of evangelism, although a church must have these to become great. It wasn't even the deacons or a great staff of assistant pastors, although those are necessary to build a great church. The First Baptist Church is a great church because of the Sunday school and the multitude of dedicated Sunday school teachers that went all over the city of Dallas evangelizing the lost and then teaching them the Bible every Sunday morning. Remember, "Visit every home until we reach every person."[12]

Criswell told me that he was a close friend with A.V. Washburn, who eventually became the leader of the Sunday School Board in Nashville, Tennessee. It was Washburn who gave Criswell a passion for Sunday school, not necessarily the classes he took at seminary. Criswell explained that Washburn studied for a religion education degree at Southwestern Baptist Theological Seminary rather than taking traditional pastors' courses because he didn't want to take Greek and Hebrew. Criswell commented that his friends teased him, telling him he could never pastor a great church because in seminary he didn't take Greek, Hebrew and homiletics.[13]

After graduation, Washburn became pastor of a small Southern Baptist church in rural Texas. The next thing Criswell heard was that the church was averaging more than 1,000 in attendance. Then Criswell heard that Washburn had been invited to give the keynote sermon at the Southern Baptist Convention in Houston, Texas. Criswell told me he laughed and said, "Ha . . . A.V. Washburn can't preach! What's he doing addressing the convention?"[14]

Washburn began his sermon by saying anyone could build a great church from approximately 50 to almost 1,000 just as he did if they were to follow the laws of Sunday school growth. That day, Washburn's sermon included the five Sunday school laws. Criswell exclaimed, "Preachers everywhere wiped the sneers off their faces and reached for paper to begin writing down the secret formula of growth."[15] This is an outline of the sermon that Washburn preached:

1. There must be one Sunday school class for every 10 pupils.
2. There must be one Sunday school teacher for every 10 pupils.
3. Enrollment and attendance increases when classes are divided and/or new classes added.
4. There must be a class for each age group from birth to adulthood, and these classes must be divided between boys and girls.
5. Enrollment and attendance increase in proportion to evangelistic visitation. It takes eight visits to get one visitor to attend Sunday school.[16]

I learned the hard way about Criswell's commitment to evangelistic visitation. Every Sunday in the worship service I attended, Criswell would announce Monday night visitation by saying something like this: "I want everyone who believes people are lost without Jesus. . . I want everyone who believes that Jesus saves from sin. . . I want everyone who loves God, loves this church, and loves this pastor. . . to STAND UP!"[17]

Who would resist that invitation? I would stand, and an usher would put a reservation card in my hand. It registered me for visitation dinner at the church the following Monday evening. Then, to make sure people didn't back out of the dinner, Criswell would announce, "If you don't show up for visitation, someone will have to visit you at your home. . . and that will take away from our soul-winning outreach."[18]

I don't know if that happened, but I went on visitations for my Sunday school class, and I wasn't a teacher. As a matter of fact, I inwardly grumbled because I had Greek and Hebrew lessons the next day. I wouldn't get finished with the visitations until approximately 9:00 PM, and then I would have to stay up and study past 1:00 AM. My sacrifice was typical of many others. It was that type of dedication that God used to build First Baptist Church into a great church.

In 1954, I walked into the nursery department (six to nine months of age) to observe the dynamics of building a great nursery ministry. I saw a couple handing their child to a nursery worker. The teacher, in turn, gave the couple an offering envelope to register their baby. The parents filled out the Sunday school attendance information slip for their baby and placed an offering for their child in the envelope. Some may criticize this method and say a child wouldn't be aware of giving money to the Sunday school. Criswell responded, "Everyone gets registered, and we teach everyone to give to God an offering...everyone. We teach everyone to give to God, even before a baby knows what he's doing so he will grow up with an awareness of his responsibility to God."

When someone complained that babies couldn't hold an envelope in their tiny hands, Criswell laughed and said, "Pin it on their diaper."[19]

W.A. Criswell

Criswell was born in El Dorado, Oklahoma, and was given the initials "W.A." for his name, which was the custom of the people in that part of the country. When Criswell later applied for an American passport, he needed a first and second name, so he inserted his father's names, "Wally Amos." However, he has always been known as "W.A. Criswell."

Criswell was converted at a revival meeting when he was 10 years old. Two years later he publicly committed himself to gospel ministry. He was licensed to preach when he was 17, and while a student at Baylor University he held two part-time positions in churches in Texas. After graduation, he went to Southern Baptist Theological Seminary in Louisville, Kentucky, where he completed his ministerial degrees. He was pastoring the First Baptist Church in Muskogee, Oklahoma, when he was called to be pastor of the First Baptist Church in Dallas in 1944. He remained the church's senior pastor until 1990 and then became pastor emeritus until his death in 2002.

History of the Southern Baptist Convention

The Southern Baptist Convention separated from the American Baptist Convention in 1845 because the larger population in the north controlled those churches. The northern voters would not allow any slave owner to be appointed as a missionary and/or hold office on denominational committees, so the southern churches broke away. They held their meeting in Curtis Baptist Church in Augusta, Georgia, and at the time had 351,951 members, including 130,000 blacks who left shortly after the Civil War. Today, there are approximately 16 million Southern Baptists located in all 50 states, making it the largest non-Catholic denomination in the United States.

The SBC pulpits have traditionally emphasized evangelism, being driven by a strong commitment to lay evangelistic outreach through organized Sunday school visitation. The Convention is theologically conservative—more so in recent years because of a conservative-fundamentalist revolt against liberals who had taken control of denominational committees. In 1963, the SBC adopted the "Baptist Faith and Message" as a "non-creedal" guide to their beliefs. The denomination used this document to determine eligibility for appointments to Southern Baptist committees and employment in SBC agencies. The trustees in the six denominational seminaries were filled with conservatives, and any liberal theologian employee or professor not able to sign the Baptist Faith and Message was released.

Beginning at the seminaries and working down through agencies and churches, the SBC renewed its commitment to the fundamentals of the faith. Its members have the conviction that all people are lost, only Jesus Christ can save, and that after a person is born again, he or she must be immersed in water as an entrance into local church membership. Whereas some mainline denominations count children who are automatically baptized (sprinkled) into church membership, Southern Baptists only record those who have confessed a born-again experience, thus making the Southern Baptist statistics even more impressive when compared to other mainline denominations that count their children.

Strengths and Weaknesses

The first obvious strength of using the Southern Baptist Sunday school system is that laypeople are unleashed for ministry. Southern Baptist churches put laypeople into ministry, allowing them to be used of God. While John Wesley learned of lay involvement in small groups from the Brethren of the Common Life and used it for growth in the early Methodist churches, it was the Southern Baptists who perfected a lay system of ministry, organized it, built it into Sunday school goals, and through it built the largest Protestant denomination in the world.

A second strength of the SBC Sunday school is its age-graded, all-encompassing scope. It aims to teach Scripture from the cradle to the grave and produce age-level learning. It divides the church into need-focused groups based on the chronological age of each person. While there may be other needs not represented in age classification, at least SBC standardizes its teaching outreach for an objective basis.

The third strength of SBC Sunday school is the diminishing perimeter of ministry. Because of the principle of "dividing classes to add new ones," new Sunday school classes can always have new outreach into the community and locate new groups of people to which it can present the gospel. As SBC Sunday schools grow, so do their churches. As their churches grow, so does the denomination.

A fourth strength is the applied disciple (i.e., discipleship) that the Southern Baptists bring to each pupil in their Sunday school system. Students are taught at a young age to bring offerings in envelopes each week. Through the envelope system they can assess themselves in faithfulness, and every student has a standardized criteria by which they can measure their spiritual growth.

A fifth strength is the objective standards for teachers that involve preparation and presentation as well as learning goals and outcomes. Every church's organization is supported by LifeWay in Nashville, Tennessee, which has produced Sunday school material with some of the highest standards in the Sunday school publishing industry. Not only is Sunday school organized on a week-to-week basis, but also there are several planned events throughout the church year, such as special days (e.g., Christmas, Easter, Thanksgiving) and other events designed to help each church carry out a well-rounded program of evangelism, education, worship, service and outreach. All of these programs are integrated into the Sunday school literature to involve every pupil in the local church.

There are some weaknesses seen in the SBC Sunday school organization. First, laypeople are motivated to a front-line outreach of evangelism and education, but they may be untrained, untaught and unable to perform the expected tasks of evangelism or teaching. As such, errors can creep into a local church, such as excessive legalism and/or antinomianism and errors concerning doctrine and local church expectations.

Another weakness is that if an age-graded teacher does not have an acceptable ministry, those in that age grade may be shunned, ignored and/or never enter the church membership (or leave the church altogether) because of the barrier created by that weak teacher. If there is any weakness in any Sunday school teacher, that weakness will influence that class and/or the whole church.

A third weakness is facilities.[20] Because a new room (cubical or facilities) must be provided for every new Sunday school class, evangelism and outreach may be stymied by lack of available buildings and/or teaching space. Growth could be hindered by lack of money, resources or space. David Yonggi Cho, who built the largest church in the world, said, "I could have never built the largest church in the world if I had to build a Sunday school class for each of my small groups."[21]

Perhaps there is a fourth weakness in the Southern Baptist structure. The class is driven by a curriculum that gives a consistent, systematic and complete coverage of Scripture. Therefore, individual needs of certain students may be overlooked and/or neglected by an assigned lesson for any given Sunday. As an illustration, a class on tithing from the book of Malachi may not meet the needs of students who feel alienation in their public schools because of their stand for Christ.

Wrap Up

Dr. Criswell replaced the elegant pulpiteer, George Truett, who had pastored the church from 1897 to 1944. Truett built church attendance but only had an average Sunday school that was populated by the children of parents who came to hear him preach. Criswell used a reverse strategy. His Sunday school commitment was the engine that drove the church to become the largest Baptist church in the world.

Year after year, Criswell continued to buy up buildings in downtown Dallas, converting them into Sunday school rooms. Year after year new classes were created, and year after year Criswell motivated Sunday school teachers to visit absentees and non-church members, thus increasing the attendance more and more. It was through the Sunday school that offerings were taken, and many felt the financial giving at First Baptist Dallas was probably the largest of any church in the nation.

Criswell followed the Sunday school strategy of Arthur Flake, A.V. Washburn and countless other SBC pastors who had also built growing churches through their Sunday school. He was chosen to represent the trend of building a church through the Sunday school not because he was the first or the fountainhead of the movement, but because of the energy he employed in the strategy as he drove his church to perfect the Sunday school model.

Scofield Memorial Church
(Present Location) Dallas, Texas*

C.I. Scofield*

A Change to Bible Teaching Instead of Traditional Pulpit Ministry

Scofield Memorial Church

Dallas, Texas

Originally founded as the First Congregational Church in Dallas, Texas, in 1877, C.I. Scofield was called as their pastor in 1882. He began to establish a Bible-expositional teaching ministry from the pulpit that spread across the world to influence the way pastors delivered their Sunday morning sermons. Scofield's fame and influence was also spread throughout the world through the *Scofield Reference Bible,* which became the bestselling Christian book in the 1900s. Slowly, Scofield developed his pulpit ministry to reflect the teaching he had delivered during the summers at some of the greatest Bible conferences in America and Great

Britain. Located only two blocks away was the new Dallas Theological Seminary. The church influenced thousands of Dallas Seminary graduates who went all over the world with a Bible-expositional preaching ministry in their Sunday morning pulpits.

A desire for universal education for the masses swept Western civilization in the past 200 years. This brought about explosive educational advances in technology and the sciences. At the same time, the Christian church grew in its passion to teach biblical knowledge. That desire was perhaps first seen in the establishment of the Sunday School Movement in 1870. Eventually, it influenced the pulpit and changed the traditional sermon in some churches from a devotional, motivational and liturgical sermon to a biblical teaching ministry. Today, many Bible-teaching sermons include explanations of original Hebrew and Greek, analyses of biblical backgrounds, biblical exegesis, and applications based on an understanding of the biblical text.

While not well known outside the evangelical church community in Dallas, Texas, Scofield Memorial Church became one of the most influential churches in the past 100 years. As the church's fifth pastor, C.I. Scofield, brought to the pulpit the teaching ministries he enjoyed during the great Bible conferences of America and Britain. He began offering the same ministry he developed across the nation in the regular Sunday preaching services. American vacationers had flocked to hear Scofield teach in Bible conferences the biblical intricacies of dispensationalism and a premillennial interpretation of Scripture. During his first term of ministry at the church, from 1882 to 1883, attendance grew from 14 members to approximately 800, after which time he left to become the pastor of D.L. Moody's church, the Trinitarian Congregational Church of East Northfield in Massachusetts.[1]

Scofield Memorial Church grew and became influential without evangelistic crusades, programs of outreach, or the use of advertisement. Also, there was no hint of revival awakening or any extraordinary movement of the Holy Spirit. Observers did not experience deep worship or other exciting victories that were happening in Azusa Street or other places in the world. Scofield Memorial Church had simple Bible teaching with no shouts of "Hallelujah" or "Amen." Because the Word of God was changing lives inwardly, attenders told their friends and neighbors, who then attended with them and grew the church.

Scofield spread his message of dispensationalism and premillennialism around the Christian world through the content in the *Scofield Reference Bible*. In addition, many enrolled in his highly successful Scofield Bible Correspondence Course. But it was not just the content of dispensationalism and premillennialism that initiated a revolutionary trend; it was also the innovative methodology of turning the Sunday pulpit into a teaching experience. This trend spread beyond "Bible churches" to influence Presbyterian, Pentecostal, Methodist, Evangelical Free and

Baptist churches, to name a few denominations. Because statistics on the number of these churches were not gathered, or kept, no one knows how widespread was this trend. But church authorities recognized that something was happening in many pulpits in America.[2]

Historical Background of Bible Teaching

In the late 1800s, a Bible conference movement began in England and spread to America. As a result of this "Second Great Awakening," many Christians were thirsty to know more of the Bible. That thirst was not being satisfied in traditional mainline denominational pulpits, nor was it being quenched in the growing Methodist churches. Bible conferences such as Keswick in 1875 sprang up in the vacation resort town in England on the Irish Sea by that same name. These Bible-hungry believers spent their holidays (Americans called it "vacation") to hear the eminent Bible teachers of their day. At first Keswick was known for its teaching on the deeper victorious life, but later emphasis was placed on premillennialism, dispensationalism and prophecy.

The Bible conference ministry leaped the Atlantic Ocean, and the Niagara Bible Conference began in 1878 in upstate New York. Then, in 1886, the Northfield Bible Conference began on a farm owned by Dwight L. Moody in Massachusetts. Then the Winona Lake Bible Conference began in Indiana in 1900. Scofield became an influential Bible teacher in these conferences.

The influence of these conferences trickled down to the local level, and in almost every metropolitan area there emerged "Bible-teaching centers" where well-known Bible teachers traveled to teach the Word of God on Sunday afternoons and evenings. Average Christians attended Sunday morning worship, but in the afternoon they also went to Bible centers to hear inspiring Bible teaching.[3] Some of those who traveled from city to city included C.I. Scofield, R.A. Torrey, A.C. Gaebelein, William Pettingill, James M. Gray and A.T. Pierson. Over time, the leaders of many of these "Bible-teaching centers" organized them into local churches, and then they planted mission churches that offered a teaching ministry like their own.

These conferences demonstrated that some in the Christian public were ready for a change in Sunday morning pulpits. What they really wanted was preaching from the Word of God that explained what God had said in the text. Because of the growing educational sophistication of the American church attender, they wanted more than Bible pabulum (i.e., three-point sermons) spoon-fed to them. They wanted more than an evangelistic sermon to get lost people saved. Scofield supplied a Bible-based, yet theological synthesized, approach to Scripture where people could hear and understand biblical data and then interpret it for themselves.

Cyrus Ingersoll Scofield

Cyrus Ingersoll Scofield was born in 1843. His mother died during childbirth, so his stepmother raised him. The next records we have indicate he was raised in the home of his sister Laura and her husband in Lebanon, Tennessee, in 1860. He first enlisted in the Confederate Army but later deserted and escaped behind Union lines in Bowling Green, Kentucky, where he took an oath of allegiance to the United States and fought for the North.

Scofield ended up in St. Louis, Missouri, where he apprenticed in a law office of his brother-in-law and then moved to Kansas in 1869. Twice he was elected to the Kansas House of Representatives and worked for the election of a senator, and after the election was successful, Scofield was appointed by President Ulysses Grant to the office of district attorney for the District of Kansas.

Some dark shadows lurk in Scofield's past. He was accused of theft, and there are reports he was indicted and/or tried, though there are no confirming records. He then returned to St. Louis, where he appears to have sunken into a life of drunkenness and thievery, never to practice law again. He was converted to Jesus Christ in 1879, but still periodically lapsed back into his alcohol addiction. Each time, he returned in repentance to Jesus Christ.

Scofield's life was changed when Pastor James Brooks of the Walnut Street Presbyterian Church in St. Louis began to mentor him in his faith. Immediately, he became extremely active in Christian work. Brooks was an early teacher of dispensationalism, and his deep theological lessons transformed Scofield.

When Dwight L. Moody preached an evangelistic crusade in St. Louis in 1879-1880, Scofield switched to the Plymouth Congregational Church of that city, where he was later licensed to preach. Then, for a short period of time, he pastored High Park Congregational Church of St. Louis. In 1882, he was sent to candidate at a small mission church of the Congregational denomination in Dallas, Texas. The small work of 14 people grew rapidly, and within a few years he was preaching to 400 people on a regular basis.

Scofield's influence increased rapidly in the city of Dallas and throughout the Southwest. After 1887, he began to appear regularly in Northfield at the Niagara Bible Conferences. The people clamored to sit under his teaching ability. In 1888, he published the immensely popular book *Rightly Dividing the Word of Truth*, which explained how to interpret the Bible according to a dispensational, pretribulational and premillennial approach. Scofield also organized and was president of Southwestern School of the Bible in Dallas.

In 1890, Scofield founded the Central American Mission. He had met J. Hudson Taylor at the Niagara Bible Conference and felt someone should carry the gospel to Central America, just as Taylor had obeyed the Great Commission in carrying the gospel to central China. Also in 1890, he founded a self-study Bible correspondence course called the Scofield Bible Correspondence Course. Much of the material was later placed in the Bible he edited.

In 1895, he left Dallas to become pastor of the Trinitarian Congregational Church in Northfield, Massachusetts, because his friend D.L. Moody needed someone as a teaching pastor in the pulpit of that city, the same city in which Moody had begun Northfield Schools for boys and girls. Scofield served as president of Northfield Bible Training School from 1890 to 1903.

In 1902, he began writing the notes for his *Scofield Reference Bible*, but his duties preoccupied his time. So he returned to his former pastorate in Dallas, Texas, where from 1903 to 1909 an assistant did the ministerial work while he preached only on Sundays. The Oxford University Press in England published the Bible in 1909. The academic prestige of Oxford University gave Scofield's Bible acceptance in many academic circles as well as among the Christian public. Oxford was considered perhaps the premier university in the world, and that academic reputation gave tremendous credibility to the *Scofield Reference Bible*.

In 1908, the church withdrew from the Congregational denomination because of its liberal tendencies. Scofield then became a member of the Paris, Texas, Presbytery of the Presbyterian Church USA. In 1909, Scofield resigned from the Dallas church that one day would bear his name. He was granted the status of pastor emeritus from 1910 to the time of his death in 1921. In 1923, Lewis Sperry Chafer became pastor of the church, and he led it to rename itself the Scofield Memorial Church. Dr. Chafer founded Dallas Theological Seminary in 1924.

During his later years, Scofield wrote a number of pamphlets and continued to travel and teach in the Bible conferences of America. He wrote extensively for the *Sunday School Times*, which was published weekly by the American Sunday School Union. It had the largest circulation of any publication in the United States. Again, this platform extended the influence of dispensationalism and premillennialism in America. The *Sunday School Times* printed the International Uniform Sunday School Lesson each week, and a vast majority of Sunday school teachers taught from this magazine. As a result, Scofield became even more influential to lay teachers as well as pastoral teachers.

Scofield was a major influence in establishing, growing or directing some of the major Bible colleges in America. As stated earlier, he was president of Southwestern School of the Bible in Dallas, and he presided over the Northfield Bible Training School in Massachusetts. Also, he founded the New York City School of the Bible and the Philadelphia School of the Bible (later called Philadelphia College of the Bible, then Philadelphia Biblical University, and now Cairns University).

Scofield's Theology

While Scofield was converted in a Presbyterian church, and later during his middle adult years served at a Congregational church, his ordination was finally transferred back to the Presbyterian Church USA. But it was not the Reformed or Calvinistic view of Presbyterianism for which Scofield is known. People do not remember him as a Presbyterian, but they do remember his commitment to the universal church—the body of Christ. Scofield was also not known for election or predestination of believers, but he is remembered for his indisputable commitment to the doctrine of redemption through Christ's blood—and that those who place their faith in Christ are born again.

Scofield was known for his eschatology, or the teaching of the events that will occur at the end of time. To Scofield, dispensationalism emphasized the difference between the Old Testament kingdom and the New Testament church. He divided up the Bible into seven distinct eras in which God dealt with people in unique ways. He taught that these seven dispensations were the framework in which the Bible should be interpreted. Popular Bible teachers such as Hal Lindsey[4] and Tim LaHaye[5] would later accept his interpretation of Scripture.

The continued influence of Scofield is seen through the ministry of Dallas Theological Seminary, which during the 2013–2014 school year had almost 2,000 students. For years the seminary was located two blocks from Scofield Memorial Church. Scofield met Lewis Sperry Chafer, founder of the seminary, in 1901 when he was leading music at a conference at the Northfield Training School. Later, Chafer said, "Up until that time, I had never heard a real Bible teacher. . . I was changed for life."[6] After Scofield died, Chafer wrote of him:

For twenty years I have enjoyed the closest heart-fellowship with him and the incalculable benefit of his personal counsel. The fruit of that mentoring relationship was the founding of Dallas Seminary as the fulfillment of the dream of Scofield's.[7]

Why Scofield Church Is Listed Among the 10 Most Influential Churches

Obviously, many effective ministers taught the Bible from the pulpit long before Scofield's time. During the Protestant Reformation, Martin Luther (1483–1546) was a preacher of the grace of God and justification by faith. John Calvin (1509–1564) was a scholar-theologian who wrote on the sovereignty of God and the election of believers to eternal life. Both preachers were known for the content of their preaching, not their style or method of delivery of sermons. While Scofield was known for the content of his preaching—dispensationalism and premillennialism—it was the method of delivering a sermon that characterized his influence on many "Bible-type" churches.

True, many follow Scofield's theology, but many more preachers have become teachers of the Word because of him. His method of delivery of sermons began the modern trend that influences the preaching of many contemporary pastors. Before the Reformation, the Brethren of the Common Life preached the Word of God to its members. Coming out of that influence was John Nelson Darby (1800–1882), who became influential among a group called Plymouth Brethren. He is usually identified as the first dispensationalist preacher. In St. Louis, Missouri, Scofield attended Walnut Street Presbyterian Church, where Pastor James H. Brooks was an early dispensational premillennialist.[8]

The idea of editing a reference Bible came to Scofield in 1902, and Oxford University Press published the *Scofield Reference Bible* in 1909, with revisions in 1917. Within 30 years more than two million copies had been sold, leading to a generation of Bible students and pastors who believed the dispensational view. They in turn taught it in adult Sunday school classes and preached it from their pulpits, giving a theological foundation to the rising Fundamentalist movement.

Dallas Theological Seminary trained a new generation of Bible scholars whose intent was to preach and teach the Word of God in the pulpits of America. In 2013, the seminary claimed among its graduates 68 presidents of Bible colleges, Christian colleges and seminaries, thus spreading even wider the influence of Scofield's dispensationalism and premillennialism. Also, there were many leaders of other educational institutions among its graduates.

Other churches known for Bible teaching that could be identified with this trend include Grace Community Church in Sun Valley, California, pastored by John MacArthur, a popular radio and television Bible teacher whose books, pamphlets and articles have influenced a number of pastors to develop a Bible-teaching ministry. To that list could be added Harry Ironside (1876–1951) of Moody Memorial Church in Chicago, Illinois; J. Vernon McGee (1904–1988) of Church of the Open Door in Los Angeles, California; and "Chuck" Swindoll (1934–) of First Evangelical Free Church in Fullerton, California. Swindoll served as president of Dallas Theological Seminary from 1994 to 2001 and now pastors at Stonebriar Community Church in Frisco, Texas.

Chuck Smith (1927–2013), founder of the Calvary Chapel movement, was also influenced by this trend. His movement could be seen as an example of a Bible-teaching pulpit because Smith followed a verse-by-verse explanation of the Word of God beginning in Genesis that continued for several years until he finished the book of Revelation. However, Smith was known primarily for his charismatic expression, not his dispensationalism and premillennialism, which he also believed.

Scofield Memorial Church is included in this volume not for its size, its popularity or the impact it made on its immediate city but because of its pastor—a pastor who taught dispensationalism and premillennialism in an understandable way and then wrote his findings in a reference Bible that influenced the doctrinal thinking of the world and changed the way premillennial pastors presented their sermons.

Scofield Memorial Church recently celebrated 135 years of ministry in a magnificent facility located in northeast Dallas. Harlan J. Roper succeeded Dr. Chafer and pastored the church for 44 years. Dr. Roper was a man of faith and vision under whose leadership dozens of new ministries were established throughout the city. In 1970, the church called R. Neil Ashcraft from California to be an associate pastor, and in 1972 to be the senior pastor, a position he held for the next 25 years. During Dr. Ashcraft's ministry, the church experienced its largest numerical growth, the already large missionary program expanded literally to around the world, and the local evangelistic program reached throughout the city of Dallas.

Dr. Ashcraft's ministry was followed by Dr. Matthew R. St. John, and then by Dr. Jeffrey VanGothem, who presently serves as pastor. The influence of Dallas Theological Seminary continues to shape the theology and preaching of Scofield Memorial Church.

Strengths and Weaknesses

The very nature of a teaching pulpit—as opposed to a motivational pulpit—suggests that Christians will be presented with Bible content and theological doctrine in a complete and comprehensive manner. Just as a school is built on its curriculum, so the teaching church is built on education that is communicated through sermons. Rather than using sermons to motivate to do right, parishioners are grounded in Scripture that gives them a foundation for doing right. Rather than exhorting listeners to live for Christ, that goal is embedded in the sermon's teaching content. The teaching pulpit is illustrated by the message in Proverbs 4:7: "Wisdom is the principle thing; therefore get wisdom. And in all your getting, get understanding." Or, in the modern vernacular, "right thinking leads to right living."

A second strength is that a teaching pulpit is reflected in biblical illustrations of preaching. Many see Nehemiah 8:1-13 as a perfect example of biblical preaching. The leaders stood on a platform high above the people as the congregation worshiped God first. Then "they [the leaders] read from the Book of the Law of God and clearly explained the meaning of what was being read, helping the people understand each passage" (Neh. 8:8, *NLT*). The same illustration is seen in Peter's sermon on Pentecost. While Peter did not read from one passage, he quoted from several verses in the Old Testament, explaining, "But this is that which was spoken by the prophet Joel" (Acts 2:16, *KJV*).

A third strength is that a teaching pulpit sets the Christian church apart from cults and other world religions. A teaching pulpit focuses almost exclusively on Bible exposition. Believers are given a basis of what they believe and why it is credible, and proofs are grounded in the Word of God. Cults and world religions are not based on Scripture, and if they appeal to Scripture, it is a "proof text" but not a clear explanation of the meaning of the text. As a result, Christians who are taught in Bible-teaching churches should be able to "always be ready to give a defense to everyone who asks you a reason for the hope that is in you" (1 Pet. 3:15).

A fourth strength of Bible teaching is that it more than likely guarantees a legitimate conversion of sinners. While the teaching church may not get as many emotional decisions of those seeking salvation, those who are saved are probably more grounded in Scripture. The teaching church appeals primarily to the intellectual's understanding of Scripture. The Word of God becomes the basis for any Christian action that is taken, including responding to Jesus Christ in salvation. The opposite results with emotional appeals. Many have an outward profession of

Christianity when they are motivated by guilt, shame, the enticement of heaven, fear of hell or any other motivation. Many of these emotional converts have not really been saved, or they have dropped out, or they have turned away from Jesus.

Remember, conversion involves a total response from the total personality of the person seeking salvation. That involves their intellect, emotion and will. A person must know (intellectual) that they are lost and that Christ has paid the price for their sins. Then they are moved (emotionally) with love toward God and gratitude for Christ's death, and they embrace Him with all their hearts. This final decision is an act of the will and may involve repentance, but it surely involves fully turning to Christ. Strong intellectual Bible teaching may prohibit some from making ineffective decisions for Jesus Christ, but at the same time it lays a strong biblical foundation for an authentic conversion experience.

At the same time, there are weaknesses in a Bible-teaching pulpit. A Bible-teaching church teaches a biblical explanation of salvation. Some may hear the Word of God and understand it in their heads, but without the motivation of emotions, they may not be moved to full salvation. Is this case, they only "tasted the good word of God" (Heb. 6:5). So, to rectify that weakness, Paul would say, "Examine yourselves as to whether you are in the faith" (2 Cor. 13:5).

A second weakness with the teaching church is that just knowing about Christianity does not necessary produce godly Christians nor active and effective servants. In the law of diminishing response, older Christians sometimes know much about Christianity, but they do less to serve the Lord.

A third weakness is that a teaching pulpit appeals primarily to the dedicated and/or motivated Christians, who will seek strong Bible teaching and apply its message to their lives. But what about the person who is just saved and still is influenced by his or her old fleshly nature? A teaching pulpit can become a barrier to those who are not spiritual or mature. They may complain that the sermon is boring, not relevant and does not meet their needs. Because the teaching pulpit may not reach beyond the perimeter of Christianity, it thwarts the full ministry of the Word of God to all in a congregation.

Another weakness is that a Bible-teaching church must be careful to maintain balance. If a teaching church only emphasizes knowledge, there is a danger of becoming proud of one's knowledge. It is easy for such a church to become judgmental, argumentative, legalistic and lacking in compassion and love for all people.

This leads to the next weakness, which has to do with evangelism. Those who lead Bible churches usually have a weak program of evangelism; i.e., sermons are not pointed to the lost, invitations are not given to receive Christ, and soul-winners are not organized to go out on evangelism. Outsiders judge a church by its pulpit message, so they perceive that the teaching church is not an evangelistic church. But to be fair, the Bible church's defense is that its strategy is to give its members a strong basis for their faith so they will live the Word of God, and that will motivate them to go share Christ with their friends in personal evangelism.

Wrap Up

The Scofield Memorial Church never made a sensational mark on the city of Dallas, but its influence has been seen in changed lives in the city—perhaps because of its restrained Bible-teaching pulpit. The pastor(s) focused on getting listeners into the Bible so it would change their lives.

Scofield's ministry was part of the birth and spread of Bible churches. From Scofield Church came the birth of Dallas Seminary, which was foundational and key in the expansion of the Bible church movement. The Bible church movement has not only spread across America but has also gained worldwide influence through the Dallas Seminary missionaries who gave their lives to translate the Bible into the languages of the people and then taught the Bible to the masses. The emphasis on Bible-teaching pulpits has also grown through the Bible colleges and Christian colleges and seminaries started, staffed and led by Dallas Seminary men. These include Talbot Theological Seminary in greater Los Angeles, California; Multnomah University in Portland, Oregon; Detroit Bible College in Detroit, Michigan; and Liberty University in Lynchburg, Virginia. Bible-teaching pulpits have also reached into many denominations. Some good examples would include the Presbyterian churches, Southern Baptist churches and Evangelical Free churches.

A church doesn't have to be large or well known to be influential. Through the influence of the writings of Scofield, the *Scofield Reference Bible*, and the Bible college expositors from Dallas Theological Seminary, Scofield Memorial Church has become one of the most influential churches in the past 100 years by instituting a Bible-teaching trend that continues to grow to this day.

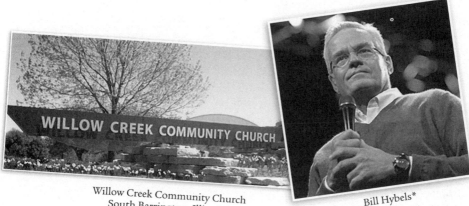

Willow Creek Community Church
South Barrington, Illinois*

Bill Hybels*

7

A Seeker-Model Church Designed for the Unchurched

Willow Creek Community Church
South Barrington, Illinois

Willow Creek Community Church in South Barrington, Illinois, is designed to give the unsaved person a safe environment where he or she can seek God and find salvation. It is the original church to use the method and term "seeker evangelism."[1] Bill Hybels began this church in 1975 in the Willow Creek Movie Theater, which he rented for Sunday services. He was frustrated with the dead rituals of the traditional church and its meaningless liturgy and plummeting attendance, so he built a "seeker service" where people could come to an exciting church built on contemporary music, drama and preaching to meet the contemporary needs of their lives. They could seek God and salvation in their integrity. Also, the church is built on marketing. The church conducted surveys to find the needs of the people and then planned to meet those needs, thus removing any barriers to the unsaved in following Christ.

Located 30 miles from downtown Chicago, the church looks more like a civic center than a sanctuary, and the grounds look more like a landscape park than a church campus. The church is a comfortable non-threating environment for the unchurched clientele. People do not sit in pews but in individual theater seats. They do not see robes or hear choirs and organ music but listen to the Word of God in a contemporary setting.

Throughout the past 35-plus years, Bill Hybels, the elders and leaders of Willow Creek have never lost sight of that original vision of being an Acts 2 church. The church's mission, to turn irreligious people into fully devoted followers of Jesus Christ, remains its singular passion.

Today, more than 20,000 people worship at one of Willow Creek's six regional campuses each weekend. Churches from around the world look to see what God is up to at Willow Creek, and to find encouragement and equipping for their own ministries. Willow Creek remains, above all else, a local church of Christ followers—a place where people matter to God, where together they seek to live out God's vision of being an Acts 2 church.

Rick Warren of Saddleback Church in Lake Forest, California, later adapted the seeker-driven strategy of Bill Hybels into a *seeker-sensitive* church that was sensitive to unsaved people but not driven by their appetites. Warren brings a traditional Baptist flavor to his morning service while remaining in the seeker tradition.

After World War II, there was a decline in church membership and attendance in America, including a decline in income and new ministers entering the ministry. Yet the couples moving to America's suburbs had a "distant memory" of the Christianity they learned from Sunday school or perhaps from the Christian influence they received in the public schools. Bill Hybels determined to build a church by reconstituting the Sunday morning worship service into an appealing place where people seeking salvation could be comfortable. It would be a service where the message of salvation was adapted to their needs.

Bill Hybels has been the only pastor of Willow Creek Community Church, a congregation with an average attendance of nearly 24,000 in 2012 that has been listed by a national poll of pastors as one of the most influential churches in America.[2] The church meets in five suburban Chicago campuses. Whereas church has always been a place where Christians come together for worship, education, fellowship and a place of evangelism, Bill Hybels planned his church service for the unsaved—a radical idea, yet influential when measured by the number of churches that have followed his example.

The $30 million facility of Willow Creek Community Church is located on 120 acres in South Barrington, Illinois, approximately 30 miles from downtown Chicago. The building looks more like a civic center than a church, and the grounds look more like a landscaped park than a church campus. This is not by accident. Everything at Willow Creek—from physical surroundings, to the schedule of their services, to the selection of music and preaching—is to create a comfortable, non-threatening environment for the unchurched. The weekend services—one on Saturday night and two on Sunday morning—feature drama, multimedia presentations, a praise-worship band and backup singers who offer the best in contemporary Christian music. Bill Hybels, 61, founder and senior pastor of the church, describes the weekend services as "seeker services" designed specifically for the unchurched.

Hybels doesn't repeat the Lord's Prayer because "people don't yet have a personal relationship with Jesus Christ and can't honestly pray, 'Our Father who art in heaven.'" Also, he doesn't use traditional hymns because he feels they are out of date. Again, Hybels says, "People can't honestly sing, 'Oh, how I love Jesus,' because they're not Christians."

Entering the Sunday morning service at Willow Creek is quite different than entering the traditional American Protestant church. The worshiper sits in individual theater seats rather than in pews. There is no organ music or robed choir, and the church is designed not to look like a sanctuary but a contemporary auditorium. Bill Hybels is dressed business casual, as is most everyone in the audience. No one is expected to put on their "Sunday best" to attend Willow Creek.

Listening to Hybels preach is like listening to an executive in the Chicago group conducting a sales meeting, yet he is committed to the inerrancy of Scripture and the essentials of Christianity. His sermons are more like listening to a marketing specialist than a preacher. He communicates Scripture, but he doesn't sound like a preacher. He doesn't point a finger or pound a fist, nor does he thunder, "Thus saith the Lord!" Yet he preaches the Bible and speaks to hearts.

Hybels believes the Bible is totally relevant, but that many times Christianity is not. He believes that media-savvy individuals want something different when they walk into a church, so he offers Jesus, the relevant twenty-first century Savior.

Unchurched Harry

To understand Willow Creek Community Church, you have to understand the motivation for its strategy. Taking a page out of a marketing book, Hybels has determined his target audience and has developed a general profile for the person Willow Creek can best reach, whom he calls "Unchurched Harry." The typical target person is a 25- to 45-year-old professional male who is married, busy in the marketplace, and disenchanted with the traditional church.

Some Unchurched Harrys may have a distant memory of Christianity—a memory that is becoming fainter all the time. As a result, Hybels reaches out cross-culturally, just as an American missionary may reach out to a tribe in the bush country of Africa or to a lost family living in the ghettos of Haiti. Thus, Willow Creek adapts to the cultural elements of the secular target audience without changing or diluting the timeless cross-cultural message of the gospel.

When Hybels talks about "Unchurched Harry" he is not being chauvinistic; he also describes "Unchurched Mary," the twenty-first century woman who more than likely has a job and has to multitask to care for her family yet find enough time to care for her own personal needs and desires.

Hybels realizes his church can't reach everyone, so doesn't try to reach everyone. He told me years ago that he is not focusing on the dump truck driver who is working a construction job, but rather is targeting middle- to upper-class white collar families. He focuses primarily on men because he knows that when he reaches men, he will also reach women.[3]

When asked why he doesn't begin with "Unchurched Mary," Hybels notes that the traditional church has focused on women and has been weakest in reaching men. He adds, "If you reach the men, you will probably also reach their wives and children."[4] John Maxwell, a leadership expert, agrees with Bill Hybels's strategy and notes, "If a pastor thinks he can reach everyone, he is probably not reaching anyone."[5]

Hybels went on to say that reaching men is not only the central thrust for the church but also the focus for the pastor. Hybels says many pastors are ineffective simply because they are trying to reach people with whom they have no natural affinity. He believes that God uses individual pastors' unique gifts and passions that enable them to reach a specific group of people—such as the inner-city poor, or the rural Midwesterner, or the university student. Hybels said that a pastor can define his appropriate target audience by determining the people with whom he would like to spend a vacation or an afternoon of recreation.

Adapting to Change

When Hybels decided to actively reach Unchurched Harry, it presented him with a unique problem. How could he edify believers while at the same time focus everything on unbelievers? He concluded he couldn't do it. The two groups are different in needs and focus. So, he designed the weekend seeker services as "Christianity 101" or "Christianity 201" and focused on contemporary Christian music, drama, media and messages geared to unchurched people. At the same time, he planned midweek services on Wednesdays and Thursdays for believers. Originally, he called this "Christianity 301" or "Christianity 401." The services were devoted to expository teaching, corporate worship and prayer. When communion is observed, it is observed during the week.

Removing Barriers

Hybels planned his seeker services so that unbelievers would not be necessarily offended. True, the Bible may offend as it points out sin and error, but methods should not be offensive. To Hybels, a method is the application of a principle to culture. As far as his culture was concerned, he was using methods that worked with contemporary young adults in the greater Chicago area. As a result, Willow Creek became a safe place for the unsaved to visit.

I interviewed a former atheist who was converted at Willow Creek. He testified that he agreed to come to Willow Creek because there were no crosses and no religious symbols, and it was informal place where he didn't feel pressured. He said, "I could investigate Christianity at my own pace." The atheist seeker attended for more than two years before accepting Christ. While Hybels called Willow Creek "a safe place to visit," he added that it is "a safe place to hear a dangerous sermon."[6]

Hybels sees the seeker service as foundational to evangelism. The church does not have a formal weeknight visitation program, nor does it have a regular evangelistic crusade, nor does it hold special evangelistic days in its ecclesiastical calendar. Rather, church members are taught to build relationships with unchurched people and use the Sunday services as a tool. They should share the plan of salvation both before and after they bring a friend. Hybels says, "More people are won to Christ in the parking lot by a friend than some churches that give an invitation to come forward for salvation."[7]

Hybels believes that most churches place unrealistic expectations on Unchurched Harry. These churches expect a lost person who has been totally secular for 20 to 40 years to completely change his whole way of thinking after one hour of preaching. Willow Creek accepts the fact that many people have a slower process of conversion. Most unsaved Harry's at Willow Creek attend services for six to eight months before accepting Christ.[8]

Bill Hybels

Bill Hybels was a student at Trinity College (now called Trinity International University) in Deerfield, Illinois, in the early 1970s when a lecturer named Gilbert Bilezikian challenged the class to build a church according to the model found in Acts 2. That vision captured Hybels, and he gave up his ambition to go into business and follow in his father's footsteps, who was a successful businessman.

Hybels became a youth pastor at South Park Church in Park Ridge, Illinois. He decided to call his youth group "Son City" and have contemporary music, drama and multimedia, all based on the Word of God. He used contemporary language and ideas, and the group grew from 25 to more than 1,200 in just three years.

On one occasion in May 1974, more than 300 young people gave their hearts to Jesus Christ. It was at that time that Hybels began dreaming about starting a new church. Using marketing ideas, Hybels began surveying the community of South Barrington, Illinois, going door to door and asking people why they didn't attend or join a local church. He categorized the following answers or criticisms he received, which directed the formation of his new church:

1. Churches are always asking for money
2. Churches ask people to stand up, speak up, and give up their name and address
3. Pastors preach down at people
4. Church is boring
5. People have to dress up to attend church[9]

Hybels decided to address these barriers and construct a church service that would overcome them. First, instead of passing an offering plate, Hybels planned to place a box or plate in the foyer and have people leave money if they desired. Second, because most unchurched people thought church music was out of date, he decided to use contemporary music with a contemporary band and a contemporary praise group rather than the traditional church choir in robes. Third, rather than preaching what he considered a traditional "boring" sermon, Hybels decided to "answer the questions that people ask in the bars, or the questions they deal with on popular television afternoon talk shows." So, he focused his sermons on their questions but gave answers from the Word of God.

The church held its first service in Palatine's Willow Creek Theatre on October 12, 1975, and had 125 in attendance. Teenagers sold 1,200 baskets of tomatoes door to door to cover the rent and other costs. Within two years, the church reached more than 2,000 in attendance. In 1981, the congregation occupied new facilities at its current location in South Barrington, Illinois. Within the next 20 years, more than 15,000 were attending the weekly services that met in six different weekend services.

The church built a new worship center in 2004 that seated 7,000 people. The church boasted one of the largest state-of-the-art theatres in the United States, and at present averages more than 24,000 worshipers per week.

Reaching Saddleback Sam

Many have thought that Rick Warren, pastor of Saddleback Church in Lake Forest, California, should have been the focus of this chapter on "church for the unsaved." Warren is a fourth-generation Southern Baptist pastor whose great-grandfather was converted under Dr. Charles Spurgeon, the famed pastor of London, England, in the 1800s. Warren moved to greater Los Angeles with his wife, Kay, and their four-month-old daughter, Amy, in January 1980. They packed everything they owned into a U-Haul trailer and met the afternoon Southern California gridlock.

Not knowing what to do, Warren went straight to a real estate office in Orange County and met Don Dale. "I'm here to start a church," he announced. "I need a place to live, and I don't have any money!" Within a couple of hours, Dale found a condominium for the Warren family that was rent-free for the first month. The following Friday, Dale and Warren met for Bible study at what was to become Saddleback Church.

Some of the great evangelical churches of America were within 25 miles of the place where Rick Warren started his church, including Robert Schuller at Crystal Cathedral, Chuck Smith at Calvary Chapel of Costal Mesa, and Charles Swindoll of the Evangelical Free Church in Fullerton. Like Hybels, Warren went door to door asking why people did not attend church.[10] The answers he received from people included:

- Sermons were boring and not relevant to their lives
- Churches were unfriendly to visitors
- Churches were more interested in money than in people
- Churches did not provide quality childcare

Almost immediately, Warren developed a four-fold strategy to answer these objections from the Orange County residents. First, he implemented quality childcare to attract young families. Second, he preached humorous sermons that were practical to the peoples' lives and solved their problems. These sermons were based on biblical answers. Third, he organized the church to be friendly and told people to "shake hands with 75 people." Fourth, he made it known that visitors would not be asked to contribute financially but would be asked to fill out cards to receive a free tape of the service.[11]

Whereas Bill Hybels had "Unchurched Harry," Rick Warren called his average target person "Saddleback Sam." As far as Warren was concerned, Saddleback Sam believed in God but didn't attend church. He made good money but did not make enough to acquire everything he wanted. He was a nice guy, but he was stressed out and searching for answers in life. Also, even though Warren's church was affiliated with the Southern Baptist Convention, he didn't use the word "Baptist" because many thought that would imply it was a Southern-cultured church.[12]

The church service featured the pulsating beat of drums, with contemporary rock music but decidedly Christian lyrics. The people sang, swayed, clapped their hands and enjoyed themselves. But, being Southern Californian, they came dressed in sports shirts, Reeboks and blue jeans.

Before long, shorts were definitely in. At first, Warren sometimes wore a coat with no tie. Then he became known for his audacious Hawaiian shirts, which he wore with the shirttail out.

Warren's early strategy was to invest money into staff and people, but not construct buildings. As a result, he rented any public facilities he could find. In the first 13 years, the church used 57 different buildings. Baptisms were performed in swimming pools and whirlpools, causing Warren to coin the phrase, "Jacuzzis for Jesus." More than 70 percent of the members of Saddleback were converted and baptized into the church. Saddleback grew in the early days primarily by conversion rather than transfer growth.[13]

In the early days, Warren visited one of the largest Southern Baptist churches that had one of the most expensive Sunday school facilities but came away discouraged. He did not want to spend millions on buildings that would only be used one hour each week. He used a number of different classes to reach people for Christ, then cause them to grow in Christ, and then eventually become involved in service. He used the metaphor of a baseball diamond and spoke about going to first base (committed to membership), then to second base (committed to maturity), then to third base (committed to ministry), and finally to home plate (committed to missions).[14]

The Five Circles of Commitment

In the early days, Warren used the Five Circles of Commitment to represent the strategy to move a person from his or her first visit to the church to ultimately service.[15]

The Inner Circles: Core and Committed. Warren estimates he had approximately 1,000 people in the early days who were considered core members. The second circle included those identifiable lay ministers who were involved in approximately 69 different ministries of the church. To keep this coordinated, two people were put in charge of job placements and plugged people into the 69 different places of ministry. The people in the core ministry went through the four "base" classes (of the baseball diamond) to learn skills and maturity. They signed a ministry covenant and were involved in ministering to others.[16]

Third Circle: Congregation. These people were the official adult members of the church who committed to its membership. These adult members went through a four-and-a-half-hour membership class and signed the membership covenant. In this class, they were taught the strategy and structure of the church. When the church reached approximately 3,000

Saddleback's Program to Help You Grow Through Christian Life and Service Seminars

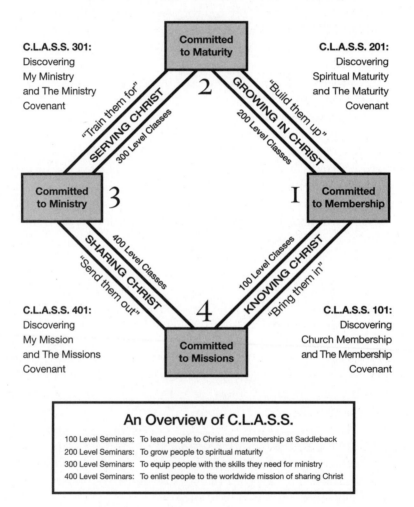

C.L.A.S.S. 301:
Discovering
My Ministry
and The Ministry
Covenant

C.L.A.S.S. 201:
Discovering
Spiritual Maturity
and The Maturity
Covenant

Committed to Maturity

Committed to Ministry

Committed to Membership

Committed to Missions

"Train them for" SERVING CHRIST
300 Level Classes

GROWING IN CHRIST *"Build them up"*
200 Level Classes

SHARING CHRIST *"Send them out"*
400 Level Classes

100 Level Classes
KNOWING CHRIST *"Bring them in"*

C.L.A.S.S. 401:
Discovering
My Mission
and The Missions
Covenant

C.L.A.S.S. 101:
Discovering
Church Membership
and The Membership
Covenant

An Overview of C.L.A.S.S.

100 Level Seminars: To lead people to Christ and membership at Saddleback
200 Level Seminars: To grow people to spiritual maturity
300 Level Seminars: To equip people with the skills they need for ministry
400 Level Seminars: To enlist people to the worldwide mission of sharing Christ

Ministry Application

SADDLEBACK
5 CIRCLES OF COMMITMENT

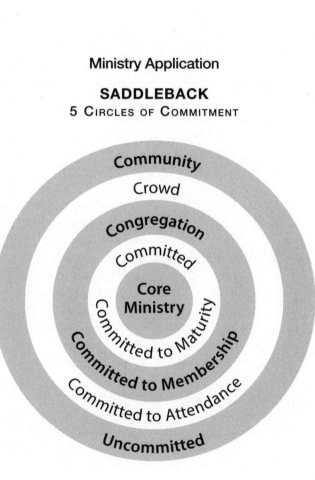

adult members, Warren noted, "We do not count children or non-residents." Each year people were taken off the roll if they were not active. "We remove several hundred names each year," Warren said. In the first 10 years of the church, approximately 4,000 people joined. Warren observed, "We are interested in a small membership that really means something rather than having a large number of names on the list."[17]

Fourth Circle: Crowd. Warren described the fourth group as the people who showed up on Sunday morning for the worship service. They were the "regular attenders." There were approximately 5,000 to 7,000 in the crowd who attended each Sunday, depending on the week. The strategy was to move casual attendees in the crowd to a commitment membership. Many in the crowd were not yet believers. Warren says, "A crowd is not a church. But you can turn a crowd into a church, and if you want a large church, you must attract a large crowd first."[18]

Fifth Circle: Community. Warren indicated that the largest group was the community they wanted to reach. Two elements were involved the community: "First, the community is the uncommitted and non-attenders whom we want to reach for Jesus Christ. We target our ministry to the 'Saddleback Sams and Samanthas.' More specifically, we consider the community as anyone who attended at least four times a year; i.e., Easter, Christmas, Mother's Day and on other occasions."

The church had approximately 18,000 who attended at least four times in 1992. "We needed a specific strategy to meet the spiritual needs of those in each circle to help move each closer to God." Warren felt that the average church had a shotgun strategy that aimed at all people instead of targeting the different levels of commitment into which people may fall. He states, "Our strategy is to get neighbors and business associates into the crowd; that means we must get them attending every week. We preach practical sermons, directed toward their needs, and contemporary music is provided." The entire service was designed to move people from being spectators to participants.

The next strategy was to move the crowd into the congregation. This meant they had to get people committed to Christ and His church. "The difference between an attender and a member is commitment," said Warren. "It's like the difference between a man and woman just living together and their actually getting married. Everything we do at Saddleback is aimed at moving people through the circles of commitment to get every person into the core where they have a ministry in the church and a mission in the world."[19]

Over the years, the tools of Saddleback have changed, as well as its methods. Warren talked about originally using "advertisements" with card decks for direct mailing to reach people. Now he says advertising has become less and less effective. He explains that America is an over-advertised society and people are bombarded with thousands of messages, until eventually no one pays attention to them. Warren mentions that he began the church with direct mail, but today people do not read direct mail. Now he uses social media to contact people.

Four Defining Innovations

According to Warren, the first innovative method the church used was the CLASS discipleship program. He was able to move people from where they were to where they should be. CLASS gave people a track to run on and evaluated their spiritual growth in the process. He mentions his motive was to "move them around the bases."[20]

The second innovation was launching the Spiritual Growth Campaign, which helped people grow spiritually—internally—through every phase of life.

The third innovation was when Warren shut down the midweek prayer service and began involving people in small groups throughout Southern California. He mentions that today they have more than 6,000 small groups spread out over 169 cities in Southern California with approximately 32,000 people attending weekly. Warren is proud of the fact that more people attend small-group Bible studies than come to hear him preach on the weekends.

The fourth innovation was the PEACE plan. Warren's ambition was for his church to look like heaven. He mentions that he began his church with young, white suburbanites, but the PEACE plan changed everything. He mentions, "Today we speak 67 languages in our church family. We have become a church of the nations and for the nations."[21]

What have these four innovations accomplished? Warren wants to produce a purpose-driven church, not a personality-driven church. He feels that these programs are self-sustaining because approximately 18,000 volunteers are ministering through these programs.[22]

Strengths and Weaknesses

The most obvious strength of the seeker church is that lost people are confronted with the gospel and given an opportunity to believe in Jesus Christ. Whereas many churches focus on Bible study, or devotionals, or worship, or many of the other excellent purposes of Christianity, the seeker church focuses on evangelism and lost people. "Woe is me if I do not preach the gospel" (1 Cor. 9:16).

A second strength is that seeker churches remove barriers that keep lost people from coming to salvation. Seeker churches look at a Sunday morning church service the way unsaved people do. Whether they employ marketing, or survey, or focus groups, they identify and remove barriers that make it difficult for unsaved people to respond to the gospel. They would identify with Donald McGavran, father of the Church Growth movement, who said on many occasions, "People like to become Christians without crossing racial, linguistic, or cultural barriers."[23] Seeker churches also remove symbolic barriers of dead orthodoxy (e.g., church choir, organ music, rote prayers), or religious symbols in a church building, or even the traditional "Sunday morning dress" that seem to be required in many churches.

A third strength of the seeker church is *acculturated Christianity*. Christianity was revealed in a Jewish context; i.e., "first to the Jew, then to the Gentile" (see Rom. 1:16). But the gospel successfully acculturated into the Mediterranean-Roman culture of non-Jews so that Christians wore the dress of that day, ate the food of that day, and lived within their culture. The gospel is transcultural and trans-temporal; thus, the truth of the gospel appeals to every generation and every culture. The seeker church has acculturated the message of Jesus Christ into the life of modern twenty-first century ministers and Christians. It does not make Christians adaptable to the 1950s, nor does it form its patterns by the residual memories found in the lives of Christians who tend to live in the past. The seeker church is twenty-first century Christianity acculturated.

A fourth strength is the implied success of the movement. Because seeker churches are seeking the unsaved or unchurched, when they reach people for Christ, they carry out the purpose of the Great Commission. Implied is their success in numbers, strength and vitality. One of the criticisms against seeker churches is that they are seeking numbers. But even when they go after numbers, should they be criticized for carrying out New Testament goals?

There are both strengths and weaknesses in the seeker model or church for the unsaved. One of the first criticisms is that these churches use "slick" or "Hollywood" type methods to draw people into their church. While there is some truth in this criticism, there is also an embryonic rebuttal. Advocates answer that the most important aspect of any church is the salvation of individuals. Therefore, they will use methods to reach people for Jesus Christ, and if people go to heaven as a result, that justifies their attempt to use the programs that are similar to those of the world.

A second criticism is that seeker churches are only interested in numbers. It is said that they use elaborate spectacles that come from secular culture to draw big crowds into the church. For example, they use rock music, drama and, at times, questionable plots in their drama to build numbers or keep up the numbers. The advocates answer that every person is a number, and numbers count. They point out that the Bible counts believers in numbers (see Acts 1:16; 2:41; 4:4; 5:14; 6:1,7). They also point out that God is interested in numbers. The shepherd left his 99 sheep in the field and went to seek and save the one lost sheep because every number counts. Remember, there is a book in the Bible called *Numbers*, and every individual who is born again represents a number in God's church.

A third criticism of the seeker church is that it attempts to avoid the "negative" aspects of preaching. This is another way of saying that seeker churches usually do not preach on sin, because many seeker churches see the message of repentance from outward sins as being a barrier to reaching the unsaved person. By focusing on the positive results of Christianity and not preaching the total message of the gospel, it is possible seeker churches weaken the gospel and produce weak Christians.

A fourth weakness is the accusation that the church has surrendered its values to culture. A web posting on the *Berean Call* says:

> They mimic what's popular in our culture: Top 40 and performance-style music, theatrical productions, stimulating multimedia presentations, and thirty-minutes-or-less positive messages. The latter, more often than not, are topical, therapeutic, and centered in self-fulfillment—how the Lord can meet one's need and help solve one's problems.[24]

There are those who say the weakest point of the seeker movement is that it is questionable Christianity and contains and/or teaches errors. Author Don Koenig makes the following observation:

> The movement in reality has become a clearinghouse for all who believe in the basic goodness of man, for those who think that all paths lead to God, for those who hold their theology that does not take the prophetic future in any real, literal sense, for those who do not know the Scriptures, for those who pick and choose words of Scripture out of context to make them say what they want them to say.[25]

The last argument against seeker churches is the "dumbing down" of Christianity. Critics argue that the seeker church feeds on popular music and modern Christian praise-worship music that have rhyming verses, not the deep theological intent of hymns of previous generations. They indicate that sermons are need-centered and aimed at the thinking of modern-day Americans, rather than based on the exposition of what God has said in His Word. Seeker churches don't explain biblical doctrine and the requirement of discipleship.[26]

Wrap Up

It is only natural that someone would eventually conceive of a church for the unsaved. Think of all the positive contributors since World War II that would make it possible to reach the unsaved in America. First, Americans had a rich Christian heritage where prayer and Bible reading were preached in public school. People expected successful politicians and businesspeople to exhibit the values and attitudes of a positive Christian life. Laws were enacted based on Christian principles, and the Declaration of Independence recognized God as the Creator.

Then secularism crept into the American environment. Many left the church, but some had a distant memory of church and returned. Others desired the "good old days," and that experience was offered in church experiences. Still others knew of the benefits of Christianity. So it was only natural to create church for these unchurched individuals. With the explosion of communication and transportation, unchurched people heard about this church for them. Modern highways and cars made it possible for them to travel long distances to park in great parking lots and attend church in huge auditoriums. Radio and television gave them information about the church.

By understanding the pressures of anonymity and lostness in modern sprawls and megatropolises, seeker churches could provide a comfortable place that was designed to meet the needs of the unchurched. But, more importantly, they could remove barriers and give attention to the message. The seeker church was born out of a passion for New Testament Christianity to reach the modern "Unchurched Harry."

C. Peter Wagner, professor of church growth at Fuller Theological Seminary, once said, "Bill Hybels is *seeker driven*, while Rick Warren is *seeker friendly*."[27] By that explanation, he meant Hybels was focused primarily on the unchurched, while Warren was focused on building a church of Christians that would reach the unsaved. Therefore, the first and purest form of a seeker church was begun and grown by Bill Hybels. That's why he is the focus of this chapter.

There were probably some who designed a church for the unsaved before Bill Hybels, and there were churches that effectively reached people like "Unchurched Harry" before Willow Creek Community Church. But the church's location in a Chicago suburb and the attention given to it by the *Chicago Tribune*[28] and *TIME* magazine,[29] with a focus on Bill Hybels, made Willow Creek the defining church for the movement.

Calvary Chapel
Costa Mesa, California*

Chuck Smith*

8

A New Church Culture
Initiated by Baby Boomers

Calvary Chapel

Costa Mesa, California

Calvary Chapel was the launching pad for the great revival among the Jesus People, or those called the "Jesus Freaks." Chuck Smith, a preacher in the Four Square denomination, began preaching in Southern California, winning those called "hippies" to Jesus Christ and then baptizing them in the Pacific Ocean.

Just as young people rebelled against the empty meaningless lifestyles of America's middle class after World War II and began following Jesus Christ, they also rebelled against the empty "formalism" of affluent churches that only offered a form of Christianity without Jesus. These Jesus Freaks hated powerless religion but loved its founder, Jesus Christ. They began worshiping Jesus with their contemporary guitars and drums, rejecting church organs, choirs and European-composed hymns.

Young people came dressed in everyday garb—not the expected "best Sunday clothes." They didn't embrace the traditional church programs and organization—no evangelistic crusades, organized visitations, board meetings or other forms of infrastructure. They just wanted to come to church to meet Jesus.

They met in homes for Bible studies. Whereas traditional Sunday school was built on a structured curriculum and led by a teacher, their small groups were built on relationships and solving problems of those in attendance. Their Christian faith was simple; i.e., the way they lived.

Calvary Chapel made a difference in the way the American church worshiped and served God. It made a difference in the way Christians dressed and fellowshipped, in the Christian songs they sang, and in the way they lifted hands to praise God. In Calvary Chapel the "Jesus People" embraced Christ as their Savior but did not abandon their subculture. Their churches included informal dress, rock music, casual speech and simple living. While the Jesus People rejected the sins of hippies, they adapted many aspects of their counterculture to their Christian living. Instead of adapting their lifestyle to the culture they found in Christian churches, they did the opposite: they adapted Christianity into their counterculture. From this arose a new culture within Christianity—a new culture of worshiping God. It was the beginning of new values and attitudes that would pervade all of Christianity. It was a new church culture initiated by Calvary Chapel, and that culture slowly spread to many other churches.

After World War II, there were 20 years of prosperity called the "golden years." During these years, Americans reached all the dreams of the servicemen who fought in World War II. In 1960, America inaugurated a youthful president, John F. Kennedy, and his elegant wife, Jacqueline. The time was Camelot, and the Kennedys reigned over the United States much like a king and queen in England.

But in the bloom of Camelot, society quickly fell apart. Many disillusioned teenagers fled their Midwest homes to California. The U.S. Supreme Court removed Bibles and outlawed prayer from the public schools and then legalized abortion. Couples began living together without marriage, and homosexuality gained public acceptance. From our universities came humanism, liberalism and hedonism.

America was rocked with the assassination of John F. Kennedy, the one in whom many youth had put their dreams. A few years later, his brother Bobby Kennedy was gunned down. Then Martin Luther King, Jr. was assassinated. The dreams of many young people were dashed, and they began demonstrating against the "establishment." There were deadly riots against Vietnam and deadly riots after the assassination of Martin Luther King, Jr. Young people wanted America to get out of Vietnam. African-Americans wanted "freedom now." Out of these demonstrations grew a counterculture that was personified as the hippie movement.

Young people rebelled against the war into which they were drafted and shipped to Vietnam, a place they hated. Many other young people took refuge on the beaches of California. Others fled to Canada. The new youth culture became wedded to a non-traditional value system that was unknown to their parents. Hippies gave themselves to promiscuity and illicit drugs, and they wanted to live free. They became anti-materialistic, anti-education, antisocial, anti-business and, of course, anti-Christian.

Many young people sought answers in ancient or Eastern religions, even searching out modified versions of the occult. Eastern mysticism prevailed, spread abroad by the Beatles. Paul Baker, a news reporter, said of this generation:

> When it came to spiritual values, the young people were more disillusioned than ever. Their motto "In God We Trust" seemed to them not a creed, but a mockery. The youth were convinced that there must be a better way to do things.[1]

The hippie movement captured the attention of the world in 1969 at the famous Woodstock Musical Festival in upper New York State. There 32 musical acts performed over the course of four days, including some of the best-known groups in the nation: Sweetwater; Arlo Guthrie; Joan Baez; Santana; The Grateful Dead; Creedence Clearwater Revival; Janice Joplin; The Who; Jefferson Airplane; Joe Cocker; Blood, Sweat and Tears; Crosby, Stills, Nash and Young; and Jimi Hendrix. What did we know about Woodstock? The attenders were determined to change America, and they were committed to their own value system—not the one that had previously controlled America.

It seemed as if Christian leaders didn't know what to do with the youth rebellion. Norman Vincent Peale, known as a positive thinker, had this to say:

> For years we watched a spiritual vacuum growing in our young people. All the signs were there: dissatisfaction with a material-istic and affluent society, impatience with old forms of worship, a groping for fulfillment—first in rock music, then in various kinds of mysticism, finally in drugs. . . . We saw all this happen-ing. But did we reach out eagerly and offer the seekers a solution they could accept—in terms they could understand? I'm afraid many didn't.[2]

At the end of World War II, two vastly different and opposing cul-tures emerged in the United States between parents and their children. The parents represented a generation who had fought the greatest war in history and were victorious. They wanted to settle in to enjoy the fruits of their victory. Their children were called "Baby Boomers," a title given them by *Life* magazine. After V-J (Victory in Japan) Day in August 1945,

Johnnie came marching home. Nine months later, there were more babies born in the U.S. than any other month in the history of the United States. *Life* displayed a full-page photograph of a hospital nursery full of babies, with a nurse in her white cap holding twin babies. The caption under the photo said "*BABY BOOM.*" The name stuck.

It was the golden age of prosperity in the United States, and the parents had it all. Their young had not fought against evil and had not won any battles. They rebelled against the hypocrisy they saw in churches, and in business, and in the churches. They were disillusioned with the United States. Woodstock was a sociological rebellion against the American way of life, and the young found strength in the masses that agreed with them.

Television accentuated their new frenzy. The young were called the Pepsi Generation because Pepsi realized the money that could be made off them. Quickly, more advertisers catered to them. Their parents gave them a vast amount of money, and most advertisements focused on getting it. Older Americans were motivated to think young. . . buy young. . . wear young. . . act young. . . drive young . . . and do whatever "young" was. The young moved into the driver's seat and became intoxicated with their power. Quickly, America became a nation ruled from the bottom—by kids.

They became the "we" generation. They focused on themselves and their friends, but not their families, their churches and their pending obligations. So the young protested with "Youth Power." Drugs were a way of escape. Because Dad—and, many times, Mom—worked, they became latchkey kids, which led to dysfunctional families.

It is said that these young people became a narcissistic generation. Boomers fell in love with themselves, just like the Greek mythological Narcissus, who saw himself in a pool and fell so in love with himself that he could not love anyone else. The result was extreme individualism. The young lived for themselves and not for their families, or for love of their country, or for love of the church, or even for love of Christ. They felt that society was not freeing them but shackling them, so they rebelled. Someone said that the youth "did not want to be a part of a society that was corrupt, materialistic, repressive, closed, and fatalistic." The young people loved their rock and roll, and the more adults hated their music, the better they loved it. Adults rejected the hip-shaking Elvis Presley and long-haired hippy Beatles, so the young embraced them.

There were no heroes in Vietnam; it was a war into which the young were drafted to fight, but which they hated. They fought in the streets of America—marching, protesting, occupying the personal offices of the powerful, and burning down their symbols of hatred. Their heroes were Abby Hoffman, Tom Hayden and the Black Panthers.

Out of that counterculture arose Calvary Chapel, a church that rebelled against the traditional church, just as the youth had done. For the most part, the traditional church was weak and worldly, and Chuck Smith's ambition was to let the traditional church die. The rebels joined him and left traditional Christianity. When the young people heard about the hypocrisies of those who called themselves Christians, they rejected Christianity—some of them with justification. Many of the churches were guilty of hypocrisies, pomp and sin, and these churches deserved the condemnation that was hurled at them by the hippies.

But the young people who rejected the American church would have liked its founder, Jesus Christ. He was as anti-bureaucratic as they were. So was Chuck Smith. Jesus condemned religious shams of His day, as did the young and Chuck Smith. Jesus was anti-bureaucratic both in teaching and His lifestyle. In a real sense, Jesus was revolutionary, and Chuck Smith made them fall in love with a revolutionary Jesus.

A continuing problem is that most churches that grew from a "Jesus revolution" usually went through an inevitable cycle within 100 years . . . just as dead Judaism did in the day of Jesus. As one generation of churches die—just as the generation did before them—so young people of the future will rebel against the church of the past. They will create a new rebellious church that eventually becomes a traditional church, and it too will die. The streets of Southern California were littered with the half-filled replicas of dying traditional churches, but Chuck Smith built a new vibrant church called Calvary Chapel.

Jesus People Burst on the Scene

Chuck Smith was the pastor of a Pentecostal church in Costa Mesa, California, during the mid-1960s. One afternoon, he took his wife out for coffee on the Palisades overlooking Huntington Beach in southern California. Sitting by a large picture window, they could see a multitude of young people stretched out on the beach for miles in each direction—Baby Boomers soaking up the sun and enjoying the water. It looked like 3,000 people—the size of the crowd on the day of Pentecost.

Smith's wife said to him, "Why don't you go down there and preach Jesus to them?"

"You don't do that," Smith told her, and then promptly forgot about her suggestion. But that evening, as he was praying before going to bed, Smith heard the Holy Spirit say to him, "Why don't you go down there and preach Jesus to them?"

Again, he put the idea out of his head. Nothing happened until he began praying the next morning. Then, he again heard the Holy Spirit say, "Why don't you go down there and preach Jesus to them?"

That afternoon, Chuck Smith took off his suit, tie and white shirt, and with a golf shirt, khakis and tennis shoes, he took his Bible to the beach and found a group of about 20 kids sitting together. He preached Jesus to them. After about an hour someone said, "Here is water; can we be baptized?"

Smith took off his shoes, waded into the Pacific, and began to baptize young believers. Suddenly, curious young people came running from all directions. Smith preached Jesus to them, and the youth revival that is called Calvary Chapel began. That day, more than 200 young people professed Jesus Christ and were baptized. The next day, the same thing happened again.

Smith invited them to his church in Costa Mesa, and on Sunday morning "Jesus People" showed up with long, bleached hair and jeans. The girls wore unapologetically simple attire. They seemed out of place with the traditional Pentecostal Christians who were dressed in their Sunday-go-to-meeting clothes. For a while the Sunday morning worship remained the same, but during the nights a number of "Jesus Worshipers" came to Calvary Chapel to sing their newly composed songs for three to four hours. They prayed and devoted themselves to serious Bible study.

Calvary Chapel grew under Smith's preaching. Soon the church had to erect a tent to hold meetings while a new building was constructed. Many of the Jesus People were now writing their own music and singing with guitars, following after the influence of the folk music of the day; i.e., Peter, Paul, and Mary; Janice Joplin; and others. Out of their music came Christian rock concerts, which were held in sports arenas, just like the world. Maranatha Music was eventually formed to publish and promote the music. Soon, music from Calvary Chapel was spread to Christian bookstores across the nation.

Two young people in the church, Lonnie Frisbee and his wife, Connie, met John Higgins, who had a Bible study for the young people. They introduced the Frisbees to Chuck Smith. These young people began a Christian commune movement called "The House of Mercy." Eventually, there were at least 35 such homes in Orange County, each with 12 or more converted hippies. The news of the Jesus People spread across America when *TIME* magazine covered the story. It included a picture of Chuck Smith baptizing a new convert in the Pacific Ocean, the young boy's long blond hair splashing in the surf. In 1969, *TIME*'s person of the year was "the young single adult."

In 1967, I wrote a cover story on the Jesus People for *Christian Life* magazine, because I was the Sunday school editor/writer. I met six or seven hippies at a picnic table high on the Palisades of Huntington Beach, California, and interviewed them for more than an hour. All had blue chiffon robes and flip-flops. They spent their days witnessing to people on the beach, or they would go out to the intersection of two main streets where there was a four-way stop sign. They passed out gospel tracts or threw them into the cars through the windows of those who stopped briefly (there was no air-conditioning in the cars in those days, so people drove with their windows open).

I probed their lifestyle. They told me of living in a large old beach home, carefully reminding me the boys lived in separate rooms from the girls. There was no water or lights in the house, so they bathed at public shower rooms, and each evening they sang gospel songs, prayed and had Bible study until the sun went down. For food, they witnessed to restaurant owners on the beach and ate when given food. If they were not given food, they fasted. When I asked them how they made money, they asked, "Why do we need money?" This reflected an utter rejection of the American way of life, and their wholehearted devotion to their newfound challenge in Jesus Christ.

It was a simple life of loving Jesus, following Jesus, praying to Jesus, and getting up the next day to do the same thing again. They did not live for tomorrow, for jobs or for houses, nor were they controlled by the restraints of their past. Most of them melted into the youth culture of the day and influenced the American way of life, as it in turn influenced them.

By the early 1970s, Calvary Chapels began to appear across California and the West. There were several musical groups from Calvary Chapel that represented the Jesus People Movement. These groups went from church to church, singing and holding "rock concerts."

In 1982, a break occurred in Calvary Chapel between Chuck Smith and John Wimber. Wimber, a Calvary Chapel pastor, had been putting more emphasis on spiritual manifestations; i.e., evidences of Pentecostalism in his meetings. At the same time, Chuck Smith was moving away from the outward signs of Pentecostalism. So the two decided to split. Wimber formed a network of churches that was called the Association of Vineyard Churches.

Chuck Smith

Charles Ward (Chuck) Smith was born in Ventura, California, in 1927. He graduated from LIFE Bible College and was ordained in the Church of the Foursquare. He was pastoring a pre-existing church called Calvary

Chapel in Costa Mesa, California, when the great hippie revival broke out and the church began to grow exponentially.

Smith had been senior pastor of Calvary Chapel since 1965. That church and its name became the foundation of the Calvary Chapel movement, which now had more than 1,200 churches across the United States and many more worldwide. Today, some of the Calvary Chapel congregations are among the largest churches in the United States. Individual Calvary Chapels do not report their membership to Costa Mesa; therefore, the total number of people attending Calvary Chapel churches is not known. However, it's fair to say the association influences millions.[3]

Outreach Magazine, which publishes the 100 largest churches in America, lists Costa Mesa as having 9,500 members, making it the thirty-ninth largest church in America.[4] Smith has been called "the most influential Christian pastor in Southern California."[5]

Preaching and the Church

Chuck Smith began a new form of preaching among the Calvary Chapel churches. He preferred expositional sermons to topical, devotional or evangelistic ones. Smith began at Genesis 1:1 and preached verse by verse, chapter by chapter, and book by book from the beginning to the end of the Bible.

There are many advantages to this type of preaching. Parishioners learn the Bible first, and as issues come up, they are related to biblical backgrounds. Also, it keeps the pastor from emphasizing a certain type of sermon or a certain topic. Calvary Chapel pastors naturally cover what appears next in the Scriptures. But there's a third reason: expositional preaching tends to bring the saints to maturity, which is the focus of the Calvary Chapel movement. Therefore, many of them have said, "God sets the agenda in our churches, not the pastor or the denomination."[6]

The Calvary Chapel movement does not employ one of the three traditional forms of ecclesiastical government; i.e., congregational (Baptist), representative (Presbyterian), or episcopal (Methodist). Rather, they use what is called a "Moses Model." Under this system, God is the head of the people and, as Moses was God's leader of the people, so the pastor of a Calvary Chapel is leader of the people. Moses also had a priesthood praying for the people and delivering God's message, but he had 70 elders to support his leadership. The Calvary Chapel movement believes their pastors have a Moses-like leadership, and their board of elders supports that ministry.

Each Calvary Chapel is independent, self-governing and not controlled by the Calvary Chapel Association. They allow churches to fellowship with other churches of the movement, but not control one another. The word "fellowship" means that a church can choose to come and fellowship or to not fellowship. Those who don't fellowship are dropped from the fellowship.

Strengths and Weaknesses

There are several strengths of a church of the young that acculturated its revolutionary lifestyle and values into church, life and ministry. Technically, every time one generation passes onto the scene, a new generation brings its strengths and values into the church. So, the first strength is that the Calvary Chapel movement reflected pure Christianity. It stripped off the traditional facades and got rid of programs that were outdated and perhaps no longer worked.

There were "barnacles" attached to worship services that represented a day long passed. Calvary Chapel began with a clean slate and created churches that were reflective of true biblical Christianity. However, these churches were driven by the lifestyle and values of the youth who inhabited their pews and led their services. They brought their new music and cast out the old. They came dressed casually as they worked and played—it was their simple approach to God. Because they were children of rock concerts, they initiated Christian rock concerts. Because they were a visual generation, they introduced drama. Announcements were made through PowerPoint presentations. Calvary Chapel ushered in a new day and worshiped in a new way, but all for the same eternal biblical purposes.

Another way of expressing their strength was drinking wine out of "new wineskins." It was a new method that came out of the lifestyle of the young people who were influenced by Jesus Christ. Preaching was no longer devotional, as by a three-point sermon. Rather, the preaching of Chuck Smith set a new standard for Bible exposition, verse by verse, chapter by chapter, book by book, covering the whole Bible from Genesis to Revelation.

But there were some weaknesses in the new, as there always are with new things. Sometimes the broom that sweeps the old closet clean stirs up unintended consequences when it does away with that which is necessary. First, they got rid of programs that were necessary for traditional churches—programs an older generation considered biblical. There were reasons why the traditional church had the programs they did, and the organization they used, as well as they buildings they built. The embryonic strengths of the past were swept away with the new broom, and with it went away old loyalties.

There is a second problem: unintended financial consequences. When young people begin a church from scratch, they operate within the boundaries of the money they have. There is nothing wrong with this, but when the young take over a traditional church and try to infuse it with Christian rock, new styles of worship and new expressions of love to Jesus Christ, what about the old traditional Christians in these churches? They fought a losing battle and left, taking their pocketbooks with them.

Years ago, I wrote a book called *Putting an End to Worship Wars*.[7] This book described churches in which the young people took over. The elderly (with money) left, and the church survived for a while. But, in some cases, it faced bankruptcy. That leads to a fourth implied problem. On many occasions, the new youth-driven church has been oblivious to the needs of the elderly traditional Christians. Perhaps it is retaliation for the past, when the elderly were oblivious to needs of the young. Just as the young left the church when their needs were not addressed, so the elderly are walking out of churches when they lose control.

Wrap Up

When you look at the Calvary Chapel movement, you find large megachurches tend to dominate it. When the disciples of Chuck Smith went out to plant churches, they never intended to plant a small, traditional single-celled church. They envisioned a large church filled with young people. They planned to plant a megachurch, and everything they did was focused on being a huge congregation that would reach a huge amount of people for Christ. They planned big, acted big and prayed big, and as a result, they grew big churches. But they also had a big influence on the rest of Christianity.

Their Baby Boomer churches influenced normal American churches. Then normal American Baby Boomers influenced traditional American churches. When the American culture began to change, the American churches eventually changed. Calvary Chapels and the "hippies" who had been converted under the ministry of Chuck Smith were probably one of the first churches to be acculturated by the changes in the American lifestyle.

Hillsong Church
Sydney, Australia*

Brian Houston
Founder, Senior Pastor

Darlene Zschech
Pastor, Hope Unlimited Church*

9

Initiating Praise-Worship in Worship Services

Hillsong Church
Sydney, Australia

Christian music has evolved from generation to generation. Christians express their worship of God and testimony to others through the music of their culture. Sometimes Christian music has molded secular culture, while at other times culture has influenced the way Christians sing. There was an obvious change in Christian music during the last part of the twentieth century, when Christians began singing to God in a personal and intimate way. Believers had always sung to God corporately in the church, which could be characterized as praise and adoration. But in this latest revolution, many in Christianity began singing personal worship to God; i.e., praise-worship music.

Hillsong Church in Sydney, Australia, may not be the first to use contemporary praise-worship music, but the church pioneered the movement in Australia and took the lead in teaching the church to worship the Lord through it. Darlene Zschech became the implied leader of this movement with her song "Shout to the Lord." The historian Kenneth Scott Latourette wrote that one of the obvious characteristics of a biblical revival was when the lay people began singing their new Christian expressions in the cultural music of the people.[1] The growth of a new hymnology suggests there is an implied revival in many churches as revealed by praise-worship music, or a revival that grew out of this new music.

*Photo from historical sources found on the Internet.
*Wikipedia, The Free Encyclopedia http://creativecommons.org/licenses/by-sa/3.0/

O ne of the most obvious trends to emerge in the last 100 years in the evangelical church service has been the sweeping change to praise-worship music during Sunday morning services. Traditionally, American churches have used an organ, piano and a robed choir for worship, and maybe included a vocal soloist. If groups were added, it was usually a trio or quartet. However, a praise-worship format has taken center stage in our churches, and with it has come worship teams that usually include vocals, electronic guitars, keyboards and drums. Not only is praise-worship music sung to a different pulsating rhythm, but there has also been an abundant cascade of new music written that has spread through churches in America and abroad.

Recently, I asked a class of 54 doctoral students at Liberty Baptist Theological Seminary what individual church is responsible for the tidal wave of praise-worship music. Without batting an eye, and to a student, they all agreed that it was Hillsong Church in Sydney, Australia, with Darlene Zschech and her song, "Shout to the Lord."[2] Thus, the symbolic church representing this movement is Hillsong Church. However, an earlier pioneer was Jack Hayford, pastor of The Church On The Way in Van Nuys, California, and his symbolic song "Worship His Majesty," written in 1981.[3]

Some trace the rise of this type of Christian music to the early 1960s and the Jesus People Movement, primarily in California. They had two sounds. First, their "Jesus rock and roll" was slanted toward evangelism and/or entertainment. Their second sound had a mellower beat that incorporated worship and was more a reflection of folk music and/or the feel of a prayer meeting.

Perhaps the original source of praise-worship music came out of Calvary Chapel in Costa Mesa, California, and Pastor Chuck Smith. I attended a Sunday night service in 1968 and noted that these Jesus People liked to sit on the floor, as close to the platform as they could get. Most of these Jesus hippies had long blond hair and were wearing ragged jeans and T-shirts. Many were runaway teenagers from the Midwest. Chuck Smith set up a number of communal houses (men living with men and women living with women), and out of these houses came a new music they composed and sang. Then, Mike MacIntosh, one of the converts, began making records and selling them to bookstores under the title Maranatha Music. The records flew off the shelves.[4]

Throughout these communes, young people were humming and singing new songs to express their love to Jesus Christ. They didn't sing about God or their new devotion to God; they sang to Jesus Christ who saved them. Their new songs were not a reflection of traditional

Christian hymnody; they sounded more like a Pepsi-Cola commercial and the rhythm or beat they heard on the radio.

In the 1970s, Hiley Ward, religious editor for the *Detroit Free Press*, took a nationwide tour of Jesus People communes and observed that they were singing a "new music."[5] He might have been the first national observer to call attention to the rise of praise-worship music. He wrote, "Rarely do you hear any of the old-time hymns. They write their own."[6]

The one song that personified the movement was "Shout to the Lord." Contestants sang it on the popular television show *American Idol*. On April 9, 2008, eight contestants sang it for the closing song, but changed the name "Jesus" to "Shepherd." There was such an outcry from the public that during the next show they sang it again—but this time including the word "Jesus." The chorus has been charted #43 on the Billboard Hot 100, based on digital download sales alone. This song established Darlene Zschech as the influential leader of the movement. The lyrics are as follows:

> *My Jesus, my Savior*
> *Lord, there is none like You*
> *All of my days, I want to praise*
> *The wonders of Your mighty love*
> *My comfort, my shelter*
> *Tower of refuge and strength*
> *Let every breath, all that I am*
> *Never cease to worship You*
> *Shout to the Lord, all the earth, let us sing*
> *Power and majesty, praise to the King*
> *Mountains bow down and the seas will roar*
> *At the sound of Your name*
> *I sing for joy at the work of Your hands*
> *Forever I'll love You, forever I'll stand*
> *Nothing compares to the promise I have in You*
> *I sing for joy at the work of Your hands*
> *Forever I'll love You, forever I'll stand*
> *Nothing compares to the promise I have in You*
> *Nothing compares to the promise I have in You*
> *Nothing compares to the promise I have in You*[7]

The worship leaders at Hillsong—Geoff Bullock, Russell Fargar, Reuben Morgan and internationally known Darlene Zschech—contributed and/or produced other praise-worship music that was life-changing and church-lifting, such as "Worthy Is the Lamb," "Lord I Give You

My Heart," "Holy Spirit Rain Down" and "The Potter's Hands." These became standard repertoire for worship in churches around the world.

Today, Zschech is known all over the world as a singer, worship leader and composer of new praise music. To that she has added the ministry of speaking and writing books. In the beginning, she was involved with Hillsong Church in Sydney, Australia, and from that platform she achieved several gold albums. Her songs have been sung in several nations in many different languages.

Eventually, Darlene and her husband, Mark, became senior pastors of Hope Unlimited Church on the central coast of New South Wales, Australia. However, she still returns to Hillsong for special music events and conferences, and she extends her ministry through Hillsong.[8] But it wasn't just her great music that came out of Australia. Darlene Zschech has become passionate about training worship leaders and teens to go to other nations to lead in a revival of praise-worship music ministry.

Some may think praise-worship music is a Pentecostal or Charismatic phenomenon, but that is not the case. It's used in denominational and interdenominational churches as well as in traditional mainline churches such as Presbyterian and Methodist. It is even finding its way into Episcopal and Roman Catholic churches.

Hillsong Church

Hillsong Church is a world-class Pentecostal megachurch located in Sydney, New South Wales, Australia, with more than 35,000 worshipers in attendance each week. It is part of the Australian Christian Churches movement (ACC). Brian and Bobbi Houston began the church in 1983 as Hills Christian Life Center in Baulkham Hill, which they later merged with Sydney Christian Life Center to become Hillsong.

Hillsong is a multisite church with ten locations around the metropolitan area of Sydney, Brisbane and Melbourne. The latest site was located in Melbourne, Victoria. In addition to the sites, Hillsong has 9 "extension services" across Sydney that rely on Hillsong as the source for their worship and/or music. They have offshoots in London, England; the Ukraine; Cape Town and Pretoria, South Africa; Stockholm, Sweden; Paris, France; Amsterdam, the Netherlands; Moscow, Russia; Copenhagen, Konstanz, Germany, Barcelona, Los Angeles and New York City.

The initial congregation in 1983 consisted of 45 people, and services were held in a warehouse. In 1994, the church moved to "The Hills Center." Then, in 1997, it moved into its new building at Baulkham Hills, Northwest Business Park. The church leaders realized the name

"Hillsong" was better known than Hills Christian Center, so they changed the name in 1999. John Howard, the Prime Minister of Australia, opened the church's new convention center on October 19, 2002.

The Church On The Way

Before Hillsong, Jack Hayford, pastor of The Church On The Way in Van Nuys, California, prophesied that there would be a coming worship revolution. He noted that the Protestant Reformation led by Martin Luther in Germany transformed the church's theology back to the New Testament. But Hayford saw coming a new and greater reformation in music that would transform the church's worship.

Jack Hayford is the author of more than 50 books and nearly 600 gospel songs. He emphasized issues of the heart more than the rhythm, beat or methodology. When asked why his approach to worship was so effective, Hayford said, "Worship changes the worshiper into the image of the One worshiped."[9]

To Hayford, worship is a pursuit of God's presence, not simply an exercise in praiseful song. He said, "We pursue the pathway of worship *unto* God as intended to arrive at *meeting* Him; not only introductorily or ceremonially, but we seek *Him*—personally, to encounter His presence as we exalt His Person." Hayford notes that the heart and quest David reveals in the psalms he wrote are filled with the call and the reward of earnest, worshipful "seeking" (see, e.g., Ps. 24:3-6; 27:4-8; 40:16; 63:1-4; 69:30-32; 70:4). "Moreover," Hayford noted, "the Psalms *are* the Bible's 'song book of *and on* worship!'—a veritable handbook on the 'hows and whys' of worship."[10]

In addition to his compositions, Hayford's writings on worship have spread globally: *The Reward of Worship, Worship His Majesty* and *The Heart of Praise* evidence his biblical theology and sense of passion concerning "the Church at worship."[11] In writing about his approach to worship, he said:

> Worship is intended as an *encounter,* not merely an exercise. Psalm 115 describes the potential of worship to *transform* a person; to turn their focus for the spirit of the world and open to the Spirit of God. Music is a great gift, and powerful as a means of worship, but "music" and "worship" are not the same things: music may provide the *means,* but its purpose is to lead us into a *meeting* with the Lord Himself.[12]

Hayford saw praise and worship as a foundational key to evangelism, "opening hearts to hear and receive God's Word, drawing believers unto transformation and unbelievers unto a decision for Christ." He describes worship as "the priority that *leads* the way" and attests to "worship welcoming and opening [people] to God's presence" and preaching/teaching as "finding more ready receptivity and fruitfulness because the Holy Spirit, through worship, has prepared the people to *respond to God, not simply to the preacher.*" Hayford attributed the constant stream of decisions for Christ and the resulting growth of the church to the fact that God drew near to them as they drew near to Him. He notes, "We lived in an atmosphere where people constantly sense, '*God is in the house!*'"[13] Accordingly, he adds:

> Worship is a transcendent priority—we will never sacrifice worship on the altar of conventionality or convenience. We will be [unhesitatingly] joyful, refreshing, and unashamed in our worship. Yet, we'll also be tender and healing in our expressions. In being worshipers, we have nothing to prove, yet everything to give to God who has given us so much.[14]

Hayford states that Martin Luther didn't bring his new theology into his new Lutheran church but inserted the old worship of the Roman Catholic Church into it. The original Lutherans believed the new theology of Reformation but worshiped with the old liturgy, perhaps stunting any numerical growth in evangelism. However, Hayford saw that praise-worship music could grow a church exponentially and actually explode its influence and outreach throughout the neighborhood and the world.

Technically, Jack Hayford became pastor of the church in 1969 when there were only 18 members. At the time, the church met in a small wooden building on Sherman Way in the Los Angeles suburb of Van Nuys. It was called the Van Nuys Foursquare Church. Hayford changed the name to The Church On The Way because it was located on Sherman Way and because he wanted a name that would identify with Jesus, who called Himself "the Way" (see Acts 9:2; 19:23; 24:14). He also wanted a name that would let people know there's only one way to Jesus. The ministry of "worship and the Word"—i.e., "in spirit and truth" (John 4:24)— nurtured a growth in the church to more than 10,000 constituents (6,500 average weekly attendance) before Hayford transferred the lead pastoral role to his principle associate in order to found The King's College and Seminary (now The King's University—central campus at Gateway Church in Dallas).

Jack Hayford had been teaching at Life Bible College in Los Angeles and had been the national youth director of the Foursquare Church.

He admits that he had been "promotion-oriented" when he came to the church outreach. But when Hayford came to The Church On The Way, he decided not to use any high-pressure promotion, contests or guilt to get the people to serve the Lord. He decided, "The Church On The Way would be a happy place, but not a sensational place. Our growth will be with biblical substance and Spirit-filled worship."[15]

In 1977, Hayford and his wife, Anna, took a vacation to England and rented a small car to tour the countryside. He writes:

> On a side trip we made into Oxfordshire, an elusive sense of "the grand, the regal and the noble" came by surprise, and included a lesson I hadn't expected and resulted in a song I hadn't sought. . . .
>
> Blenheim Palace is the massive estate built at Queen Anne's orders in the early eighteenth century. She presented it to John Churchill, the first duke of Marlborough, in honor of his leadership in the military victories against Spain. Two centuries later, Winston Churchill would be born and raised here, frequently retiring to this site for rest from the rigors of leadership during World War II. It was at Blenheim that many of his stirring speeches were written, speeches that successfully inspired the English people to sustain their efforts at staving off Hitler's Luftwaffe. . . .
>
> After we passed outside and surveyed the sprawling grounds so meticulously groomed and magnificently flowered, the undefined "feel" now surfaced and blossomed into a clear, complete thought. While overlooking the palace and grounds from the southwest and contemplating Churchill's former presence on the paths and fields, I mused aloud: "Being raised in such an environment would certainly make it far more credible for a person to conceive of himself as a person of destiny."
>
> Then a second thought exploded: this is the essence of the relationship Jesus wants us to have with His church! He wants the fullness of His power, the richness of His nature, the authority of His office and the wealth of His resources to ennoble our identity and determine our destiny! Notwithstanding the deep emotion filling my soul, a holy calm and genuine joy possessed me.
>
> "Honey," [I said to my wife], "I can hardly describe to you all the things which this setting evokes in me. There is something of a *majesty* in all this, and I believe it has a great deal to do with

why people who lived here have been of such consequence in the shaping of history."

As we continued our walk, I spoke further of my concerns, with which she agreed. She felt, as I did, a pastoral longing for people to understand the fullness of Jesus, to perceive His high destiny for each of them; to see that our self-realization only comes through a real-realization of Him! How completely and unselfishly He invites us to partnership with Him in His Kingdom. How much of His Kingdom authority He wants to transmit to and through us as a flow of His life, love and healing to a hopeless and hurting world.

Now something expanding and deepening that understanding was welling up within me.

Majesty.

The word was crisp in my mind.

Majesty, I thought. It's the quality of Christ's royalty and Kingdom glory that not only displays His excellence, but which lifts us by His sheer grace and power, allowing us to identify with and share in His wonder.

As Queen Elizabeth's throne somehow dignifies every Englishman and makes multitudes of others partakers in a commonwealth of royal heritage, our ascended Savior sits enthroned and offers His regal resources to each of us.

Majesty.

"Let's go, Honey," I said, and we started for the car. My soul was still resonating to the sound of a distant chord struck in heaven. . . . As Anna and I drove along the narrow highway, I said to her, "Take the notebook and write down some words, will you, babe?" I began to dictate the key, the musical notes, the time value of each and the lyrics (and she still insists that *she* wrote the song!):

Majesty, worship His Majesty!
Unto Jesus be all glory, honor and praise.
Majesty, Kingdom authority,
Flows from His Throne, unto His own,
His anthem raise.
So exalt, lift up on high the Name of Jesus.
Magnify, come glorify, Christ Jesus the King.
Majesty, worship His Majesty.
Jesus who died, now glorified,
King of all kings.[16]

Worship for the Nonbeliever

Originally, Hayford thought that worship was only for believers, but slowly God began to change his thinking. When he saw commands that called for the unsaved to praise God, he began to look at worship differently: "Make a joyful noise unto the Lord, all ye lands" (Ps. 100:1, *KJV*). Therefore, when the unchurched enters a worship service, he wants them to participate with believers in meeting God and exalting God.

Hayford does not apologize for asking unsaved people to sing praise-worship music. As a matter of fact, he sees worship not only as a celebration or exaltation but also as an invitation to God's "manifest presence" in the services; that is, a sense of certainty that rises collectively—a knowing that God is in the house! This exceeds emotion—and where worshipers are simply yet sensitively led from the earlier celebrative tempo to a slower more pensive tempo, the mood moves from a bright exaltation of the Lord to a tender welcome of His presence and touch. This is *not* a matter of attempting to manipulate emotions. Rather, it is something of a spiritual "take your shoes off, Moses" approach, as the congregation is led to "stand on holy ground," worshiping with a more seeking and sober (not somber) sense of sincerely seeking a person-to-person meeting with God.

As a result, The Church On The Way grew steadily without evangelistic crusades, visitation programs or other strategies commonly employed by churches for outreach. Hayford used virtually no advertising or marketing, but simply used the in-house communications of the congregation to clarify objectives of forthcoming events and to capacitate the congregation to communicate to friends, neighbors and associates as they chose. Others exhibited care and personal warmth. Hayford's pastoral conviction was that when God is magnified and His *presence* is regularly verified among the people, the people of the congregation—knowing the beauty and order their visiting friends will experience—will be self-verifying; an experience virtually all will perceive and enjoy, and to which many will become open to God's Word and be born again.

Hayford says we should not return to traditional liturgy, because that is mostly dead and does not express the heart of believers, nor does it attract the unsaved. Rather, Hayford says we must "refine, unwrap, and unseal" worship and return it to its original power and outreach. By "redefining" worship, we must do more than praise and adore God; we must create an intimacy between the worshiper and God Himself.

By using the word "unwrapping," Hayford said that when people lift their heads and hands to God, they must no longer think of it as a sign of a Charismatic church. Rather, it is a way of lifting our hearts to

God. By using the word "unsealing," Hayford said that "worship is an expression of the whole person who is offering 'worthy worship' because God deserves to be worshiped. It's not about what the worshiper gets out of the service; it's what God get out of our worship."[17]

Hayford refers to the Old Testament sacrifice as the act of worship. He points out that sacrifice cost the animal its life, and so our worship must include the offering of our life to Jesus Christ. He goes on to say, "As much as we want beauty and as beautiful as worship may be, again beauty is always secondary—life precedes loveliness."[18]

During the 1990s, whenever I was in greater Los Angeles for the weekend, I always attended Jack Hayford's worship service. I felt the Lord was there, and my heart was lifted by the service to a new intimate relationship with the Lord. Just as God works His power in a sermon in a greater way when a man of God is completely yielded to Him, so God uses worship in a more powerful way when the worship leader is completely committed to God. When Jack Hayford stepped into the pulpit to lead worship, there was a new spark that hadn't been felt in the service.

So, what did Hayford do that made such a difference? Hayford was not there to lead people in singing, or even lead them in praising. Hayford went into the pulpit to worship God for himself while being supported by the worship team, who were discipled with the common convictions expressed there. Hayford said, "As we worship, the congregation is led in more than song—they detect the fact that the worship team is neither 'performing' nor 'simply leading in music.'"

Hayford adds, "More—far more than 'doing worship'—they, with the pastor, are 'igniting worship' with a holy fire brought from their own rehearsals; geared to unite with the congregation; leading so as to bid the whole assembly, to come to a higher level. . . into the Courts of God's Kingdom realm; to bow hearts and mind before Him—opening to His peace, His purposes and His gracious power."[19]

One Sunday when I was there, Hayford told the audience, "Turn to the person next to you and say, 'You'll love this worship service—you'll meet God in a new way.'" I did love the service, and I did meet God in a new way.

Quite often on Saturday night, when Jack Hayford was praying and preparing his sermon, God gave him a new song. He wrote out the music and words, and then on Sunday morning he announced, "This is one of those mornings when we must learn a new song."[20] Then he proceeded to teach it line by line, and the audience sang along with him in praise to God. I loved it, because the new music he wrote usually focused on the sermon he was about to preach.

Jack Hayford did not use the traditional choir to lead in worship, although he did have a choir as part of his church life. He answered why: "First, we are not a platform-oriented church. We are people-oriented and the Bible commands 'sing unto yourselves.' So we do not have the choir sing to us and do our worship for us."[21]

Strengths and Weaknesses

There are many reasons why praise-worship music is sweeping the country. The first is because people are doing something they've never done: they're worshiping God. Perhaps there's been a vacuum of worship. Howard Hendricks, former teacher at Dallas Theological Seminary, called worship "the lost chord of Christianity."[22] He often mentioned that worship was something that evangelical churches didn't understand. Therefore, these new worship songs opened up the experience of worship, even ushering God's presence into the worship experiences.

Second, there's a great use of Scripture in the modern praise-worship songs. Whereas historically churches have used devotional literature in singing praise to God, today much of the praise-worship music is Scripture put to rhythm, melody and chords. The Bible amplifies the need for worship, and Scripture is the best expression of the worshiper's heart to God.

Third, the new praise-worship music is easy to sing, because people understand its rhythm and beat. There's an assumption that says, "People will sing music for the rest of their lives that they learn when they go through puberty, (i.e., early teens)." Why is that? Because when young people go through puberty, they are establishing their core values, attitudes and outlook on life. Therefore, young people who previously listened to and sang contemporary music will now express their values and attitudes to God in contemporary praise-worship music.

Fourth, we must not forget that a strength of praise-worship music is the Holy Spirit Himself. Yes, there is a human worship leader up front, a worship team, and a worship band, but the Holy Spirit is doing a new work in the church today. In Acts 15, God promised, "After this I will return and will rebuild the tabernacle of David, which has fallen down" (Acts 15:16). David didn't have a tabernacle like Moses had in the wilderness. The tabernacle of Moses, Joshua and the succeeding generations was a place of sacrifice and forgiveness of sins. However, when David brought the Ark of the Covenant into Jerusalem, he put it on Mount Zion next to his home (the tabernacle for sacrificial offerings was not in Jerusalem at the time, but in the Valley of Aijalon).

In Psalm 134:1-2, the psalmist describes the people of Israel, who were worshiping in a similar manner to contemporary praise-worship services: "Stand in the house of the LORD! Lift up your hands in the sanctuary, and bless the LORD." That refers to the way Israel worshiped during the time of David and is a reflection of today's praise-worship music. It seems as the day of Christ approaches, and the end times also are near, the Holy Spirit is fulfilling this prophecy by raising up new praise-worship music to bless the name of the Lord. He is raising up the tabernacle of David in our churches.

Critics have noted several weakness of the new praise-worship music. First, some feel that it is too intimate and that the language expresses a relationship with God that is not taught in Scripture. The term "you," used for God, and "I," used for the worshiper, seems to be empty and projects onto God the emotions of people. Rather, they say praise-worship music has ignored the great statements of God's sovereignty, power, omnipresence and omnipotence in nature; or the fact that we are joined to God's mercy, benevolence, long-suffering and beneficence. These qualities are usually missing in praise-worship music. Rather, God is treated as the other part of a love relationship.

Some have criticized statements in praise-worship songs such as "hungry I come to you," or, "Your love does not run dry," or, "I'm desperate for You." While the praise-worship music demonstrates a friendly, informal and personal relationship to God, some feel it goes too far in lines such as, "I will dance, I will sing, to be mad for my King." Just as secular pop and rock music features relationships and feelings as its central thrust, so praise-worship music has the same thrust and expression. Many feel that the traditional hymns carry lofty themes such as freedom in Christ, His life and death, His power and sacrifice, and His suffering and depravation. The critics claim these are not generally found in praise-worship music.

Another criticism has to do with the volume of the music that many times drowns out congregational singing. It's not that high volume is wrong, but it works against ministry to the worshipers and their corporate fellowship of worship with others. When volume overrides everything else, it tends to make music a performance rather than an act of worship to God. Many people look to Ephesians 5:19, where Paul says we should sing or speak to one another with psalms, hymns and songs of the Spirit. Notice the phrase "speak to one another." In much of contemporary praise-worship music, there is not much communication with one another.

A third criticism is that many contemporary worship songs reflect individualism, with a focus on the worshiper rather than on God. What's left out is the corporate church; i.e., the church body, which is a community. Christians do not sing together, and many times new music does not focus on building community. Christian apologist J.P. Holding states that the song "I Can Only Imagine" is an example of people's desire for fulfillment rather than focusing on the holiness of God.[23]

Another criticism is that praise-worship music opens the door for contemporary popular music to enter the church. The use of contemporary instruments is commonplace, and critics feel that praise-worship music is "worldly" music that is more associated with a secular or ungodly lifestyle.

There are also those who oppose praise-worship music because they think it comes from Pentecostal or Charismatic theology and lifestyles, which they oppose. They point out that praise-worship music contains musical expressions that are Charismatic or Pentecostal in nature, such as raising of hands, clapping, dancing or expressions used by Pentecostals or Charismatics that invite the Holy Spirit to manifest Himself.

Wrap Up

Don Koenig claims that at least 400,000 churches use praise-worship music in their church services.[24] That's a majority of American churches. If his statistics are correct, it represents a sizable slice of Christianity. So, to judge the effectiveness of praise-worship music, we need only look at worshipers using it to praise God. They weep, lift hands, shout loudly for joy, stomp their feet and dance. But most of all, the focus is on God and worshiping Him. Their churches are lively and their numbers are growing.

I spoke to 8,000 Pentecostal preachers at Playa del Mar, Argentina, in 2004. They were packed into a basketball gymnasium, and the room was "rocking" with loud trumpets from a Mariachi band. Before I went out to the platform, I interviewed the Minister of the Interior for all of Argentina. He told me the evangelical population of Argentina was a reported 18 percent of the nation. Twenty-five years earlier, it had been perhaps one percent.

I asked, "Why are so many Argentineans becoming Pentecostal?" The official threw his arms into the air and replied in broken English, "Why, man? Can't you hear them. . . they're happy." To make a point, he then asked me, "Have you ever been to a Roman Catholic Church?" I replied, "No, not lately." The government official put his hands to his face and said, "Roman Catholic churches are so sad. . . there's no life there."

He was describing the typical liturgical service. The official's eyes then lit up as he said, "Listen to the happiness!" Hispanics loved to laugh and smile. "I'd love to be a Pentecostal. . . just to be that happy."

The bottom line of the comments of this high-ranking government official is that praise-worship music is sweeping churches because through it people experience happiness and joy. Isn't that one of the things that's missing in our modern stress-filled life?

But happiness is not enough reason to adopt praise-worship music in a church. It's sweeping the church because it's focused on God and is about Jesus Christ. Christianity is not a human-centered religion; it's Christ-centered. "For me, to live is Christ" (Phil. 1:21).

Thomas Road Baptist Church
Lynchburg, Virginia*

Jerry Falwell*

10

Using Media and Marketing
to Extend the Influence
of a Church

Thomas Road Baptist Church

Lynchburg, Virginia

Thomas Road Baptist Church in Lynchburg, Virginia, used media and marketing to build one of the largest church congregations in America and the largest Christian university in the world. In the exploding era of advertising, this church first communicated its message to Lynchburg, Virginia, and then to the entire United States. Jerry Falwell planted the church in 1956 and caused it to grow with his innovative concept of *saturation evangelism*, "reaching every available person, at every available time, with every available means [methods]."[1]

Falwell organized a Sunday school strategy yet based his outreach on a heavy use of advertising to saturate his community and eventually market the gospel of Jesus Christ to all America. He built the ninth largest church in America. The dynamics of the aggressive outreach was imprinted on Liberty University, begun by Falwell in the summer of 1971. Just as the church became one of the largest in the nation, his university has now become one of the largest in the world.

In the past 100 years commercial media and marketing have exploded in the United States and around the world and have become an influence that impacted the church. The reputation of Thomas Road Baptist Church, located in the small town of Lynchburg, Virginia (population 60,000+), spread around the globe by marketing. The church became a megachurch, and then Liberty University used the marketing principles of Falwell to become the largest private Christian university in the world, with a one billion dollar yearly budget and 103,000 students enrolled in 2013.

In the last 100 years advertising has exploded in the United States, being driven by scientific discoveries and the development of expansive areas of media. Advertisers communicate their messages by radio, television, the Internet, billboards, phones, mailings, newspapers and magazines—to mention just a few means. And with that growth of media has come a growing sophistication of marketing, which includes writing advertising copy, using psychological principles of motivation, employing the latest technological presentations, and a scientific discovery of where, when and how receptive audiences can be effectively reached.

Naturally, churches got into marketing to get their message out, just as the business world used it to make sales and expand its profits. As marketing and advertising exploded in the business world to improve its bottom line, the church has ventured into this area to carry out the Great Commission and make its message heard.

The church has always used advertising, which is nothing more than publicizing its message to as many people as possible. Preachers did it verbally by preaching in the marketplace. Then the message was advertised nonverbally by constructing tall steeples on churches that pointed people to God. Also, they did it by erecting crosses high on a hill to remind people of the death of Christ. When I walked the ancient streets of the ruins of Ephesus, I saw two places where a fish symbol was carved into street stones. Just as I saw advertisements for a tavern and a house of prostitution, I saw the fish symbol. The letters of the Greek word *ichthus* stood for Jesus Christ, Son of God, and Savior. The Ephesus church was advertising Jesus.

But advertising is not the same as marketing, and marketing is not the same as media. *Advertising* simply communicates a message. *Marketing* finds potential customers through scientific research, focus groups, surveys and other means. Its aim is to determine what the customer will purchase and how much and also when, where or how to advertise. Marketing also uses advertisements to create a desire in customers for the product when they didn't previously know about or "need" the product. *Media* is the means to communicate the message to the masses.

Why Choose Jerry Falwell?

America has always had large influential churches advertising the gospel and ministry over radio, television and the Internet. These large church leaders include Aimee Semple McPherson, who was one of the pioneers who built an early megachurch, the Angelus Temple in Los Angeles, California. She purchased time on various stations across the country, and eventually her church owned its own station in the early 1920s.

S. Parks Cadman began on the radio in 1923 with a weekly broadcast on NBC radio affiliates across the nation. He had an audience of five million listeners.[2] J. Frank Norris built a radio station in First Baptist Church in Fort Worth, Texas, and his sermons were played on stations in the Southwest and Midwest.[3] The Roman Catholic Father Charles Coughlin was an anti-communist radio preacher in the 1930s and 1940s whose messages reached millions of listeners.[4] *The Lutheran Hour* (1930–present) also built loyal listeners. Charles E. Fuller went nationwide through the Mutual Broadcasting Network, and by 1951 the *Old Fashioned Revival Hour* was heard over the ABC radio network that circled the globe through 650 radio stations.[5]

On television, Rex Humbard broadcast his weekly church services from the Cathedral of Tomorrow in Akron, Ohio, beginning in 1952. He eventually reached 695 stations (radio and television) in 96 languages, and his program was said to have the largest coverage of any programs up to that time.[6] In the 1960s, when television became the center of home entertainment, a number of other "televangelists" appeared. These included Oral Roberts (135 stations), Billy Graham, Jimmy Swaggart, Jim and Tammy Faye Bakker, Pat Robertson and Robert Schuller at the Crystal Cathedral from greater Los Angeles, California.

But Jerry Falwell was chosen to represent this trend, even though some religious programs had a larger number of stations and larger viewing audience. Some were larger in offerings. Falwell and the *Old Time Gospel Hour* were not the first or the largest to use this trend, but he pioneered direct mail and built a reciprocal relationship with his faithful viewers, which he called Faith Partners. He solicited more than just requests for money; he sent out Bibles, devotional books and study books, all written by accepted evangelical writers.

Listeners identified with Falwell's various evangelistic and construction projects as he reported about his students at Liberty University and their various ministries. Television showed pictures of the students involved in humanitarian projects in Africa, South America, Thailand and in the South China Sea. The fact that his listeners remained loyal to Falwell when other ministers tanked during the late 1980s demonstrates the strength of his telecasts. Also, today those dedicated listeners to Falwell's vision are still donating finances to build the world's largest Christian university under the leadership of Jerry Falwell, Jr.

Jerry Falwell was one of the first church leaders to effectively use marketing. He hired various advertising agencies to help him effectively target the message of Jesus Christ to receptive groups.[7] Falwell involved consultants in marketing meetings (yes, he called them marketing meetings). He was one of the first to install large computers (mainframes) in his church facilities to gather data on his listeners, but he did more than use it just to create mailing lists. He learned to read and interpret computer data to focus fundraising appeals according to the interest and past giving habits of his audiences. He knew there were several different audiences of people who listened to his television program, and he focused gift-request letters to appeal to the ministry interest of each audience.

Falwell was a marketing genius who employed marketing tools and strategies to build one of the biggest television empires, eventually broadcasting on Sundays on 214 of the largest television stations in each of the 214 MIAs (media impact areas) in the United States. In these areas he reached 95 percent of America's listening audience. How effective was Falwell? In 1979, a Good Housekeeping poll named him the most-admired man in the nation. In 1983, he was named second most admired behind Ronald Reagan. In 1985, his picture appeared on the cover of *TIME* magazine. That's an honor reserved for movers, shakers and newsmakers.

Falwell was a product of the marketing generation; it could also be called the communication generation. He grew up with media, and his influence was fashioned by media. But marketing was not the secret to Falwell's success. There were several other earlier and later Christian television personalities who were as big on television as Falwell, but they didn't expand their influence beyond the TV screen or radio. The television empire Falwell built eventually became the foundation for Liberty University, the world's largest Christian University with more than 100,000 students.[8]

Falwell was drawn to marketing because he believed all people were lost without Christ, but other Christian TV personalities believed the same. He acted on his passion and sacrificed to get the message that

"Jesus Saves" to every person. He began marketing his church by making 100 front-door calls each day of the week until he reached every home within a 10-mile radius of the church.

Every morning from 6:00 AM to 7:00 AM, Falwell interceded to God for spiritual blessings on his efforts. My wife knew that if he was going to call me that day, he would do it before 6:00 AM. If I called him back, I knew he wouldn't answer until after 7:00 AM. For almost 25 years, Jerry and I prayed together over the phone every Sunday morning at 7:15 AM, asking God to bless the activities of the services at Thomas Road Baptist Church and the outreach of the *Old Time Gospel Hour*.

Falwell's prayers were effective because of his sincerity. Every Wednesday evening, more than 3,000 people gathered at Thomas Road Baptist Church for a prayer meeting. I sat with Jerry on a pew located behind the pulpit. When it came time to pray, he directed everyone in the audience to gather into groups of two (he called them dyads) or groups of three (triads). Then the two of us would kneel in prayer together. He would always begin praying, because he was the natural leader. He talked to God in a natural voice, expecting God to do what he asked. It was the same way he would talk to me, asking me to do something for the ministry—and expecting me to do it. His faith built the ministry, and his desire to reach as many people as possible motivated him to use marketing.

The Seed Was Planted

Jerry Falwell grew up with money. His father was the sheriff of Campbell County, Virginia, and owned the largest nightclub in the area. The best-known bands from New York stopped in Lynchburg; it was a railroad town where trains from three main carriers stopped. In prohibition days when towns were dry, drinks were always available at the Falwell's. As a law officer, Jerry's father confiscated illegal booze and resold it in his place. It was illegal, but who was going to arrest a sheriff?

His mother made young Jerry attend Sunday school, but when he reached the rebellious teen years, he quit and slept in on Sunday mornings. Young Falwell never drank whiskey or smoked cigarettes, but he hung out with a rough crowd in Fairview Heights. They hung out late at night at the Pickeral Café, where they sat on a low concrete wall. They were well known to the Lynchburg police as the "Wall Gang."

A mother's love and prayers will not be thwarted, so each Sunday morning Helen Falwell left the radio playing loudly tuned to the *Old Fashioned Revival Hour*. Young Jerry would yell down the stairs, "Turn off that noise!" His mother would softly answer, "Breakfast is ready."

The smell of fresh-cooked country ham and hot cakes (his favorite) would drift up the stairwell into his room. He couldn't resist his favorite breakfast, so he compromised by listening to Charles E. Fuller.

The seeds of Falwell's future church service were planted in his mind during these Sunday morning experiences. The *Old Fashioned Revival Hour* had peppy quartet music, and Rudy Atwood's catchy piano arrangements didn't sound like church music. The white keyboard was his orchestra; his music jumped and danced. Each week Charles Fuller would ask his wife, "Honey," to read letters from servicemen who had been saved listening to the gospel on the radio. Charles Fuller had been a businessman who began preaching the way he made a business deal—and a good salesman always pushed for the sale. Each week, Fuller would point to a sailor in the balcony with his hand up and waving for salvation. He would invite the sailor down to an old-fashioned altar to pray for salvation. *That's the way church ought to be*, young Falwell thought to himself. All the churches he saw in Lynchburg were dead.

One Sunday afternoon, the guys in the Wall Gang were talking church. Falwell asked, "Is there a church in town where they preach like the *Old Fashioned Revival Hour*?" Jim Moon answered, "Yeah. . . there's a new church over on Park Avenue—across from Miller Park. A lot of people go forward at the end of the preaching, just like on the radio." Then Moon added the clincher: "They've got a lot of pretty girls over there."

That night, Falwell and Moon arrived right at 7:00 but couldn't find a seat. The usher put them on the front row. Unknown to them, faithful prayer intercessors began praying for their salvation even before the sermon began.

They spied two really cute petite girls. One was playing the piano, and the other was playing the organ. Moon told Falwell, "I'm gonna take the one on the piano, and you take the blonde on the organ." Technically, Jim Moon married the opposite—the organist, Delores Clark. He later became Jerry's trusted associate pastor. Jerry married Macel Pate, who became the endearing pianist for Jerry's church. She, like Rudy Atwood, played all the keys like her personal orchestra, and she could make church music jump and dance!

Jerry and Jim knelt at the altar after the sermon was over. Garland Carey, a silver-headed soul-winner, led them to Christ. Jerry's conversion changed everything. He repented from everything that was preached against that evening. He quit cussing, dancing and going to movies. But he didn't give up his questionable friends; if anything, he tried to get them saved. He did anything possible to get them to church. Jerry wanted them to experience the same thing that had transformed him.

Jesus had told Jerry, "Follow Me." He answered, "I'll go where You want me to go, I'll say what You want me to say, I'll do what You want me to do, and I'll be what You want me to be." The day after his conversion, Jerry went to a local department store, purchased a *Scofield Reference Bible,* and began memorizing great amounts of Scripture. He went off to Baptist Bible College in Springfield, Missouri, a two-year-old unheard-of school. It wasn't known for its academics, and it wasn't accredited. It had nothing but the power of God working in teachers and students.[9] That unknown Bible college produced some pastors who planted some of the greatest churches in America.

Early Efforts at Advertising and Marketing

Jerry's pastor told him to attend the largest soul-winning church in town and get into a Sunday school class to learn how to communicate the Word of God. So, as a freshman, in the fall of 1952 Jerry began attending High Street Baptist Church, one of the early megachurches with more than 2,000 people in attendance. He went up to meet its pastor, W.E. Dowell, who suggested that Falwell volunteer to teach Sunday school in the junior department.

When Jerry Falwell walked into the junior department, Max Hawkins, the junior superintendent, took one look at him and decided he was not a good candidate to be a teacher. Hawkins had seen plenty of pink-cheeked Bible student volunteers begin with enthusiasm but quit when the work became tedious. He told Jerry outright, "I don't have much hope for you Bible-student types. You start strong but fade fast." Jerry stood his ground, insisting he wanted to teach a Sunday school class. Hawkins gave in. "Okay, Falwell," he conceded. "You can have one 11-year-old boy." One of Hawkins's aides hung a curtain around a table and two chairs in the corner of the general assembly room in the basement—Falwell didn't even get a classroom. He was to teach there, and Hawkins would be watching in the wings.

On his first Sunday, Jerry met Daryl, a rather shy young man with dark brown eyes, large blotchy freckles, and curly blond hair. Daryl was his first real congregation. But nothing happened, and the class didn't grow. After six Sundays, Jerry approached Max Hawkins to tell him he was quitting. "Give me back the roll book then," Mr. Hawkins said, reaching out for the book. "I didn't want to give you the class in the first place. I did it against my better judgment."

"No," Jerry responded with some anger and hurt. "I'm not going to quit." He pulled the roll book away. Hawkins just shrugged his shoulders and walked away.

Jerry asked the dean of students for a key to an empty dorm room on the first floor of the men's dormitory. It had no windows, just an Army cot without a mattress. Each afternoon for the remainder of the year, Jerry went and prayed from 1:00 to 5:00 PM, stretching his body over the springs. God broke his heart over his failure of the small Sunday school class. Jerry realized if he were unfaithful in little things, God would never bless him in big things.

In that room, Jerry read authors who wrote books that motivated him to greater prayer challenges. The writings of Andrew Murray, George Mueller, Hannah Whitall Smith and E.M. Bounds enlarged his world. Falwell found himself wanting to reach a whole city for God. Then, why not a state... a nation... the world? These authors and their books challenged Falwell to pray for big results. When Jerry learned to pray big, the enlarged vision changed his whole attitude toward serving Christ. Obviously, this was the foundation for using every available advertisement to reach every available person at every available time.[10]

The next Saturday morning, Jerry got Daryl and went looking for his buddies and friends—anyone who was 11 years old. They cut a swath across every playground and empty lot, seeking 11-year-old boys. Jerry did everything he could to invite as many of them as he could to come to his Sunday school class.

Every Sunday, Jerry loaded his '41 Plymouth with boys and drove them to High Street Baptist Church. The Sunday pickup route soon outgrew his vintage Plymouth, so he organized two roommates with cars to help transport children to Sunday school. Each Sunday morning, like a long snake, they wound a path through the neighborhoods of Springfield, picking up as many 11-year-old boys as the cars would hold.

At the end of the first school year, Jerry had 56 regular members, and attendance in special class activities often swelled to more than 100 boys. Every boy in the class made a commitment to Christ, and many of their mothers, dads and friends did also. Jerry realized for the first time that if he prayed and worked hard, he had unlimited potential in the service of Christ.[11]

The greatest thing about that experience was not the great number of boys who attended and were saved. It wasn't that young Falwell acquired marketing skills or even conceived an advertising plan and made it work. Falwell learned how to touch God in that small empty dorm room. He learned to intercede and unleash the power of God. In turn, God began to use the young boy with a heart totally dedicated to doing His will.

Marketing Works for a Church

Falwell returned to Lynchburg, Virginia, in June 1956 to begin a church. Jerry organized 52 people into what he called Thomas Road Baptist Church, because it met in a small cinderblock building on a street with that name. The 30' x 60' building was the former bottling plant for Donald Duck Cola, which had gone bankrupt, so it was referred to as the Donald Duck Baptist Church.

Falwell tacked a map of Lynchburg on the wall over his desk. Beginning at the church, he drew a circle representing every mile out of the town into the county. Then, beginning at a home across from the church, he determined to visit every home. He planned to visit 100 homes every day for five days each week.

Falwell wrote down the names and addresses of all the prospects he met, and at the end of each week typed out an 8½" x 14" newsletter and mailed it to everyone. The newsletter didn't include messages or devotionals but exciting news of last week's victories. Falwell printed the names of visitors in the newsletter as well as attendance records and the amount of the offerings. People wanted to read the flimsy newsletter to experience the excitement at the Donald Duck Baptist Church.

When Falwell visited people's homes, he realized they were listening to country and western music on their radios. He took Macel Pate on a date, and as they were standing on a peak at Riverview Park, he saw a new radio tower being built in Madison Heights across the James River. He said, "That's a new country and western station, WBRG. I want to use that station to tell listeners about the new church."

Mr. Epperson, the owner, told Jerry, "I'm looking for someone to open the station every morning beginning at 6:00 AM." He was excited to find out Jerry was connected to the type of people he wanted to reach with his station. "I'll sell you 30 minutes for $7 a program," Epperson said.

Preaching at the station for the next 20 years established Jerry's habit of arising early. He didn't just preach; he told the exciting things happening at the church, including the names of those who were being saved and baptized. The young church became the most exciting event in Lynchburg. People were buzzing in barbershops and beauty shops.

Within six months, Jerry noted a new response when visiting homes. Previously, people turned off the radio. But television was different. They were glued to the television screen, and they tried to listen to him and watch the screen at the same time. Falwell found people were offended if he told them to turn off the TV. Jerry concluded that if television captivated peoples' attention, then he had to preach on the tube. So, he negotiated a contract with the new ABC station located in downtown Lynchburg for $90 for 30 minutes. His program aired live on Sunday evenings from 5:30 PM to 6:00 PM, just before the evening news.

Again, Jerry told stories of what was happening at Thomas Road, giving names, attendance figures and updates on the beginning of construction to double the size of the building. Macel played the piano, and Bill Brooks, a member from a local Methodist church, sang a solo. Jerry always ended with, "You've got an hour to get a glass of milk and eat a peanut butter sandwich, and I'll meet you at the front door to shake your hand." The invitation was too good to turn down. Attendance at the new church exploded, with 864 present on the first anniversary.

During the second year, Falwell took a vacation to the Caribbean with a group of preachers. On one Sunday morning he heard Kenneth Strachan, president of Latin American Mission, preach about conquering a nation for Christ. Strachan called it "evangelism-in-depth." He indicated big evangelistic crusades wouldn't get the job done, nor would big-name evangelists or big-name singers.[12]

Strachan laid out a plan to saturate every nation in Central and South America, plus the Caribbean, with the gospel. The strategy began at the bottom where people were located and did not use big meetings and big-name evangelists. Strachan believed "trickle-down, big crusades" didn't work. He went from nation to nation in South America promoting a "bubble up approach to evangelism."

Strachan asked every evangelical church to kick off the year by holding a big parade in every city where groups from every church would march, youth groups would enter floats, and the Salvation Army band would play marching music to gather attention. The year would focus on a Vacation Bible School in every neighborhood, a Christian film shown at night in the piazza, and musical concerts offered by local talent. They planned to visit every home in every nation and leave gospel literature and a testimony.

As Falwell sat in that meeting, he crafted a definition of the principles of evangelism that would characterize his ministry for the rest of his life. He called it "saturation evangelism" instead of in-depth evangelism. While Strachan planned to organize all the churches to reach a nation, Falwell planned to organize his church to "reach every available person, at every available time, with every available method."[13] He came home to saturate Lynchburg with the gospel, and then he would take on America. Maybe the world!

Falwell maintained that every person would call on God in his or her desperate hour. Falwell wanted people in Lynchburg to know about the ministry of Thomas Road Baptist Church when their desperate hour came. He wanted sinners to remember his church and phone him.

In the 1960s, the son of a local businessman crashed his motorcycle on the Lynchburg Expressway and slid on raw concrete, peeling the skin off every place in his body. When the father, G.D. Smith, walked into the emergency room at the hospital, he was overwhelmed with the bleeding body of his teenage son. He retreated to the dimly lit hallway to lift his fist to heaven and say, "Oh, God, if You'll save my son, I'll do anything."

In his hour of desperation, G.D. remembered the name Thomas Road Baptist Church. Smith looked up the name of Jerry Falwell in the phone book and called him. The young pastor was there in only a few minutes. In that dimly lit hallway, G.D. Smith repented of every sin and was saved. Later, he taught Sunday school and became a deacon at the church. G.D. owned several enterprises and used his finances for several projects at the church.[14]

Falwell sophisticated his saturation evangelism plans. In the fall of 1971, he planned to have the largest attended Sunday school in history. He began by tearing the 107 pages out of the phone book and asked 107 people to call every person in Lynchburg and invite them to attend the largest and most exciting Sunday school in history. The church made three mailings to every home: a newsletter, a letter, and then a postcard reminding them of the time, place and address. Next, the church placed a full-page advertisement in the local paper on Thursdays, Fridays and Saturdays before the target date. Then the church aired 60 one-minute long commercials on all 13 radio stations and the one TV station in Lynchburg.

The high school students tacked more than 10,000 posters on as many light poles as they could find. The junior high students placed 12,000 flyers under every windshield wiper on every car in Lynchburg. More than 200 workers were marshaled to knock on every door on Saturday to invite people to attend the following day. Every Sunday school class sponsored an attendance contest with prizes to those bringing the most people to the event. Steve Wingfield brought 49 visitors and won a new *Scofield Reference Bible*.

The city's fire marshal attended to make sure the safety code was enforced, so Jerry got him to count attendance. No one would doubt the accuracy of his count. When Falwell announced that 10,187 people were in attendance, the audience cheered wildly—not so much because the record was broken, but because each person had been part of the victory.

But Falwell was not content just marketing the gospel to his city. Next, the young pastor took on the world. He announced in the spring of 1972 that the church would preach the gospel to everyone in the world on the same day. He arranged to buy time with all the super Christian radio stations that broadcasted its radio beams in all languages into all nations.[15] Then he arranged for the radio and television programs to translate his sermon into every language in which they broadcasted. Then they broadcasted his sermon into every available language on the same day.

Next, Falwell called for a one-day Yom Kippur fast by all the church members and all the students at the young Liberty University. He instructed them to pray for souls to be saved and money to pay for the endeavor. Falwell planned big events during his early days.

But Falwell didn't want to saturate just Lynchburg or the state of Virginia—he wanted to saturate the nation. He assembled a mailing list that was dedicated to the ministry of the *Old Time Gospel Hour*. He tied it to the new Liberty University that was originally named Lynchburg Baptist College. Jerry planned to build a huge college. He told me, "Elmer, you hire the teachers, write the catalog and schedule the classes. I'll recruit the students, raise the money, and construct the buildings. Together, we'll build the biggest evangelical college in the world."[16]

I showed up for work on June 1, 1971. Later that day, I put on his desk a proposed budget for the college year of $154,000 to $158,000. Then I said, "I'll need a $5,000 check for seed money."

"I don't have any money," Falwell answered. "We're broke every Monday."

"There was $12,000 in the collection yesterday," I said.

"I spent that three weeks ago," Jerry laughed, explaining that they ran to the bank every Monday morning to cover the paychecks issued the previous Friday afternoon.

"What's the college going to do for money?" I asked rhetorically.

"Let's go get it tonight . . ."

Jerry and I left the church around 4:00 PM and drove 100 miles west to a large Southern Baptist church up in the Blue Ridge Mountains: the Mountain View Baptist Church. Doug Oldham, the gospel singer, met us there in his bus and already had records out in the foyer for sale that evening.

Around 7:00 PM, Doug sang a concert for 30 minutes; he was the reason the people came. I took 10 minutes to cast a vision of a new college that would change the world. Then Jerry turned in his Bible to Psalm 84 and read, "I'd rather be a doorkeeper in the house of the Lord."

He explained that a Doorkeeper could hold the door open to preach the gospel on television and train young people to capture the world. Jerry asked people to be a Doorkeeper by donating $1 a week to partner with him in reaching the world though the airwaves and training young "Champions for Christ" who would go out to capture a town for Christ.[17]

"Dr. Towns is going to give you a packet of 52 envelopes," Jerry explained. "Put a dollar in the first envelope and give it back to him." That evening, I walked up and down the aisle distributing Doorkeeper packets and collecting envelopes.

"How much did you get?" Jerry asked me on the way home.

"We got $75," I answered.

"No... we got $3,900. A dollar a week times 52 weeks from 75 people amounts to $3,900."

The names on the donor list who gave a dollar a week were called Doorkeepers. Then the IRS determined the ministry had to issue a receipt after each $1 was received—the ministry couldn't just give one total receipt for each donor at the end of the year. So Jerry changed the program to ask for $10 per month. Almost everyone made the switch. Their new names were Faith Partners. Then inflation hit during the 1970s and 1980s, and Jerry asked for $15 per month and then $20. His supporters stayed with him, and the list of names increased to 100,000 people. Liberty soon began constructing one building after another. Many Faith Partners didn't want to pay for buildings; they just wanted to make monthly donations for the ministry.

Earlier, I referred to the four large black machines called mainframe computers. The mailing list was kept on hundreds of thousands of IBM cards. Jerry studied his supporters and found they fell into five categories. Those who gave to one project remained faithful to that project, and most would not give to projects in other areas. I later wrote and published an article about this called "The 5 Pockets of Stewardship."[18] This was Jerry's research into marketing that enabled him to focus a request letter to donors who were interested only in that area. Falwell saved advertising money and increased effectiveness. He found 75 to 80 percent of our donors gave faithfully to their area of interest and didn't respond to other appeals.

In 1979, Jerry moved into the political arena to support the election of Ronald Reagan. Before that happened, the church transferred all the donor files to a digital file. Now names were kept on large rolls of magnetic tape instead of IBM cards. When Jerry began the Moral Majority to counteract the spread of secularism, he found another pocket of stewardship. The people in this stewardship pocket made up a different file

The Five Pockets of Stewardship

1. Light bill money—given to help pay normal bills
2. Brick and mortar money—given to construction projects
3. Missions money—given to support foreign missions
4. Ivy wall money—given to higher education
5. Humanitarian money—given for clean water, clothing, shelter and so forth to people in need

completely. They were born-again activists who were dedicated to political conservatism. When Falwell preached on conservative politics, his five pockets of stewardship didn't respond in giving, but the giving in the political file went up.

Building a Mailing List

As editor-in-chief of Jerry Falwell's publications, I began the *Journal Champion* newspaper. Because the mailing list had grown so large, the paper was mailed biweekly to more than one million homes. Approximately 100,000 copies were mailed to pastors. The power of the press gave Jerry tremendous political leverage. Most observers think that coverage from the Moral Majority helped put Ronald Reagan into the presidency. Obviously, there were many other forces that got President Reagan elected.

The marketing world for Christian television crashed in March 1987 when the *Charlotte Observer* printed a story and the name of a young lady who had a sexual alliance with Jim Bakker, host of the daily PTL television program. Along with sexual sins, the newspapers printed stories about financial mismanagements. The night before the story broke, Jerry gathered a number of the church and Liberty University leaders and told about the story that would break the following morning. He was a prophet predicting the future, telling us the story would cripple his television empire—but not only his. It would also impact Billy Graham, Robert Schuller and the Crystal Cathedral—every one of them. "This news will turn off financial giving," he said. "They won't trust anyone."

Within a year, financial giving to the *Old Time Gospel Hour* dropped $24 million per year, leaving about $3 million in income, which came primarily from Faith Partners paying basic bills. Money dried up for foreign missions, new college buildings and humanitarian projects. Jerry continued preaching on 210 television station across America, and the ministry began falling into debt. Thousands of religious television programs went off the air and out of existence. Those churches that paid for television time out of their plate offerings stayed on the air, but usually televised only their Sunday morning service.

Jerry found large gifts of $100 evaporating, as well as smaller $10 or $20 gifts. Gifts were based on trust, and no one seemed to trust television preachers. Jerry began selling off church and college assets to pay salaries and bills. First, a shopping center went, and then acreage on Liberty Mountain, and then the nationwide television network was sold. Liberty had acquired the international headquarters of Craddock-Terry Shoe Company, which also was sold. The ministry's debt, which had exploded up to $104 million, was reduced to $52 million.

Before the financial cliff, Jerry had begun selling Liberty Home Bible Institute's 1,200 audiotapes and workbooks for $1,000. He eventually sold 100,000 programs. He repackaged that into shorter certificate courses, and then he bought expensive Bibles for 10 percent of their value and sold them at full price. This strategy helped keep the ministry afloat.

A wealthy businessman had made payroll several times. He sent four CPAs to do a manpower audit, determining how much each employee cost the university and how much money each employee brought in. This was a complete cost-estimate evaluation of the total ministry. About a third of the faculty, staff and maintenance crew were released on a "Black Friday." University majors were cut, courses were dropped, and faculty members were released. Expenses were reduced below the level of income. Within a short period of time, Liberty was taking in more money that it was spending. Every part of the ministry had to be reduced and everything slowed down.

Just about the same time Jim Bakker's episodes began to cripple the Christian television ministry, Liberty began LUSLLL (Liberty University School of Life-Long Learning). College courses and degrees were sold so that an individual could earn an accredited degree at home. At first distant students viewed courses on a VCR, supported by work text and textbooks. Eventually, LUSLLL was digitized and students learned via the computer and Internet. Selling courses through media was another financial solution to Liberty's problems.

Liberty spent 25 years perfecting its online programs. After Black Friday, there were 3,400 students left in the university. Today there are more than 13,000 resident students and more than 90,000 online students. The budget is no longer measured in millions but in billions.

Strengths and Weaknesses of Marketing/Media Churches

The strength of the marketing/media church is its commitment to carry out the Great Commission. Jesus attached several commands to the Great Commission, "Go. . . preach. . . disciple. . . all the world" (see Matt. 28:19; Mark 16:15; Acts 1:8). Marketing/media churches claim that they are outward-focused and can reach people who are not already in their church or in their neighborhood. This is quite the opposite of most local churches that are tradition bound, program focused and maintenance minded.

The marketing/media church points to abundant illustrations in the Scriptures that focus on reaching out to unsaved people. Remember the man out of whom 2,000 evil spirits were cast (see Mark 5:5)? After Jesus healed him, the man begged to go with Jesus. But instead, Jesus told him to go home and tell his friends, and he shared his story throughout the cities of the Decapolis (see Mark 5:18-20). And what about the illustration of Andrew meeting Jesus Christ? "He first found his own brother Simon [Peter], and said to him, 'We have found the Messiah'" (John 1:41).

Again, we have the woman whose life was changed by Jesus at the well. She immediately went and told all the men of the city about Jesus—some of whom might have been the men she sinned with—"Come, see a Man who told me all things that I ever did. Could this be the Christ?" (John 4:29). And then, don't forget on the day of Pentecost, "the multitude came together" (Acts 2:6). They wanted to know about the excitement of the phenomena they heard from the upper room. That seemed to be a use of advertising the gospel.

As you go through the book of Acts, you find other illustrations such as, "A multitude gathered from the surrounding cities to Jerusalem, bringing sick people and those who were tormented by unclean spirits, and they were all healed" (Acts 5:16). Then, when Peter and John healed a lame man in Jesus' name, a large crowd gathered and they preached to them (see Acts 3:11-12). Fast-forward 2,000 years and you see the marketing/media church in action. These churches attempted to get the message out to the multitudes.

In Scripture, churches used whatever means they had, and today churches use whatever media is available. This includes radio, television, social media and the Internet. There are hundreds of Christian radio stations where people can hear the gospel, and again there are hundreds of Christian television programs where the gospel is proclaimed.

There are several weaknesses with marketing/media churches. First, they may tend to trivialize the message of Christianity. Because they have such a strong outreach message to the lost, they may not put equal emphasis on discipleship and building up the saints who are already under their ministry. Because they are attracting the unsaved and are using their pulpits to emphasize the gospel, they may minimize the command of Christ, who said, "Take up [your] cross daily, and follow Me" (Luke 9:23). Because the main message from these churches is "Jesus saves," those who are born again may not feel any expectation to go beyond the gospel to follow Jesus daily. As a result, media/marketing churches produce a lower level of commitment to Jesus Christ than they desire. They may produce people who make decisions for Christ but do not become disciples of Jesus Christ.

A second criticism is that these churches are in the "attraction business." They are so committed to attracting listeners that they do not get out the message about God in the Bible. When churches focus on attraction, they tend to be less focused on God, His holiness, justice and worship of Him. Obviously, churches with strong media and marketing outreach are those most commonly found among growing churches or large megachurches. In one sense, all churches should work toward being more evangelistic, while tradition-bound churches might be committed to a broader biblical curriculum.

A third weakness of media/marketing churches is that a pastor who is a dynamic communicator must lead them. The greater the communicator, the greater the church growth and the more likely it will become a megachurch. However, not all great communicators are Bible expositors, and not all communicators make pastoral visits in the hospital and other daily pastoral requirements. Nor are they all intercessors who pray for results or are anointed to weep with those who weep at funerals. Therefore, not everyone can pastor a marketing/media church, because all are not gifted in that area. What does this mean? Not all churches will be marketing/media churches.

However, many people equate church growth with marketing/media. And what do they expect? They expect all churches to have an aggressive advertising campaign, to understand marketing, and to immediately communicate the gospel through many forms of media. But many churches do not have the technical ability or technicians to use media. They don't have the finances to invest in all the technical equipment to make advertising possible. A media/marketing church must make a tremendous commitment to purchase equipment, learn communication skills, stay up to date on the latest trends in marketing, and continually raise enough money to keep the media "empire" running. There are very few pastors who will make that commitment; therefore, there will be only a few effective media/marketing churches.

Another question must be asked. If the audience "out there" gets saved, how can they experience Christian community? How can they fulfill their obligation to a local church? How can the local church look after them? The marketing/media church must ask the question, "Once people receive and believe our message, but cannot attend our church physically, what then?" That seems to be an issue that is seldom raised or effectively handled by the marketing/media church.

Finally, media/marketing churches can get caught up in the techniques of the world and cheapen the gospel. Rather than attracting unbelievers, they may actually repel them. Today, some churches give out free Sunday lunches at a local restaurant, some give key chains, and others give out gifts for attendance. Just as Hollywood is known for its advertising, the First Presbyterian Church in Hollywood, California, brought the famous horse Trigger and its rider, Roy Rogers, to Sunday school to attract visitors. Many other churches use well-known guest speakers—sports figures, politicians and movie stars—to attract people to their services.

The attractional church is not a new phenomenon in Christianity; it's just that with the explosion of media and marketing, the church has been caught up in its euphoria. But can they use the same methods and media to advertise Jesus Christ?

Wrap Up

After World War II, there was an electronic explosion in methods of communication that resulted in all types of ways for people to communicate with other people. But more importantly, there arose giants in the communication industry; i.e., radio, television, movies, telephones, telegraph and, eventually, an explosion of electronic gadgets that produced all types of social media.

It was only natural that churches would use as many methods of communication as possible to get their message out to as many people as possible. Jerry Falwell was just one of the many Christian leaders who tried to master as many methods of communication as possible for gospel expansion. There were many who effectively used radio and television to preach to the masses. But Jerry Falwell based his outreach to one local church in a small media outlet (60,000 population), and because God blesses the church, God was able to use Jerry Falwell in an unusual way. He personifies the media ministry of the twentieth century.

Part Two

Other Churches and Trends

First Presbyterian Church
Hollywood, California*

11

Henrietta Mears
Director of Christian Education*

Bible Teaching for Every Age Through Sunday School

First Presbyterian Church, Hollywood, California

The First Presbyterian Church of Hollywood, California, was established in 1903 and developed a Bible-teaching ministry through Sunday school and other Christian education church programs. Henrietta Mears, the director of Christian education, wrote the entire Sunday school curriculum. Today, that curriculum is Gospel Light Publications, and it influences thousands of other churches that use it.

Mears taught a young adult Bible class of more than 400 people that produced evangelical leaders for the next 50 years in the United States. Some of her students included Dawson Trotman, founder of the Navigators; Bob Pierce, founder of World Vision; Bill and Vonette Bright, founders of Campus Crusade for Christ; and Billy Graham, of whom her influence is well documented. Henrietta Mears took over a Sunday school with 175 in attendance and built it to more than 4,000 weekly attenders. Hundreds of Hollywood stars came to know Jesus Christ, including Roy Rogers, Dale Evans and radio superstar Stuart Hamblen, who went on to write the ever-popular Christian song, "It Is No Secret What God Can Do."

*Photo from historical sources found on the Internet.
*Wikipedia, The Free Encyclopedia http://creativecommons.org/licenses/by-sa/3.0/

Crystal Cathedral
Garden Grove, California*

Robert Schuller
Pastor*

12

The Influence of Positive Thinking and Financial Prosperity on Churches

Crystal Cathedral, Garden Grove, California

In 1955, Robert Schuller began a church in a drive-in theater, appealing to the people's informality of worshiping from their cars. When he finally built the 3,000-seat Crystal Cathedral, he asked 10,000 people to donate $1,000 each to buy a large pane of glass that made up the walls of the building (my wife and I bought one pane of glass). Schuller's inspiration for the church ministry came from a book by Dr. Norman Vincent Peale of Marble Collegiate Church in Manhattan, New York, called *The Power of Positive Thinking*.[1]

While "positive thinking" was associated with some mainline and evangelical churches, "prosperity theology" is more associated with Charismatic/Pentecostal churches and ministers, such as Fred Price of the Christian Crenshaw Center in greater Los Angeles, California. The current personification of both positive thinking and prosperity theology is seen in the ministry of Lakewood Church in Houston, Texas, where Joel Osteen preaches to more than 26,000 people in the large auditorium that was once the home to the Houston Rockets basketball team.

Coral Ridge Presbyterian Church
Coral Ridge, Florida*

D. James Kennedy
Pastor*

13

Churches Built on a Systematic Approach to Personal Soul-Winning

Coral Ridge Presbyterian Church, Coral Ridge, Florida

Dr. D. James Kennedy began Coral Ridge Presbyterian Church in 1958 and built it on door-to-door visitation, winning people to Christ in their living rooms and bringing them into the church. The church followed traditional mainline worship liturgy and church calendar sequence. It did not feature evangelistic preaching, an altar invitation to receive Christ, or traditional revival meeting. At Kennedy's funeral in 2007, several millionaires gave testimony that he had led them to Christ in their homes using an evangelistic program that became known as "evangelism explosion," a worldwide program of teaching and organizing personal soul-winning that extended to every country in the world.

People's Church
Toronto, Canada*

Oswald Smith
Pastor*

14

Churches Organized and Focused as Foreign Mission Endeavors

The People's Church, Toronto, Canada

Oswald Smith began The People's Church in Toronto, Canada, with a strong evangelistic pulpit. Over time, the primary thrust of the church became supporting foreign missions, including finances, prayer and trips to involve its members in foreign missions. The church became the first to give one million dollars to foreign missions, and later it was the first church to give two million dollars to foreign missions. Smith became a worldwide ambassador for foreign missions, both visiting missionaries and preaching in local church foreign mission conferences.

Vineyard Church
Cincinnati, Ohio*

Steve Sjogren
Founding Pastor*

15

An Aggressive Initiative of Servanthood Evangelism

Vineyard Church, Cincinnati, Ohio

Steve Sjogren is the founding pastor of Vineyard Cincinnati in Cincinnati, Ohio, a church that grew from 5 people to more than 7,500 in weekly attendance. After two years of struggling to get the church off the ground, Sjogren decided to give everything away. He asked, "How many people can we serve, love and show generosity to?" He developed the slogan, "Servant evangelism: random acts of kindness done in a small way with great love will change the world." Through servant evangelism, Sjogren and his church sought to do good works to gain an entrance into people's lives to present the gospel. Sjogren became famous for his book *Conspiracy of Kindness*. In it, he says, "Kindness builds the bridge for the person to receive a touch of love from God."[1]

Sjogren organized his church to systematically do acts of kindness throughout the neighborhood and, in so doing, attract the unsaved to the church where they could be converted. Sjogren himself went to gas stations and convenience stores to wash and clean restrooms—something unheard of for pastors. With an international organization and a national prayer to propagate his idea, thousands of churches have incorporated servant evangelism—previously known as the social gospel—into their outreach.

*Photos provided by Vineyard Church. Used by permission

Northwood Church
Keller, Texas*

Bob Roberts
Pastor*

16

A Church-Planting Strategy
of Evangelism

Northwood Church, Keller, Texas

Bob Roberts, Jr. planted Northwood Church in Keller, Texas, in 1985. Instead of just doing evangelism through the typical methods, Bob and the church of 2,000 in weekly attendance chose to do church multiplication by church planting. The church has planted more than 200 churches. Rather than building a single, oversized megachurch, they have planted 20 churches within a 10-mile radius of their own campus.

Roberts, who wrote *The Multiplying Church*, has a program in Northwood to annually train more than a dozen future husband-and-wife church planting teams.[1] To make sure the church is evangelizing different racial communities, as mandated in Matthew 28:19, Roberts seeks to train half of the church planters with non-Anglo backgrounds, both in the United States and abroad. Roberts does not insist that church planters begin a church in keeping with the Northwood model. Instead, he supports many models, including house churches, traditional churches, and others. He states, "We want to embed. . . a DNA that we believe is essential for the planting of churches that will transform people and the world."[2]

Other church-planting churches include Redeemer Presbyterian Church in New York (100 planted); Mars Hill Church in Seattle, Washington (100 churches); and Perimeter Church (Presbyterian) in Duluth, Georgia (22 churches). Perimeter Church in North Atlanta, Georgia, could be considered a pioneer in multiplying churches, as Randy Pope, the founding pastor, announced a goal of beginning 100 churches that would surround Atlanta, Georgia, located on its perimeter beltway (hence the name "Perimeter").

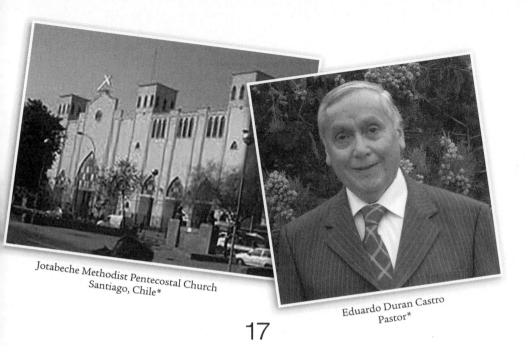

Jotabeche Methodist Pentecostal Church
Santiago, Chile*

Eduardo Duran Castro
Pastor*

17

A Multisite Church Meeting in Multiple Locations

Jotabeche Methodist Pentecostal Church, Santiago, Chile

The Jotabeche Methodist Pentecostal Church in Santiago, Chile, began as a Methodist church that grew out of the foreign mission endeavors of that denomination. But its early Pentecostal manifestations resulted in it becoming independent. Today, it fellowships with the Pentecostal Holiness denominations. It was one of the first large sanctuaries built in this modern era, seating 19,000 with more than 100,000 in attendance. It is a Pentecostal church that is organized as one church in many locations (multisite). There is one main downtown location called The Cathedral, with 65 surrounding churches called Temples, dozens of local churches, and even more Sunday school missions. It has more than 100,000 in total weekly attendance. Founded in 1903, it is among the first multisite churches operating under one pastor, with many associate pastors and one administrative board. Only members are counted who attend The Cathedral on Good Friday to take Communion (served only once each year).

Young Nak Presbyterian Church
Seoul, South Korea*

Kyung Chik Han
Pastor*

18

A Leadership Church that Influenced a Large Denomination

Young Nak Presbyterian Church, Seoul, South Korea

Pastor Han, an ordained Presbyterian minister, was defrocked after World War II because he bowed to the Japanese Shinto shrines in post offices and government buildings during the war. But he felt called of God, so he repented of his sins and begged the Presbyterians for a ministry. They sent him to the Young Nak Valley, where radical political refugees were pouring in from North Korea following the communist takeover of that nation.

Han began the church in a tent borrowed from the U.S. Army. As his flock grew, he expanded the size of the tent until it could seat 2,400. Han challenged his people to sacrifice and not build their homes—even though all the other Koreans were building their homes—and instead put God first by building the church sanctuary first. The giant church sanctuary that came about as a result is reflective of the size and design of Westminster in London, England. John Foster Dulles, the Secretary of State and a Presbyterian layman, dedicated the church in May 1950.

The communists of North Korea invaded South Korea the following month and attempted to burn the building, but the sanctuary did not catch fire. Han said, "God in heaven saw the sacrifice of the people who first built the church and would not let the sanctuary burn." The church became the largest Presbyterian church in the world, with more than 50,000 members (other Presbyterian churches eventually became larger). At its zenith, it had seven Sunday services. Young Nak Presbyterian Church became a leader-church because of its explosive growth after World War II.

Seacoast Community Church
Greater Charleston, South Carolina*

Greg Surratt
Pastor*

19

A Video-Venue
Multisite Church

Seacoast Community Church, Greater Charleston, South Carolina

Seacoast Church in Mount Pleasant, South Carolina, was one of the first to effectively use a video-venue in multisite locations to reach people for Christ. Greg Surratt, a Pentecostal minister, was building a traditional local church, but it could not expand because it was hemmed in by a suburban neighborhood with only a two-lane road leading to the church's location. So Surratt began satellite churches and preached in them via video venue, recording his Saturday evening sermon and playing it in all other churches throughout South Carolina, North Carolina and Georgia. At the present time, there are 29 weekend worship services at 13 locations. The church also began the Association of Related Churches (ARC), which is a church-planting network of 400 congregations across the United States. This church reflects the explosion of multisite churches in the twenty-first century.

Glory of Zion International Ministries
Corinth, Texas

Chuck Pierce
Apostle*

20

An International
Interactive Congregation
Built on the Internet

Glory of Zion International Ministries, Corinth, Texas

Glory of Zion International Ministries in Corinth, Texas, has 1,500 worshipers in residence each weekend but includes another 30,000 who worship online. All worshipers also minister to one another via the Internet. All members have been through membership classes online, and they also experience baptism and communion online.

Apostle Chuck Pierce planted this church in Denton, Texas, and added Internet outreach in 2004. There are 5,000 Internet house churches organized with a leader-shepherd who oversees a group of believers who gather to view the Sunday services via computer. The house church averages 2 to 25 believers (more than a biological family). While some Internet churches claim a larger viewership, this church is influential because viewers have made a commitment-vow to the church through a membership class, have become regular financial givers, and have become involved in ministry for Christ through the Internet.

Another Internet church is LifeChurch, located in Oklahoma City, Oklahoma. It has 16 campuses in cities around the United States and more than 50 viewing times via the Internet in most time zones. Craig Groeschel is the founding pastor (1994), and the innovative leader is Bobby Gruenewald. The church's Internet outreach is similar to a church media ministry, while Glory of Zion attempts to tie its members into community worship and outreach ministry. In addition, Christ Fellowship in Palm Beach Gardens, Florida, has a large Internet outreach with more than 20,000 views weekly. Todd Mullins is the pastor. The church counts loyalty by the amount of offerings received, which are around $4 per viewer.

Afterthought

What Can We Learn from These Churches?

Every pastor and all church workers should want their church to be more influential than it is. Therefore, those reading this book should ask the following questions: What can I learn about influence from these churches? What will be my church's main influence? How can I influence more people in my church? How can my church influence other churches? How can I have the greatest possible circle of influence?

I have divided the principles that we can learn from these churches into two areas: (1) What we can learn from the pastors of these churches, and (2) what we can learn from the methods used by these churches.

What We Can Learn from the Pastors of These Churches

I spent my life studying great church leaders, both men and women. For more than 10 years I listed in *Christian Life* magazine the "The 10 Largest Churches in America, 1967–1976," and for 10 years "The 10 Fastest Growing Churches in America, 1975–1984." Usually, we cannot disassociate the greatness of a church from the greatness of its leader. Sometimes I learned of a church's greatness by studying the life and ministry of its leader, but other times I was perplexed why a church was great, because I didn't find the primary cause from its human leader. I probably concluded a church's great influence came from the ministry of the Holy Spirit.

1. *Leaders of great vision build great churches.* In the law of cause and effect, we learn that for every reaction there was an action. Most times there is a correlation between the size of the reaction and the force of the action. Therefore, I conclude that for every great church there is usually a great pastor who has developed and communicated a vision, and then prayed and worked to build the church that God has put on his heart.

There is an old adage that says, "You can't achieve what you can't conceive." The greatness of the churches in this book usually began in the heart and vision of its leader. We know that is true of Bill Hybels, who wanted to create a church for the unsaved. We also know that is true of David Yonggi Cho, who wanted to build a church bigger than the campus of UCLA. The same was true of Jerry Falwell and W.A. Criswell. Therefore, we know that vision is absolutely necessary to build any church of influence. However, not every pastor of vision can build the church of his dreams. It takes skill, hard work and spiritual attainment. So, we must look at the second criteria to learn other factors to build a church of great influence.

2. *Leaders with great spirituality build great churches.* Technically, I first heard the statement, "Great leaders build great churches,"[1] from Beauchamp Vick, pastor of Temple Baptist Church in Detroit, Michigan, who claimed to have the largest Sunday school in America in the 1960s. (There was a center-spread photograph in *Life* magazine, December 25, 1958, that showed 5,000 children in his Sunday school; they could be counted.)

But Vick meant something special by "great leaders." He meant great leaders walked with God, were great soul-winners, and prayed to get things from God. They were great church builders because of the power of God on their lives. Vick went on to say, "Great leaders build great churches, average leaders build average churches, and weak leaders hurt churches."[2] By the term "weak leaders," Vick meant those who gave into the sins of the flesh, or those motivated by pride, or those who were lazy and didn't work diligently.

As you read the stories of these 10 churches, don't miss the leaders' relationship to God. It was evident on many occasions that they wanted to know God and/or worship Him long before they wanted to plant a church or build a church. And what does knowing God do to the leaders? It gives them purity of motive and power in their work. They will build great churches because they allowed God to work through them.

3. *Leaders have great courage.* The leaders in these churches acted on their convictions, sometimes went against the advice of people around them, and even went against the advice of the thinking of the day. Most of them planned to do something that had never been done before, and they innovated new ways to get the work of God done. Then they communicated their vision to their followers. They believed in their plans because they felt their ideas came from God. So, with determination and courage, they took great steps of faith.

The easy way in ministry is following tradition, or following the advice of friends, or even doing what your heroes are doing. But the influential pastors in this book received their marching orders from God.

They thought of a better mousetrap, designed it, built it and worked it. To be a great influencer for God, you must have the courage of your convictions and you must believe in your dreams. Great courage leads to great obedience.

4. *Leaders have great obedience.* The *pastor-influencers* in this book attempted to do something different—many times something that was never done before. Consider the story of William Seymour. He sought the baptism of the Holy Spirit in the Midwest, but then he borrowed money to go to California because he heard about a woman there who had a spiritual secret that no one else had. What if Seymour had given up? What if Seymour had not had the courage of his convictions? But he persisted, and in doing so he influenced the world of Pentecostals and Charismatics.

The great pastors of these churches were not satisfied with the way it had been done in the past, nor were they satisfied with what they saw about them. No! They saw a need and knew that God could meet that need. Consider Jerry Falwell's determination to preach the gospel to every person in the world on one Sunday. We don't know how effective it was, but look at his motivation. Look at the heart of Jerry Falwell. He wanted to carry out the command of Jesus Christ to "preach the gospel to every creature" (Mark 16:15). Could it be that the greatness of obedience characterized these great influencers?

5. *Leaders study to become great.* The secret of building a great church is not necessarily studying the great churches or even following the example of great churches. If you do that, it only makes you a follower. . . not a leader. But these pastors gave attention to learning to do the will of God in what they thought was a new and better way. They learned to apply their new method, and it gave them a platform to share with others.

6. *Leaders who have lofty dreams that influence the world also have feet of clay.* What if William Seymour had kept his agenda on the baptism of the Holy Spirit and not allowed the bitterness of racism to influence his message? Could he have let the Holy Spirit work through him more powerfully than it did through John Wesley or any other great leader in the world? Could Seymour have been the greatest leader in church history since the apostle Paul?

Martin Luther King, Jr. shook the establishment of American segregation and began to bring down walls of prejudice. But what if King had not given into the sexual sins of the flesh? Could he have had a greater spiritual impact on churches and helped end segregation more quickly? Could King have had an evangelistic influence on churches? What if King believed the verbal inspiration of the Scriptures by the Holy Spirit? Could he have unleashed the work of the Spirit of God in the hearts of listeners so they not only tore down the walls of segregation but also built churches where the Holy Spirit could work in the hearts of both whites and blacks?

David Yonggi Cho built the largest church in the history of Christianity, but could he have accomplished more if he had not wandered into a doctrinal wilderness? It appears that all great spiritual leaders have strengths that God uses for His purpose. Some may question why God would use a man with feet of clay, but as long as we are in the body—not translated into heaven—we all have a sin nature and are tempted by our weaknesses (see 1 John 1:8,10). We all have some dirt between our toes, and we all face the devil, who "walks about like a roaring lion, seeking whom he may devour" (1 Pet. 5:8).

What does that mean? Should we not glorify any man for any accomplishment that he has done on this earth? Perhaps. But the emphasis of our praise should glorify God for everything that is done. And in doing so, we should praise God for His grace and mercy to use men in spite of their foibles.

Finally, the question could be asked, "Why does God use any of us?" Because we all have weaknesses and "we have this treasure in earthen vessels" (2 Cor. 4:7), let's determine to do the most we can for God with the talents we have while we are alive. Let's determine to be the greatest influencers for God that we can be.

What We Can Learn About the Church

Remember, Christ has a love affair with His church, for the Scriptures say, "Christ also loved the church and gave Himself for her" (Eph. 5:25). Therefore, any human will be blessed of God who wants to advance the church of Jesus Christ on earth. The leaders in this book were extremely influential because they focused their ministry through churches. They didn't attack the church or abandon the church to begin a parachurch ministry. They were committed churchmen.

1. *God is not impressed with denominational labels or systems of theology.* Note the various types of denominational churches that God used to change the world. Four of the most influential churches in the past 100 years were Pentecostal, and if we really knew the makeup of the Chinese organic house churches, we would find that the majority of them were also Pentecostal. And what about the Baptists? Three of the most influential churches are Baptist in name. Two churches in the ranking 11 to 20 were Presbyterian. Three were independent churches, depending on how you want to label them. But even those independent churches created a fellowship or a wider

circle of influence that put them into a "denomination" of their own making.

What does that say about the blessing of God? God's primary blessing is not on the form of baptism, system of theology or church government. God uses churches that are committed to the Great Commission and carry out their commitment by reaching lost people for Jesus Christ.

When Paul described the three great qualities of faith, hope and love (see 1 Cor. 13:13), he was pointing out qualities that God blesses in ministry. *Faith* is absolute belief in Him. *Hope* is absolute trust in the future. *Love* is absolute acceptance of one another. It seems God blesses those who display the most trust in Him and have hope, commitment to the future, and a deep love for people. God blessed these leaders because they made themselves blessable—in other words, they had "blessability."[3]

2. *God understands culture and expects us to live our faith in the culture in which we find ourselves.* Throughout this book we have used the phrase "acculturated,"[4] which means that Christians must understand and live in the society in which they find themselves. Didn't Jesus tell us to be in the world but not of the world (see John 17:11-16)? What does that phrase mean?

Doesn't it mean that we are to dress like the people around us, yet not display our body in a lewd and enticing manner? Doesn't it mean that our dress should not call attention to itself, but we should fit in with culture so that people see beyond our clothes and see "Christ in you, the hope of glory" (Col. 1:27)? Doesn't it mean that Christians should live as those about them in work habits, relationship to friends, eating and housing? Yes, believers are to be like the culture around them, but there may be food and drink that Christians should not eat or consume simply because it destroys their physical bodies and/or their minds. Didn't Paul ask the question that leads to our separation from the world: "Know ye not that ye are the temple of God" (1 Cor. 3:16, *KJV*)?

The churches in this book first influenced the people in the church, then they influenced believers in other churches, and finally they influenced the culture around them. The believers of the house churches in China did not dress like the believers in Sidney, Australia, or the believers of a Baptist church in Lynchburg, Virginia. The believers who attended the cell meetings in the Full Gospel Church in Seoul, South Korea, did not dress like Americans. That suggests Christians were accepted within their culture yet showed themselves superior to the culture for the sake of Jesus Christ so they could influence their culture for Jesus Christ.

But what about the Jesus People, who attended Calvary Chapel barefoot and wore ragged jeans and T-shirts? Their primary intent was not to attack the traditional culture in a "dead" church; i.e., their Sunday "go to church" dress. Also, their primary intent was not to rebel against the social customs of the United States. They just attended church naturally, as they lived. They came to worship Jesus, fellowship with others and learn from the Word of God. Their worship was so authentic that they showed themselves superior to the worship of traditional churches. Eventually, through their differences, they influenced the dress in traditional churches.

3. *Churches have life cycles like all other living, organic things.* We begin with the premise that no church has continued in a state of revival into new generations and ages. Why? Because all churches have an implied life cycle, just like trees, plants, animals and people. All are born, grow, reach maturity and then atrophy gradually to the point of death. The death of a person is always sad, but it's inevitable. But is death always inevitable in churches? Isn't Jesus Christ alive forever? Doesn't the gospel continue from generation to generation? Yes! But no local church has continued without change and without eventually dying.

It seems the Azusa Revival had the shortest life span of any church in this book. It burst on the scene like holiday fireworks that lit up the night, and then, just as quickly, was extinguished. The Apostolic Faith Mission in Los Angeles had its greatest influence in three to five years, and then struggled for a dozen years. Those few years of brilliance and pure manifestations of the Holy Spirit were so bright that they continued to today and covered the world.

The book of Judges examines several cycles of "religious devotion." The cycle of life in the Old Testament was similar to New Testament local churches, and/or today's churches and denominations. God's people followed Him and worshiped Him; however, over a period of time spiritual atrophy set in and the people wandered from God.

> So the people served the LORD all the days of Joshua, and all the days of the elders who outlived Joshua, who had seen all the great works of the LORD which He had done for Israel. Now Joshua the son of Nun, the servant of the LORD, died when he was one hundred and ten years old. . . . When all that generation had been gathered to their fathers, another generation arose after them who did not know the LORD nor the work which He had done for Israel. Then the children of Israel did evil in the sight of the LORD, and served the Baals (Judg. 2:7-8, 10-11).

Examine the cycles of Judges and compare them to today's church. First, the Israelites sinned and God punished them by allowing outside nations to conquer them and put them into servitude. Second, God's people cried out in repentance over their sins. Third, God heard and forgave their sins. Fourth, God raised up a warrior-judge to deliver them from bondage. The judge led the people to fight and win over their captors.

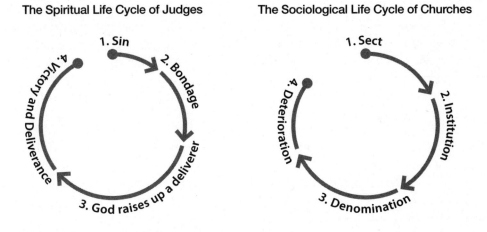

The Spiritual Life Cycle of Judges

1. Sin
2. Bondage
3. God raises up a deliverer
4. Victory and Deliverance

The Sociological Life Cycle of Churches

1. Sect
2. Institution
3. Denomination
4. Deterioration

Richard Niebuhr, a sociologist and theologian, gave the same insights into the life cycle of churches and Christian institutions. Niebuhr states:

> Children born into families of first-generation sect members begin to change the sect into a church even before they reach adulthood. With their coming, the sect must become an educational and disciplinary institution in order to make the new generation conform to its ideas and customs. The second generation holds its convictions less fervently than pioneers of the sects, whose convictions were formed in the heat of conflict and sometimes at the threat of martyrdom. With each succeeding generation, isolation from the world becomes more difficult.[5]

The problem is with the second generation, or when children are born into a congregation. The first-generation evangelistic church must become a second-generation educational church. When the original passion and vision that made the church influential changes in the second generation, it usually redirects its vision to keep the institution alive and going. It is no longer a conquering institution.

After studying the 10 innovative churches, I maintain that these churches were effective because they had the sectarian-type strengths that theologian Ernst Troeltsch described in the sociological cycle of church growth and decline. The following cycle is an elaboration of Troeltsch's original position. A church begins as a sect and moves to the second stage on the cycle, which is an institution (it begins organizing itself to carry out ministry and keep itself going). The third stage on the cycle is a fully organized entity that Troeltsch called *ecclesia,* or a denomination. The final stage is deterioration (the original passion of the church is abandoned and tradition takes over with a view of keeping the door open and the organization going.)[6]

Harvey Cox, in his controversial book *The Secular City*, explained the development (or life cycles) of churches in relationship to the socio-economic factors of society. He sees a church cycle as: (1) the tribe, (2) the town, (3) the metropolis and (4) the megalopolis.[7] His cycle has many parallel factors to Troeltsch's cycles.

What drives churches through this cycle? Churches at birth begin with great expectations and sacrifice by the founding pastor and members, but they evolve into a traditional church with traditional expectations. First, pastoral changes usually alter the church's passion. The second-generation pastor doesn't have the vision of the founding pastor. Or, if he does have it, he can't communicate it as well or carry it off as well.

Second, the church inevitability adds additional ministries. These may be needed for the church to survive, but they tend to dilute the members' commitment to the church's original purpose. Like barnacles on a boat, new additions slow it down or weigh it down.

Third, the demanding needs of children born into the church are usually different than the needs of the community and its original set of needs that provoked the church's original influential ministry. New children must be taught the purposes of the original church, but that educational process is not always effective, and second-generation Christians become less fervent than the original pioneers.

Fourth, there is the problem of money. With the rising level of wealth and affluence in the world, financial forces play a role in changing the members of an *influencer-church*. Wealth and ease can make pioneers less willing to sacrifice for the purpose of the church.

4. *There is a life cycle of methods just as there is a life cycle of churches.* At times I have called these methods that are most effective "anointed methods." Just as a leader is anointed by the Holy Spirit for effective spiritual ministry, so these are times when it seems certain methods

are more effective than any previous time in its life, and more effective than the old methods a church may have been using.

A method is the application of an eternal biblical principle to culture. Therefore, some effective methods of evangelism in one culture will not be as effective—or even work—in a different culture. We're not describing biblical principles, but a culturally related method. As an illustration, teaching the Bible to children is a principle, but organizing them into an age-graded class that is divided by grades is a method called Sunday school. It has been effective in American culture, which has dominated by compulsory public school education. It worked in the First Presbyterian Church of Hollywood, California, but wouldn't work for the Jotabeche Church of Santiago, Chile, or the underground church of China.

Therefore, when culture changes, so church methods must change. Why? Because a church method loses its effectiveness. The seeker church of Bill Hybels would not be effective in historic Christian-based England. But as England abandons its traditional Christian heritage, a seeker church for the unsaved may be effective. And as the English culture becomes more secular, a seeker church will become more effective in the future—or, as I describe it, it will become an "anointed method." Note the following statement about changing methods:

Methods are many,
    Principles are few;
Methods may change,
    But principles never do.

Also, note the following chart, which traces effective methods used by Southern Baptists in the past 100 years to build a church in the southern part of the United States:

1900–1960	Door-to-door visitation evangelism
1960–1970	Sunday school bus evangelism
1970–1980	Saturation evangelism involving advertising and mass media
1980–1990	Front-door evangelism, making Sunday morning an evangelistic service
1990–2009	Seeker evangelism
2000–2010	Worship evangelism
2010–2011	Church planting evangelism

The life cycles of churches and methods are evident when we examine the 10 most influential churches. Note the following explanation of the changing intensity of methods in these churches:

Apostolic Faith Mission	The intensity of the protracted meetings involving Holy Spirit manifestations inevitably ran its course. Meetings were shortened or cancelled.
Chinese House Church	Will this method continue when governmental persecution is lifted? Will these churches follow the route of other house churches that have become institutionalized, organized and have begun constructing church buildings?
Ebenezer Baptist Church	With the assassination of Martin Luther King, Jr. and the passage of the 1964 Civil Rights Act, there is less need for passive resistance to segregation that doesn't exist as it did in the past.
Yoido Full Gospel Church	With the retirement of David Yonggi Cho and the separating of more than 50 satellite churches from the mother church, will the second-generation pastor be challenged to be the largest and to reach new communities that could be considered unreached?
First Baptist Church (Dallas, Texas)	The worship attendance is the highest it has been in the history of the church. Additionally, the church has just completed a $135 million re-creation of their downtown campus—the largest in modern church history.
Scofield Memorial Church	Will the method of a Bible-teaching pulpit be as effective with postmodern Americans?
Willow Creek Church	The seeker method will become more effective as culture becomes more secular. However, it may become less effective as the congregation of Willow Creek becomes more mature traditional believers.

Calvary Chapel	The uniqueness of casual dress is being accepted because the Baby Boomer has taken over. The next challenge will be to reach the millennial generation.
Hillsong Church	There is a question as to whether praise-worship music has reached its apex or if there will be a new expression of music to capture the young and eventually invade the church.
Thomas Road Baptist Church	The television church seems to have had its day, and if anything, the media/marketing church of the future will be the Internet church.

Just as the "Brush Arbor Meetings" of the Second Great Awakening had great impact in their day but are rarely seen today, so some of the methods used by these churches will cool off and lose their effectiveness in the future. The challenge is to live today, present the ageless message of Jesus Christ to the next generation, and use the methods that will effectively reach them with salvation and continuing ministry.

5. *Each church used a different method to influence its members and other churches.* A church method is the application of a biblical principle to culture.[8] While all of the 10 influential churches were committed to the principles of Christianity, each church expressed itself in different methods and influenced other believers, churches and the culture in different ways. Note the differences in the methods:

Church	Method
Apostolic Mission, Los Angeles	Individual expressions of the Holy Spirit
The Organic House Church, China	Relationship, belief and practice
Ebenezer Baptist Church, Atlanta	Passive resistance to unrighteous laws
The Yoido Full Gospel Church, Seoul	Small-group ministry
First Baptist Church, Dallas	Evangelistic Sunday school classes

Scofield Memorial Church, Dallas	Expositional Bible-teaching sermons
Willow Creek, Greater Chicago	Church designed for the unsaved
Calvary Chapel, Costa Mesa	Baby Boomer culture influencing churches
Hillsong Church, Sydney	Innovative worship through contemporary praise music
Thomas Road Baptist Church, Lynchburg	Media and marketing

6. *Each church included methods found in other churches but grew by emphasizing their primary method.* While all of the 10 churches were driven by their strengths, they also employed "methods" found in other churches that contributed to their total ministry. As an illustration, Scofield Memorial Church was known for a Bible-teaching pulpit, and the pastor taught his unique interpretation of the work of the Holy Spirit in the lives of "Bible church" Christians. At the opposite extreme was the Azusa Revival at the Apostolic Faith Mission, which placed a different emphasis on the Holy Spirit.

Churches that emphasized worship music—such as Calvary Chapel and Hillsong Church—were also active in evangelism but did not express evangelism like First Baptist Church, Dallas, where soul-winning was its overriding purpose. And those who attended church services led by W.A. Criswell worshiped God even when the sermon ended in an old-fashioned gospel invitation for "sinners" to walk forward to receive Christ. All the *influencer-churches* displayed in some manner all the methods of other churches while emphasizing the strengths of their own identity.

7. *A worship experience is legitimate when God is the focus.* When God is worshiped in spirit (see John 4:23-24), He is magnified. In return, God rewards that church with His presence and power. It is authentic worship whether the worship music is sung *a capella* (as in Chinese house churches) or by 10,000 worshipers led by Darlene Zschech singing, "My Jesus, My Savior, Lord there is none like You."[9]

8. *No influencer-church has a corner on the market.* The great thing about these churches is that they share what God has done for them with others, but they are all different. That's what makes them great, and that makes them *influencer-churches.*

9. *Various strengths in the influencer-churches may be seen at different stages or times in the growth cycle of other churches.* Some people think evangelism always comes first, but that is not always the case. In praise-worship churches, unsaved people are brought to Christ as they feel intimacy with God in worship. In Southern Baptist methodology, a person must be evangelized first by preaching against sin, and salvation must be presented. The person is then asked to receive Christ as his or her Savior. Then, after salvation, they are introduced to worship. In addition, Bible-teaching pulpits begin with biblical education and, as a result, unsaved people are led to salvation. These other forms of method/ministry are then used, such as worship and fellowship.

10. *No one type of ministry meets all the needs of all people.* God uses different church ministries to bring different people to salvation. The emotional person may be reached for Christ through praise-worship music, the rational or intellectual person may be reached through Bible-teaching pulpits, and the secular postmodern may be reached through a Willow Creek type of "seeker" ministry. A Buddhist family member may not be reached with any of the above methods but will be open to the message of Jesus Christ in a cell meeting in a relative's living room in Seoul, South Korea.

11. *Because God has used different types of methods, we should not magnify or emphasize one method over another but emphasize the unity we have in Jesus Christ.* Even though churches use different methods to reach people for Christ, the focus should be on Christ. And even when we worship with different methods, and we preach with different expressions, God is still the focus of our ministry, and the Word of God is the foundation for all we do. "There is one body and one Spirit, just as you were called in one hope of your calling; one Lord, one faith, one baptism; one God and Father of all, who is above all, and through all, and in you all" (Eph. 4:4-6).

We should pray for unity as Jesus prayed "that they all may be one" (John 17:21). While Jesus prayed for unity among believers—which is a heart attitude of accepting one another as He accepts them—this unity does not mean union. "Union" means that all believers joining the same organic structure do the same thing in the same way. Union is conforming to the group as required and/or expected.

In essentials—unity
In non-essentials—liberty
And in all things—charity[10]

Appendix A

Research Techniques to Find the 10 Churches of Greatest Influence

The criteria to determine the 10 largest and/or fastest-growing churches began with objective data.[1] I used standards that were observable, measureable and repeatable to gather data from these churches. Some of these types of data involved measurements of attendance, new converts, offerings, size of auditorium, buildings and resources. However, I could not necessarily use these criteria to identify the 10 most influential churches in the past 100 years. Some influential churches were large, while others were small. Some were wealthy, while some obviously were not. Some had explosive growth, while some did not. Some had short life spans, while others endured. Therefore, before I could measure influence, I had to determine what *was* influence.

> *Influence* (in floo ens) n.v. 1. Invisible or insensible action exerted by one thing or person on another. 2. Power of producing effects by invisible or insensible means (sphere of influence). 3. A thing or person that exerts action by invisible or insensible means (beneficial influence). 4. Electrostatic induction. *Oxford Dictionary*, 1947.

The above definition suggests that influence is a force or power on someone or something else that produces a similar effect. Therefore, when trying to determine the 10 *influencer-churches,* we are looking for the following:

- An influence that is positive (not negative) that grew out of the originating churches' purpose to express the Christian message
- The originating church has purposed to do the actions that influence other churches

• The originating church was so successful in its ministry that other churches followed its example

• The ministry of the originating church was considered worth copying (emulating) by other churches

• The tie between the originating church and the churches it influences was evident enough to observe, measure and reduce to writing or measurement.

Therefore, the following seven questions guided research to determine *Ten of the Churches with Greatest Influence in the Past 100 Years:*

1. What is the essence (descriptive ministry) of the influence that a church was able to exert on its members, neighborhood or other churches?

2. How has the church's ministry influenced other churches or social institutions to have a similar or positive influence on culture?

3. What new methods or means of ministry has the church created to spread its influence? How has the church used methods, advertising, marketing and other social media to communicate its influence to as large a population as possible?

4. How has the church's ministry influenced its immediate surrounding culture? This involves the influence the church has had on community lifestyle, social values, attitudes, laws, ordinances and improving the life of the community.

5. Has the ministry of the church leader been acknowledged and/or admired by the Christian public and/or the non-Christian public? Has that acknowledgement extended past the leader's life into succeeding generations? Can the unique influence of the leader that made him influential be identified, observed, measured and recorded?

6. How has the influencer-church overcome problems, barriers and obstacles to carry out its ministry and become more influential? How has the church communicated its problem-solving successes to other churches to help them overcome their obstacles to ministry?

7. Has the influencer-church effectively communicated its successes to a second and third generation? How has the church extended its influence to other generations in other cultures?

The first step in my research was to determine the greatest area of influence (trend) in Christian churches in the past 100 years. To research this question, I used focus groups of students studying for a Doctor of Ministry degree at several evangelical seminaries. Thus, the observations came from students who were actively involved in Christian ministry (a Ph.D. focus group would probably produce suggestions from theoretical research rather than actual issues in church life). These D.Min. students represented a wide background (denomination) of theological beliefs and church practices. They also represented a wide range of age, size, economic strength, evangelistic expressions and geographical location.

I summarized these results into 20 trends that grew out of the students' observations in their churches. It was assumed that a trend would represent a broader result of many churches following a particular action or method. The following 20 trends emerged, which are not listed in logical but alphabetical order:

20 Influential Trends Among Evangelical Churches in the Past 100 Years

1. Age-graded Sunday school: Bible teaching
2. Baby Boomers: Culture in churches being changed by Baby Boomers
3. Bible-teaching sermons: Bible-teaching sermons instead of traditional pulpit ministry
4. Church planting: Church-planting strategy of evangelism
5. Foreign missions: Foreign mission endeavors by local church
6. Home cells: Used for church ministry and outreach
7. House churches: Local churches in homes; also, those that might meet in apartments, restaurants, public meeting areas and/or the underground church (persecuted church)
8. Internet churches: Internet churches that are built on community participation and loyalty
9. Lay Sunday school teachers: Used for evangelism and ministry
10. Leadership: Ministry by pastors and churches
11. Media and marketing: Used by churches for ministry
12. Multisite churches: Meeting in multiple locations
13. Pentecostalism: Its spread and growth worldwide
14. Personal soul-winning evangelism: To build a church
15. Positive thinking: Or prosperity teaching in churches
16. Praise-worship: Contemporary worship services

17. Racial integration: Non-violent changes in churches
18. Seeker-model: Church designed for the unchurched
19. Servanthood evangelism: Servanthood for outreach
20. Video venue: Multisite church

Focus groups were assembled during a period of four years for Doctor of Ministry students in theological seminaries. Each group was given these 20 trends and asked to place them in order of importance; i.e., from 1 to 20 by their opinion of the most influential trends or influences.

The Doctor of Ministry students were active pastors with a practical grasp on trends, and they should have given good guidance in finding the most influential trends. But I was wrong about their objectivity. Some who were aggressively Calvinistic would not rank "the spread of Pentecostalism worldwide" as number 1. Some non-Charismatics or anti-Charismatics ranked it low or left it off the survey all together. What happened? These students' theology influenced their ability to objectively assess trends and influences.

The same was true with some ultra-right-wing ministers. They refused to rank Martin Luther King, Jr. because of his liberal (rather than conservative) orientation to theology. Some ranked the Bible-teaching pulpit low because they might have reacted against what they viewed as "dead preaching," or they might have been against Scofield's dispensationalism. So, I couldn't accept all conclusions, but I was guided by all insights. The focus groups arrived at the following ranking:

Twenty Trends Among Evangelical Churches in Order of Importance

1. Pentecostalism: Its spread and growth worldwide
2. House churches: Local churches in homes; also, those that might meet in apartments, restaurants, public meeting areas and/or the underground church (persecuted church)
3. Racial integration: Non-violent changes in churches
4. Home cells: Used for church ministry and outreach
5. Lay Sunday school teachers: Used for evangelism and ministry
6. Bible-teaching sermons: Bible-teaching sermons instead of traditional pulpit ministry
7. Seeker-model: Church designed for the unchurched
8. Baby Boomers: Culture in churches being changed by Baby Boomers

9. Praise-worship: Contemporary worship services
10. Media and marketing: Used by churches for ministry
11. Age-graded Sunday school: Bible teaching
12. Positive thinking: Or prosperity teaching in churches
13. Personal soul-winning evangelism: To build a church
14. Foreign missions: Foreign mission endeavors by local church
15. Servanthood evangelism: Servanthood for outreach
16. Church planting: Church-planting strategy of evangelism
17. Multisite churches: Meeting in multiple locations
18. Leadership: Ministry by pastors and churches
19. Video venue: Multisite church
20. Internet churches: Internet churches that are built on community participation and loyalty

The next task was to find the primary church that could be identified with each of these trends. This was difficult. I first searched historical records to locate churches that were identified with each trend. The *influencer-church* had to give historical evidence of using a method (or methods) that began a trend, or at least have evidence that it took a trend and greatly enhanced it so that it became influential.

An illustration of this is the seeker trend. In the 2014 media market, Rick Warren created news because of his size, political involvement and some of his spectacular actions (e.g., his Hawaiian shirts). It seems the church he founded, Saddleback Church, should be identified as the *influencer-church*. But Bill Hybels and Willow Creek Community Church was historically first. *TIME* magazine featured an article on Bill Hybels and the Willow Creek Community Church he planted in 1975, and then Rick Warren five years later, in 1980. Both had innovative ingredients, but they were different from each other.

Assigning 20 churches to the 20 trends was my individual choice. I attempted to remain loyal to objectivity. This is illustrated in the fact that I placed some churches high on the listing even though they did not represent my theological beliefs. I am not Pentecostal, but traditional Baptist; yet I placed the Azusa Street Revival first and the Yoido Full Gospel Church fourth, both before fifth-place First Baptist Church of Dallas, Texas, and tenth-place Thomas Road Baptist Church in Lynchburg, Virginia. Obviously, Pentecostalism has had worldwide influence, whereas the Sunday school movement was influential primarily in the United States.

When I assigned a church to a trend, I couldn't always find a church that initiated a trend and/or was tied to the beginning of that trend.

Sometimes, I chose a church not because it existed at the beginning of a trend but because it did more to accelerate the trend than other churches. In addition, in its use of the influence, the church gave attention to the trend and accelerated the trend to a new level of achievement. Such was the case with First Baptist Church of Dallas, Texas. Technically, Arthur Flake in the early 1900s did more to give growth to the Southern Baptist Convention than any other person. Flake initiated the organized Sunday school movement among Southern Baptist churches that gave rise to a multitude of Southern Baptist churches. But W.A. Criswell built the largest individual Southern Baptist church by building the largest Sunday school. Therefore, his church and Sunday school are listed in fifth place.

I had previously published a research volume titled *The 10 Largest Sunday Schools and What Makes Them Grow*.[2] I found these Sunday schools by researching denominational statistics plus the records of state and Sunday school conventions both in the United States and Canada. These statistics were easy to identify, so there was not much conflict with the list of the 10 largest.

But statistics alone couldn't determine *Ten of the Churches with Greatest Influence in the Past 100 Years*. As mentioned earlier, some influential churches were small. The Azusa Street auditorium seated 300, and Scofield Memorial church seated 1,000. Therefore, focus groups gave me broad guidance, but they were not always authoritative. It was then I decided to use a panel to verify and establish objectivity to the final listing of the *Ten of the Churches with Greatest Influence in the Past 100 Years*.

Douglas Porter and I had also published a research volume titled *The 10 Greatest Revivals*.[3] To determine the 10 greatest revivals, we had asked a panel of 19 experts to vote their opinion of the greatest revivals in history. They represented several denominations and several theological perspectives. The credibility of the book was tied to the integrity of the panel.[4] For this reason, I presented the findings in this book to a panel of three individuals who had experience in church growth research. In addition, they had published extensively about influential churches.

Dr. Warren Bird, Director of Research and Intellectual Capital at Leadership Network, wrote *Into the Future* with me, published by Fleming Revell in 1999.[5] He also is co-author with Dr. Ed Stetzer and me on *Eleven Innovations in the Local Church*, published by Regal Books.[6] Bird understands church influence and has written other notable books, such *Better Together: Making Church Mergers Work* (San Francisco, CA: Jossey Bass, 2012), which he wrote with Jim Tomberlin and Craig Groeschel; and *The Other 80 Percent: Turning Your Church's Spectators into Active Participants* (San Francisco, CA: Jossey Bass, 2011), which he wrote with Scott Thumma.

Bird's position as director of research qualifies him to give objectivity to listing the 10 most influential churches.

Dr. Ed Stetzer, President of LifeWay Research, and I wrote *The Perimeter of Light* (Chicago, IL: Moody Press, 2004), an examination of the influence of postmodernity.[7] In addition, Ed has published the following research volumes: *Viral Churches* (San Francisco, CA: Jossey Bass, 2010), with Warren Bird; *Planting Missional Churches* (Nashville, TN: B&H Publishers, 2007); and *Transformational Church: Creating a New Scorecard for Congregations* (Nashville, TN: B&H Publishers, 2010), with Thom S. Rainier. Ed Stetzer's position as president of one of the largest research institutions also qualifies him to give objectivity to this volume.

This panel of three (including me) has taken the list of 20 *church-influencers* and put them into the order of chapters in this book. While these may not be the same order that would be arranged by researchers 50 years from now, this is the order that they chose in 2013.

What 100 Years?

Technically, this book begins with the twentieth century (1900) and extends to its publication date (2014). That's more than 100 years. The 100-year limit was extended to include some influences that extended beyond the chronological limits.

Some of these churches are older than the 100 years of this survey. Some are young churches when compared to 114 years. I was looking for the things these churches accomplished in the past 114 years that made them an *influencer-church*. Because their heritage has extended from the last century into this one, I have stretched the limits from 1900 to 2014. So, this book begins with year 1900 and includes the world-changing influences that began in 1904 with the Faith Apostolic Mission in Los Angeles, better known as the Azusa Street Revival. It extends to several modern day *church-influencers* who are just beginning to be an influence.

History and Future of Influencer-Churches

I recognize that no church is an island, so these 10 churches grew out of previous traditions and have been influenced by churches that existed before them. When churches are planted on the foundation of Scripture, they are also influenced by the content and church methods found in Scripture. So, no church comes into existence by and of itself. Therefore, I have included a sketch in each chapter of how each trend developed and its influence on the church that is the focus of the chapter. In addition, some other churches are included that also could have been noted as an influence for each trend or influence.

When I originally interviewed Bill Hybels for the book *10 Innovative Churches* in 1990, he claimed his seeker model was new and innovative and couldn't be identified with any previous church growth paradigm. In one sense he was right; other American churches had not descriptively reached contemporary unchurched America as he had. But he was wrong in that there have been other church movements throughout history that had targeted the unchurched. Of course, some of them did it much differently than Bill Hybels.

These 10 churches did not become buckets to just receive ideas from the past and use them for their self-growing ministry. No! They were innovative conduits to pass their ideas and methods onto other churches. It's like giving a farmer a new innovative wheat combine. The farmer uses his new combine to harvest wheat fields much larger than he could have done with just a plough and a mule. But he doesn't keep his ideas to himself. He communicates his new ideas to other farmers so they can be as effective as he has been. He then becomes an influencer-farmer.

When William Seymour experienced the baptism of the Holy Spirit and tongues, he passed it on to Aimee Semple McPherson, who helped plant the large Foursquare Church denomination. She, in turn, was a conduit to Chuck Smith, an ordained pastor in the Foursquare Church who began Calvary Chapel, another denomination of 1,200 churches. William Seymour became an influencer-pastor.

Therefore, the churches described in this book are part of a process. They have received something from previous generations and have passed that influence on to others. That process explains why I wrote this book. It should influence your church to pass its influence on to other churches (see Afterthought: What Can We Learn from These Churches).

The Ten Most Influential Churches in the Past 100 Years

The following individuals were given copies of the chapter that related to them. They were asked to read the chapter and then respond in three ways: (1) what changes needed to be made, (2) what strengths needed to be highlighted, and (3) what needed to be eliminated.

Title	Evaluator
Chapter 1: The Spread and Growth of Pentecostalism Worldwide	C. Peter Wagner, recognized leader among Pentecostal/ Charismatics, especially for his recent work on the spiritual gifts/office of apostles. Wagner gained fame as a professor of church growth at Fuller Theological Seminary in Pasadena, California, primarily during the 1970s and 1980s. He first wrote in the area of evangelism and church growth and then moved into prayer and spiritual factors of church health and growth.
	Steve Strang, first noticed for his work on the staff of Calvary Assembly of God (Winter Park, Florida) during its meteoric rise in size and influence. He directed church publications, and that ministry evolved into *Charisma* magazine. From that platform he has become one of the most influential publishing voices in the Pentecostal/ Charismatic world.
	James O. Davis, founder of Cutting Edge International and cofounder of the Billion Soul Network.
Chapter 2: The Unseen but Ever-Present Influence of House Churches	Dr. Christian Wei, President of Eucon University, Saipan (Island) Japan. His institution trains leaders for the Chinese house church.
Chapter 3: A Non-Violent Revolution that Led to Racial Integration in Churches	Dr. Allen McFarland, an African-America pastor at Calvary Evangelical Baptist Church in Portsmouth, Virginia. He is also president of the Fundamental Baptist Fellowship Association in Kansas City, Kansas, a fellowship of African-American pastors.
Chapter 4: Home Cells Used for Church Ministry and Outreach	David Yonggi Cho is the focus of this chapter.

Chapter 5: A Church Built on Sunday School Evangelism	Dr. Gary Waller, associate pastor of First Baptist Church in Dallas, Texas, and assistant professor Liberty University. Jerry Sutton, pastor of the rapidly growing Twin Rivers Baptist Church in Nashville, Tennessee, which is gaining an international reputation in the area of church leadership. He left the church to become a professor at Liberty Baptist Theological Seminary and then became dean at Midwestern Theological Seminary in Kansas City, Missouri.
Chapter 6: A Change to Bible Teaching Instead of Traditional Pulpit Ministry	Dr. Neil Ashcraft, pastor of Scofield Church for 27 years (1972 to 1997).
Chapter 7: A Seeker-Model Church Designed for the Unchurched	Bill Hybels, author, speaker and founding and senior pastor of Willow Creek Community Church in Barrington, Illinois.
Chapter 8: A New Church Culture Initiated by Baby Boomers	Chuck Fromm, nephew of Chuck Smith and editor at *Worship Leader Magazine* (1990–present)
Chapter 9: Initiating Praise-Worship in Worship Services	Jack Hayford, author, Pentecostal minister and founding pastor of The Church On The Way in Van Nuys, California.
Chapter 10: Using Media and Marketing to Extend the Influence of a Church	Jerry Falwell, Jr., Chancellor at Liberty University in Lynchburg, Virginia (2007–Present). Jonathan Falwell, pastor of Thomas Road Baptist Church in Lynchburg, Virginia (2007–Present).

Appendix B

The 10 Greatest Leadership-Influencers in Christian Ministry in the Past 100 Years*

1. Billy Graham: Preached to more people than any other in Christian history.
2. Billy Sunday: Won millions to Christ and was humanly responsible for the Eighteenth Amendment to the U. S. Constitution.
3. Bill Bright: Built the largest Christian ministry organization in the century with approximately 500,000 volunteers and paid workers.
4. Charles E. Fuller: The greatest radio outreach through the *Old Fashioned Revival Hour.*
5. Donald McGavran: Changed the strategy of foreign missions to church planting.
6. James Dobson: Helped strengthen families through Focus on the Family.
7. Arthur Flake: Developed a Sunday school outreach strategy that helped build the largest Protestant denomination in America.
8. Jan and Paul Crouch: Built the largest worldwide television ministry, TBN Trinity Broadcasting network.
9. John Maxwell: Taught American pastors to lead their congregations, rather than just preach and minister to them.
10. Several authors whose books influence the way Christians think: Ken Taylor, *The Living Bible*; Tim LaHaye, *The Left Behind Series*: Norman Vincent Peale, *The Power of Positive Thinking*; and Oswald Chambers, *My Utmost for His Highest.*

* These individuals have exerted influence apart from local church ministry.

Appendix C

The 15 Greatest Influences of Christian Thought in the Past 100 Years

1. Karl Barth: *Dialectical Theology*, the father of neo-orthodoxy; *Church Dogmatics* (13 volumes)
2. C.S. Lewis: *Mere Christianity, Miracles, The Problem of Pain*
3. Augustus Hopkins Strong: *Systematic Theology: A Compendium and Commonplace-Book Designed for the Use of Theological Students*
4. H. Richard Niebuhr: *Christ and Culture*
5. Emile Brunner: *Dogmatics* (three volumes, *magnum opus*)
6. Paul Tillich: *The Courage to Be, Systematic Theology* (three volumes)
7. Francis Schaeffer: *Escape from Reason, The God Who Is There, A Christian Manifesto, Whatever Happened to the Human Race?*
8. Dietrich Bonhoeffer: *The Cost of Discipleship*
9. Carl H.F. Henry: *The Uneasy Conscience of Fundamentalism, God, Revelation, and Authority*
10. Lewis Sperry Chafer: *Systematic Theology* (seven volumes)
11. Cornelius Van Til: *In Defence of the Faith* (6 volumes, systematic theology)
12. Edward J. Carnell: *An Introduction to Christian Apologetics, A Philosophy of the Christian Religion, The Case for Orthodoxy*
13. J. Gresham Machen: *Christianity and Liberalism*
14. B.B. Warfield: *The Inspiration and Authority of the Bible*
15. Reinhold Niebuhr: *Moral Man and Immoral Society, and The Irony of American History*

Endnotes

Foreword

1. "Christian Child's Prayer," words written by preacher Clare Herbert Woolston (1856–1927) [Cited July 22, 2013]. Online: http://en.wikipedia.org/wiki/Christian_child%27s_prayer.
2. Elmer L. Towns, *A Practical Encyclopedia: Evangelism and Church Growth* (Ventura, CA: Regal Books, 1995), 47.
3. "Shout to the Lord" lyrics by Darlene Zschech, *metrolyrics.com* [Cited July 22, 2013]. Online: http://www.metrolyrics.com/shout-to-the-lord-lyrics-zschech-darlene.html.

Introduction: Finding the Most Influential Churches

1. See Appendix A.
2. Ibid.
3. Definition of "cult" from Merriam Webster Online Dictionary: (1) formal religious veneration; (2) a system of religious beliefs and ritual; *also:* its body of adherents; (3) a religion regarded as unorthodox or spurious; *also* its body of adherents, [cited August 7, 2012]. Online: http://www.merriam-webster.com/dictionary/cult, s. v. *cult*.

Chapter 1: The Spread of and Growth of Pentecostalism Worldwide

1. Julia Duin, "Pentecostalists to Mark Centennial," *The Washington Times,* January 1, 2006. Online: http://www.washingtontimes.com/news/2006/jan/1/20060101-122305-1724r/ (accessed August 24, 2012).
2. "The San Francisco Earthquake, 1906," EyeWitness to History (1997). Online: www.eye witnesstohistory.com (accessed on July 22, 2012).
3. Ibid.
4. Herbert Asbury, *The Barbary Coast* (New York: Basic Books, 2002), n.p.
5. Jack Hayford and S. David Moore, *The Charismatic Century: The Enduring Impact of the Azusa Street Revival* (Nashville, TN: Faithwords, 2006), n.p.
6. William Johnson, *The Church Through the Ages* (Bethesda Books, 2003), n.p.
7. "A Brief History of Pentecostalism." Online: http://www.rapidnet.com/%jbeard/bdm/ Psychology/char/abrief.htm (accessed on January 21, 2013).
8. Elmer L. Towns and Vernon M. Whaley, *Worship Through the Ages* (Nashville, TN: B&H Academic, 2012).
9. Anonymous, *J. Wilbur Chapman, 1859–1918: Evangelist and Pastor,* 2012, Truthfulwords.org. Online: http://www.truthfulwords.org/biography/chapmantw.html (accessed on July 31, 2012).
10. Ibid.
11. Steven Ross, "Echoes from Glory: J. Wilbur Chapman," Wholesome Words. Online: www .wholesomewords.org/biography/biorpchapman.html (accessed on May 17, 2012).
12. Donald P. Hustad, *Jubilee II: Church Music in Worship and Renewal* (Carol Stream, IL: Hope Publishing, 1993), 247.
13. International visitors and Pentecostal missionaries would eventually export the revival to other nations. The first foreign Pentecostal missionaries were A.G. Garr and his wife, who were Spirit baptized at Azusa and traveled to India and later to Hong Kong [Vinson Synan, *The Holiness-Pentecostal Tradition: Charismatic Movements in the Twentieth Century* (Grand Rapids: Wm. B. Eerdmans Publishing Co, 1997), 101-1022]. Seymour influenced T.B. Barratt, a Norwegian Methodist pastor, during his tour of the United States. By December 1906, Barratt had returned to Europe and is credited with beginning the Pentecostal movement in Sweden, Norway, Denmark, Germany, France and England [ibid., 104-105]. A notable convert of Barratt was Alexander Boddy, Anglican vicar of All Saints' in Sunderland, England, who became a founder of British Pentecostalism [Ibid., 131]. Other important converts of Barratt were German minister Jonathan Paul, who founded the first German Pentecostal denomination (the Mülheim Association), and Lewi Pethrus, the Swedish Baptist minister who founded the Swedish Pentecostal movement [ibid., 131-132]. Through Durham's ministry, Italian immigrant Luigi Francescon received the Pentecostal experience in 1907 and established

Italian Pentecostal congregations in the United States, Argentina and Brazil. In 1908, Giacomo Lombardi led the first Pentecostal services in Italy [ibid., 133-134]. In November 1910, two Swedish Pentecostal missionaries arrived in Belem, Brazil, and established what would become the Assembleias de Deus (Assemblies of God of Brazil) [ibid., 134-135]. In 1908, John G. Lake, a follower of Alexander Dowie who had experienced Pentecostal Spirit baptism, traveled to South Africa and founded what would become the Apostolic Faith Mission of South Africa and the Zion Christian Church [ibid., 137-138]. As a result of this missionary zeal, nearly all Pentecostal denominations today trace their historical roots to the Azusa Street Revival [ibid., 105].

14. Michael Collins and Matthew A. Price, *The Story of Christianity: 2000 Years of Faith* (Wheaton, IL: Tyndale House, 1999), 225.

15. Ibid., 146.

16. Edith Blumhofer, "Azusa Street Revival." Online: http://www.religion-online.org/showarticle.asp?title=3321 (accessed on August 24, 2012).

17. Homer A. Rodeheaver, *Twenty Years with Billy Sunday* (Winona Lake, IN: Rodeheaver, 1936), 85.

18. Paul R. Dienstberger, *The American Republic: A Nation of Christians* (Ashland, OH: Paul R. Dienstberger, 2000), n.p. Online: http://www.prdienstberger.com/nation/Chap8wpr.htm (accessed on August 6, 2011).

19. Estrelda Y. Alexander, *Black Fire: One Hundred Years of African American Pentecostalism* (Downers Grove, IL: IVP Academic, 2011), 121.

20. Ibid., 119.

21. Ibid., 128.

22. Dienstberger, *The American Republic: A Nation of Christians*.

23. Ibid.

24. Ibid., 48-49.

25. The word "manifestation" is used in this chapter as church historians have used it throughout the decades to describe what they saw happen in supernatural outbreaks. This word does not mean the historians agree doctrinally with the phenomena they observed; it only means they objectively reported what they saw and what were the results of the supernatural events they reported. A Christian would believe the Holy Spirit was within the Spirit-indwelt person, motivating the person to action. The historians only reported the "manifestation" of what the person or people were doing. Many believers who do not practice tongues-speaking, nor believe its scriptural basis can never deny what God did at Azusa Street as the Holy Spirit worked through individuals who yielded to Him and sought His presence.

26. A.C. Valdez, Sr., with James F. Scheer, *Fire on Azusa Street* (Costa Mesa, CA: Gift Publications, 1980), 60.

27. Dienstberger, *The American Republic: A Nation of Christians,* 48-49.

28. *The Women of Azusa Street—God's Anointed Hand-Maidens—The Forgotten Legacy!* DVD (2006).

29. Elmer Towns and Douglas Porter, *The Ten Greatest Revivals Ever* (Ann Arbor, MI: Servant Publications, 2000), 28-34. This has been called the "Edwardian Revival" because Edward was king of England at the time. It also is called the Welsh Revival and the 1904 Revival. *The Ten Greatest Revivals Ever* judges this the greatest revival in history.

30. J. Edwin Orr, *The Flaming Tongue* (Chicago: Moody Press, 1973), n.p.

31. "Glossolalia," Wikipedia. Online http://en.wikipedia.org/wiki/Glossolalia (accessed September 10, 2012).

32. Dale A. Robbins, *What People Ask About the Church,* 1995. Online: http://www.victorious.org/churchbook/chur63.htm (accessed September 10, 2012).

33. Cecil M. Robeck, Jr., *The Azusa Street Mission and Revival: The Birth of the Global Pentecostal Movement* (Nashville, TN: Thomas Nelson, 2006), 119-122.

34. Floyd T. Cunningham, Diversities Within Post-War Philippine Protestantism, *page 23. Online:* http://ccfgc.cav.ph/floyd/ *(accessed September 10, 2012).*

35. Jack Zavada, "Foursquare Church Denomination," About.com. Online: http://christianity. about.com/od/Foursquare-Church/a/Foursquare-Church-Profile.htm (accessed September 10, 2012).

36. Bethany Church in Surabaya, Indonesia; Bethany World Prayer Center in Baton Rouge, Louisiana; Brooklyn Tabernacle in New York; The Congregation of Christ in Sao Paulo, Brazil; The First Assembly of God in Phoenix, Arizona; The Hillsong Church in Sydney, Australia; The IHOP in Kansas City, Missouri; The Jotabeche Church (Pentecostal Holiness) in Santiago, Chile; Lakewood Church in Houston, Texas; Mt. Paran Church of God in Atlanta, Georgia; The Potter's House in Dallas, Texas; Rhema Church in Oklahoma City, Oklahoma; and World Harvest in Columbus, Ohio.

37. Cheryl J. Sanders, "History of Women in the Pentecostal Movement," *Cyberjournal for Pentecostal Charismatic Research*, July 1997, no. 2. Online: http://www.pctii.org/cyberj/cyberj2/ sanders.html (accessed August 21, 2012).

38. Harvey Cox, Fire from Heaven (Reading, MA: Addison-Wesley, 1995), 63.

39. Larry Edward Martin and William Joseph Seymour, *The Doctrines and Discipline of the Apostolic Faith Mission* (Joplin, MO: Christian Life Books, 2000).

40. "A Glimpse of the Kingdom of Heaven (The Azusa Street Revival)," *This Far by Faith*. Online: http://www.pbs.org/thisfarbyfaith/journey_3/p_9.html (accessed August 18, 2014).

41. Duin, "Pentacostalists to Mark Centennial," *The Washington Times*, January 1, 2006.

Chapter 2: The Unseen but Ever-Present Influence of House Churches

1. In 1978 Roscoe Brewer, head of missions at Thomas Road Baptist Church, and I sneaked 20 Chinese Bibles into Beijing while we were on a "vacation tour" sponsored by the Chinese government and paid for by TRBC. We knew of one Chinese house church leader in all of Beijing and arranged to meet him at a clandestine meeting in a restaurant. He brought along a porter who worked on a passenger train from Beijing into Tibet. This porter distributed the Bibles to 20 different cities along his route. Week after week the churches would transfer the Bibles to other cities that didn't have a Bible, thus representing the nation's great hunger for the Word of God.

2. Ryan Morgan, "It's Getting Better, but Chinese Persecution of Christians Isn't Over Yet," Persecution.org [Cited on June 3, 2013]. Online: http://info.persecution.org/blog/bid/265313/ It-s-Getting-Better-but-Chinese-Persecution-of-Christians-Isn-t-Over-Yet.

3. I had been invited to lecture at Fudan University in Shanghai on October 12 to 17, 2009. I was introduced as a "world-leading authority on church growth," but I didn't want to lecture on principles of growing churches. That is information needed by those studying for the ministry. I was lecturing young people who were secular and/or communists, and probably atheistic. So I lectured on the church—the body of Christ. That's the real nature of any true New Testament church, regardless of the denomination. It also is the true nature of a house church, but I never mentioned the other house churches in my two lectures (one to undergraduates and the second to graduate students). I also spent two hours with the faculty discussing the topic.

4. This is an excerpt from Paul Brians, Mary Gallwey, Douglas Hughes, et al, *Reading About the World*, vol. 2 (Harcourt Brace Custom Books) [Cited May 14, 2013]. Online: http://public .wsu.edu/~brians/world_civ/worldcivreader/world_civ_reader_2/mao.html.

5. Copyright Society for Anglo-Chinese Understanding (SACU) 2006. Reprinted from SACU's magazine *China Now*, vol. 24, August 1972, page 10 and *China Now* vol. 27, December 1972, page 7. http://www.sacu.org/pinyinissues.html.

6. Manfred B. Sellner, "Language and Politics in Mao's China," *IIAS Newsletter*, no. 39, December 2005 [Cited May 14, 2013]. Online: http://www.iias.nl/nl/39/IIAS_NL39_26.pdf.

7. "Three-Self Patriotic Movement," Wikipedia "[Cited May 6, 2013]. Online: http://en.wikipedia .org/wiki/Three-Self_Patriotic_Movement.

8. Bob Fu, "Persecution in China Is Very Real," *Christianity Today* [Cited May 14, 2103]. Online: http://www.christianitytoday.com/ct/2013/february-web-only/persecution-in -china-is-very-real.html?start=2.

9. Neil Cole, *Organic Church: Growing Faith Where Life Happens* (San Francisco: Jossey Bass, xxii).

10. Ibid., xxv.

11. Ibid., xxiv.

12. Ibid., 27.

13. Anthony Weber, "America's Idol; China's Revival," blog post [Cited May 31, 2013]. Online: http://learningtojump.blogspot.com/2011/09/americas-idol-chinas-revival.html.

14. K. Connie Kang, "These Christians Radically Rethink What a Church Is," *Los Angeles Times*, August 2004, 14 [Cited June 5, 2013]. Online: http://articles.latimes.com/2004/aug/14/local/me-beliefs14.

15. See the website; i.e., www.theooze.com.

Chapter 3: A Non-Violent Revolution Led to Racial Integration in Church

1. Jim Cymbala, *Fresh Wind, Fresh Fire* (Grand Rapids, MI: Zondervan, 2003); *Fresh Faith* (Grand Rapids, MI: Zondervan, 2003); *Fresh Power* (Grand Rapids, MI: Zondervan, 2003).

2. "Browder v. Gayle, 352 U.S. 903 (1956)," *Martin Luther King, Jr. and the Global Freedom Struggle*, [Cited April 10, 2013]. Online: http://mlk-kpp01.stanford.edu/index.php/encyclopedia/encyclopedia/enc_browder_v_gayle.

3. Cokie Roberts and Steve Inskeep, "Lyndon Johnson's Fight for Civil Rights, 2004, npr.com [Cited April 17, 2013]. Online: http://www.npr.org/templates/story/story.php?storyId=3087021.

4. "Martin Luther King, Jr.," Wikipedia, [cited April 2, 2013]. Online: https://en.wikipedia.org/wiki/Martin_Luther_King,_Jr.

5. Ibid.

6. Ibid.

7. Ibid.

8. Ibid.

9. Ibid.

10. Martin Luther King, Jr., "To Ebenezer Baptist Church Members," *The Martin Luther King's Papers Project*, [Cited April 10, 2013]. Online: http://mlk-kpp01.stanford.edu/primary documents/Vol2/541106ToEbenezerBaptistChurchMembers.pdf.

11. "African American Baptists," *The New Georgia Encyclopedia*, [cited April 2, 2013]. Online: http://www.georgiaencyclopedia.org/nge/Article.jsp?id=h-1543.

12. Martin Luther King, Jr., "I've Been to the Mountaintop," *American Rhetoric Top 100 Speeches*, [Cited April 10, 2013]. Online: http://www.americanrhetoric.com/speeches/mlkivebeentothemountaintop.htm.

13. Elmer Towns, Ed Stetzer and Warren Bird, *11 Innovations in the Local* Church (Ventura, CA: Regal Books, 2007), 188.

14. Ibid., 189.

15. Carl Dudley, *Making the Small Church Effective* (Nashville, TN: Abingdon Press, 1978), 49. See the information on the sociological understanding of a single cell church, with its strengths and weaknesses.

16. Tobin Perry, "SBC Ethnic Congregations Up 66 Percent Since 1998," *North American Mission Board* [Cited May 31, 2013]. Online: http://www.namb.net/nambblog1.aspx?id=8590124402&blogid=8589939695.

17. Ibid.

18. Ibid.

19. Ibid.

20. Data for the Baptist, Four Square, Assemblies and Nazarene denomination found in Ed Stetzer, "The Changing Ethnic and Racial Landscape of Denominations in America," *The Lifeway Research Blog* [Cited April 11, 2013]. Online: http://www.edstetzer.com/2012/06/Monday-is-for-missiology-fred.html. Data for the Church of God from the Assemblies of God USA, AG Vital Statistics Summary 2010; see "National Percents," page 7 [Cited April 11, 2013]. Online: http://agchurches.org/Sitefiles/Default/RSS/AG.org%20TOP/AG%20Statistical%20Reports/2010%20Stats/Vital%20Stats%202010%20Sum.pdf.

21. "Race, Eric Redmond, and Ethnic Diversity in Denominations," [Cited April 10, 2013]. Online: http://www.edstetzer.com/2008/02/race_eric_redmond_and_ethnic_d.html.

22. From: http://racerelations.about.com/od/diversitymatters/a/RacialSegregationin Church.htm. See also Scott Williams, *Church Diversity: Sunday the Most Segregated Day of the Week*; Pew Forum, http://religions.pewforum.org/pdf/report-religious-landscape-study -full.pdf; Gerardo Marti, http://www.academia.edu/1097473/The_Religious_Racial _Integration_of_African_Americans_into_Diverse_Churches.)

23. Ruth Daily, "Viewpoint: Integrated Pews Without Political Diversity," Post-Gazette.com [Cited April 10, 2013]. Online: http://www.google.com/#hl=en&sclient=psy-ab&q=.+the +mighty+Brooklyn+Tabernacle%2C+a+veritable+United+Nations+of+the+gospel%2C+draws +10%2C000+members+from+the+New+York%E2%80%99s+areas+diverse+millions&oq=.+the +mighty+Brooklyn+Tabernacle%2C+a+veritable+United+Nations+of+the+gospel%2C+draws +10%2C000+members+from+the+New+York%E2%80%99s+areas+diverse+millions&gs _l=serp.12...54776.55573.1.57452.1.1.0.0.0.0.0.0...0.0...0.1...1c.1.8.psy-ab .LtxAVQaAZcw&pbx=1&bav=on.2,or.r_qf.&fp=f966bb6d3f992b43&biw=1024&bih=604.

24. Dennis Farro, "Nipping Discrimination in the Bud My Brooklyn Tabernacle Adventure," *Braille Monitor,* February 2010 [Cited April 10, 2013]. Online: https://nfb.org/images/nfb/ publications/bm/bm10/bm1002/bm100208.htm.

25. Emma Lazarus (1883), "The Statue of Liberty," The Statue of Liberty-Ellis Island Foundation [Cited April 10, 2013]. Online: http://www.statueofliberty.org/default_sol.htm.

26. David Anderson, *Multicultural Ministry: Finding Your Church's Unique Rhythm* (Grand Rapids: Zondervan, 2004).

27. The old Scottish term is "worthship," suggesting that we offer to God His worth in vocal praise and adoration.

Chapter 4: Home Cells Used for Church Ministry and Outreach

1. In 1979, I wrote a chapter titled "The Biggest Little Church in the World" in Elmer L. Towns, John Vaughan and David Seifert, *The Complete Book of Church Growth* (Wheaton, IL: Tyndale House Publishers, Inc., 1981), 61-68. This book was advertised as the first textbook for seminaries, representing most major seminaries in mainline and evangelical denominations.

2. Elmer L. Towns, David J. Seifert and John N. Vaughan, *Complete Book of Church Growth* (Carol Stream, IL: Tyndale House, 1981),

3. Ibid., 61.

4. Karen Hurston, *Growing the World's Largest Church* (Springfield, MO: Gospel Publishing House, 1994). This book tells how the Hurstons helped the church grow—a story not told by Cho or other Korean journalists.

5. Towns, Seifert and Vaughan, *Complete Book of Church Growth*, 62.

6. At first Cho was not willing to admit it was a heart attack.

7. Towns, *Complete Book of Church Growth*, 62.

8. Ibid.

9. Ibid., 63.

10. Ibid.

11. Ibid.

12. "Genesis 17," *John Calvin's Bible Commentary* [Cited April 16, 2013]. Online: http://www .ewordtoday.com/comments/genesis/calvin/genesis17.htm.

13. Elmer L. Towns, ed., et al, *A Practical Encyclopedia of Evangelism and Church Growth* (Ventura, CA: Regal Books, 1995), 329-330.

14. Elesha Coffman, "Where Did Small Groups Start?" Christian History.net [Cited April 16, 2013]. Online: http://www.christianitytoday.com/ch/asktheexpert/aug31.html.

15. James Egli and Dwight Marable, *Small Groups, Big Impact* (Saint Charles, IL: Churchsmart Resources, 2011.

16. "David Yonggi Cho," Wikipedia [Cited April 16, 2013]. Online: http://en.wikipedia.org/wiki/ David_Yonggi_Cho.

17. Ibid. Statements from Yoido Full Gospel Church, Seoul, South Korea.

18. Ibid.
19. Ibid.
20. "Yoido Full Gospel Church," Wikipedia [Cited May 31, 2013]. Online: http://en.wikipedia.org/wiki/Yoido_Full_Gospel_Church.

Chapter 5: A Church Built on Sunday School Evangelism
1. Elmer Towns, *Towns' Sunday School Encyclopedia* (Wheaton, IL: Tyndale House Publishers, Inc., 1993), 417.
2. The church originally purchased KCBI FM, and increased to the Criswell Radio Network, including KCRN FM, St. Angelo, and KSYE FM.
3. "W A. Criswell," Wikipedia [Cited June 3, 2013]. Online: http://en.wikipedia.org/wiki/W._A._Criswell.
4. Towns, *Towns' Sunday School Encyclopedia*, 543-545.
5. Bob Mayfield, "Flake's Legacy," bobmayfield.com [Cited May 7, 2013]. Online: http://www.bobmayfield.com/flakes-legacy/.
6. "Southern Baptist Convention: Sunday-School Board," Hot Springs, Arkansas, 1900, 67. Online: http://media2.sbhla.org.s3.amazonaws.com/annuals/SBC_Annual_1900.pdf.
7. "Annual of the Southern Baptist Convention," Memphis, Tennessee, 1925, 50. Online: http://media2.sbhla.org.s3.amazonaws.com/annuals/SBC_Annual_1925.pdf.
8. "Annual of the Southern Baptist Convention," Chicago, Illinois, 1950, 422. Online: http://media2.sbhla.org.s3.amazonaws.com/annuals/SBC_Annual_1950.pdf.
9. "Annual of the Southern Baptist Convention," Miami Beach, Florida, 1975, 245, 252. Online: http://media2.sbhla.org.s3.amazonaws.com/annuals/SBC_Annual_1975.pdf.
10. "Annual of the Southern Baptist Convention," Orlando, Florida, 2000, 114, 293. Online: http://media2.sbhla.org.s3.amazonaws.com/annuals/SBC_Annual_2000.pdf.
11. Dr. David Jeremiah, while preaching for the dedication service of the new worship center in April, reflected on his days at seminary and attending the church. Probably thousands of students from Dallas Theological Seminary and Southwestern Baptist Theological Seminary received their practical training at FBC Dallas and then carried the influence of this church around the world.
12. Statement made by Criswell to me at a dinner before his sermon at the National Sunday School Association Convention, Kiel Auditorium, St. Louis, Missouri, October 1960.
13. I heard this story at the dinner I had with Criswell.
14. Ibid.
15. Ibid.
16. Ibid.
17. Paraphrased statement from W.A. Criswell that I heard while attending services announcing soul-winning efforts by First Baptist Church in Dallas, Texas, 1954.
18. Ibid.
19. Paraphrased statement from W.A. Criswell that I heard while attending services encouraging registration of infants to the church rolls and beginning lessons of giving to God at First Baptist Church in Dallas, Texas, 1954.
20. This would be true until the late 1960s, when churches realized they were using most of the Sunday school rooms one time each week. After that time, churches began using multiple Sunday schools and using off-campus spaces to address the need for additional Sunday school rooms.
21. See chapter 4 for his discussion of small groups in The Yoido Full Gospel Church, Seoul, South Korea.

Chapter 6: The Change to Bible Teaching Instead of Traditional Pulpit Ministry
1. "Guide to Scofield Memorial Church Selected Records." Online: http://library.dts.edu/Pages/TL/Special/ScofieldMemChurch_CN014.pdf (accessed January 29, 2013).
2. I pastored Faith Bible Church, a mission of Scofield Memorial Church, from 1956-1958. Every Monday morning I met with Pastor Harlan Roper and the other pastors of mission

churches begun by Scofield Church. In 1957, Faith Bible Church was launched into an indigenous local church. In 1958, I became a professor at Midwest Bible College in St. Louis, Missouri. Dr. James Brooks and others founded this college (technically, it was founded as "Brooks Bible Institute" and later became "Midwest Bible and Missionary Institute," and then it became "Midwest Bible College"). The college met in the facilities of the St. Louis Gospel Center, which was a Sunday afternoon Bible-teaching center visited by great Bible teachers such as C.I. Scofield. In these two locations, I became aware of much of the history written in this chapter. Also, I am a 1958 graduate of Dallas Theological Seminary, with a major in systematic theology.

3. Some of these locations included The North Side Gospel Center in Chicago, Illinois; the Midwest Bible Center in St. Louis, Missouri; Gospel Tabernacle in Chicago, Illinois; and The Gospel Temple in Fort Wayne, Indiana.

4. Hal Lindsey, *The Late Great Planet Earth* (Grand Rapids: Zondervan Publishing Company, 1972) and *There's a New World Coming* (Eugene, OR: Harvest House Publishers, 1984).

5. The *Left Behind* series constituted eight volumes and sold more than 100 million copies, thus extending the influence of Scofield throughout the English-speaking world.

6. "Cyrus Ingersoll Scofield—Biography," *Understanding the Bible*. Online: http://www.ancientpath.net/Bible/PBU/Scofield/Scofield_Bio.htm (accessed January 22, 2013).

7. Ibid.

8. R. Todd Magnum and Mark S. Sweetnam, *The Scofield Bible: Its History and Impact on the Evangelical Church* (Colorado Springs: Paternoster, 2009), 11.

Chapter 7: A Seeker-Model Church Designed for the Unchurched

1. There are many different words used to describe this model of evangelism and worship, including "seeker-sensitive," "seeker-friendly" and "seeker-driven." See Elmer Towns, gen. ed., *A Practical Encyclopedia: Evangelism and Church Growth* (Ventura, CA: Regal Books, 1995), 141.

2. "Bill Hybels," Wikipedia [Cited April 22, 2013]. Online: http://en.wikipedia.org/wiki/Bill_Hybels.

3. Elmer L. Towns, *Ten of Today's Most Innovative Churches* [Cited April 22, 2013]. Online: http://elmertowns.com/books/online/10_innov_ch/10_of_Todays_Most_Innovative_Churches%5BETowns%5D.PDF.

4. Ibid.

5. Ibid.

6. Ibid.

7. Ibid.

8. Ibid.

9. Ibid.

10. Elmer L. Towns, *10 Sunday Schools That Dared to Change* [Cited April 22, 2013]. Online: http://elmertowns.com/books/online/10_ss_change/10_SS_That_Dared_to_Change%5BETowns%5D.PDF.

11. Ibid.

12. Ibid.

13. Ibid.

14. Elmer L. Towns, *10 Sunday Schools That Dared to Change,* (Ventura, CA: Regal Books, 1993), 70.

15. Ibid., 69.

16. Elmer L. Towns, *10 Sunday Schools That Dared to Change* [Cited April 22, 2013]. Online: http://elmertowns.com/books/online/10_ss_change/10_SS_That_Dared_to_Change%5BETowns%5D.PDF.

17. Ibid.

18. Ibid.

19. Ibid.

20. James Long, "The Outreach Interview: Rick Warren," *Outreach,* January/February 2013, 105.

21. Ibid., 106

22. Ibid., 107.

23. C. Peter Wagner, ed., Win Arn and Elmer Towns, *Church Growth State of the Art* (Wheaton, IL: Tyndale House Publishers Inc., 1986), 17.

24. T.A. McMahon, "The Seeker-Friendly Way of Doing Church," *The Berean Call* [Cited April 23, 2013]. Online: http://www.thebereancall.org/category/author/mcmahon-ta.

25. Ibid.

26. Marva J. Dawn, *Reaching Out Without Dumbing Down* (Grand Rapids, MI: Wm. B. Eerdmans Publishing Company, 1995), n.p.

27. I heard Wagner make this quote at an American Society of Church Growth conference during the late 1980s. Most would agree with this conclusion, but it has never been documented.

28. Manya A. Brachear, "Rev. Bill Hybels: The Father of Willow Creek," August 6, 2006 [Cited on June 3, 2013]. Online: http://www.chicagotribune.com/news/chi-061121 -hybelsprofile,0,2446732.story.

29. "The 25 Most Influential Evangelicals in America," *TIME*, February 7, 2005 [Cited on June 3, 2013]. Online: http://www.time.com/time/specials/packages/article/0,28804,1993235 _1993243_1993288,00.html.

Chapter 8: A New Church Culture Initiated by Baby Boomers

1. Paul Baker, *Contemporary Christian Music: Where It Came From, What It Is, Where It's Going* (Westchester, IL: Crossway books, 1985), 4.

2. Norman Vincent Peale, "The Surging Spirit," *Guideposts,* November 1971, 4. Quoted in Paul Baker, *Contemporary Christian Music*, 5 [Cited May 14, 2013]. Online: http://www.ccel.us/CCM .ch1.html.

3. "Calvary Chapel History," Jack Savada, about.com [Cited May 14, 2013]. Online: http://christianity .about.com/od/Calvary-Chapel/a/Calvary-Chapel-History.htm.

4. "Calvary Chapel Costa Mesa," Wikipedia [Cited May 14, 2013]. Online: http://en.wikipedia .org/wiki/Calvary_Chapel_Costa_Mesa.

5. Jamee Lynn Fletcher, "Calvary Chapel Founder Battling Lung Cancer," January 5, 2012, *Orange County Register* [Cited April 23, 2013]. Online: http://www.ocregister.com/articles/ smith-334349-chapel-calvary.html.

6. "Calvary Chapel," Wikipedia [Cited February 10, 2014]. Online: http://en.wikipedia.org/ wiki/Calvary_Chapel.

7. Elmer L. Towns, *Putting an End to Worship Wars: Understanding—Why People Disagree over Worship, The Six Basic Worship Styles, How to Find Balance and Make Peace* (Nashville, TN: Broadman & Holman, 1997).

Chapter 9: Initiating Praise-Worship in Worship Services

1. Kenneth Scott Latourette, *A History of Christianity* (New York: Harper & Brothers, 1953), n.p.

2. "Shout to the Lord," lyrics by Darlene Zschech, elyrics.net [Cited April 19, 2013]. Online: http://www.elyrics.net/read/d/darlene-zschech-lyrics/shout-to-the-lord-lyrics.html.

3. Worship Lyrics, "Majesty," lyricstime.com [Cited April 19, 2013]. Online: http://www.lyrics time.com/worship-majesty-lyrics.html.

4. "About Maranatha Music," Maranatha Music [Cited May 7, 2013\. Online: https://www .maranathamusic.com/about/.

5. "The 'Praise and Worship' Revolution," *Christianity Today* [Cited April 19, 2013]. Online: http://www.christianitytoday.com/ch/thepastinthepresent/storybehind/praiseworship revolution.html.

6. Ibid.

7. "Shout to the Lord" lyrics by Darlene Zshech, metrolycrics.com [Cited April 19, 2013]. Online: http://www.metrolyrics.com/shout-to-the-lord-lyrics-zschech-darlene.html.

8. "Darlene," Darlene Zschech [Cited on April 22, 2013]. Online: http://www.darlenezschech .com/biography/.

9. Elmer L. Towns and Vernon M. Whaley, *Worship Through the Ages* (Nashville, TN: B&H Publishing Group, 2012), 354.

10. Personal email from Jack Hayford sent to me on August 30, 2013, with his additions and corrections.
11. Some of Jack Hayford's books on worship include *Heart of Praise* (Ventura, CA: Regal Books, 1997); *Reward of Worship* (Grand Rapids, MI: Baker Book House, 2007; and *Worship His Majesty* (Nashville, TN: W Publishing Group, 1987).
12. Ibid.
13. Ibid.
14. Towns and Whaley, 355.
15. Elmer L. Towns, *Ten Innovative Churches* (Ventura, CA: Regal Books, 1990), 61.
16. "Majesty," by Jack Hayford, ©1981, Rocksmith Music, JackHayford.com [Cited April 22, 2013]. Online: http://www.jackhayford.com/pages/majesty_let_fire_fall.html; Elmer L. Towns, *God Encounters* [Ventura, CA: Regal Books, 2000]. Online: http://elmertowns.com/books/online/god_enctrs/God_Encounters[ETowns].pdf, (accessed April 22, 2013).
17. Towns, *Ten Innovative Churches*, 61-62.
18. Ibid., 62.
19. Personal email from Jack Hayford sent to me on August 30, 2013, with his additions and corrections.
20. Ibid., 64.
21. Ibid., 65.
22. I graduated from Dallas Theological Seminary in 1958 and often heard Hendricks make this statement.
23. J.P. Holding, "Myths About Christianity," *TEKTON Education and Apologetics Ministry* [Cited May 7, 2013]. Online: http://www.tektonics.org/af/christianmyths.html.
24. See footnote 28 in chapter 7.

Chapter 10: Using Media and Marketing to Extend the Influence of a Church
1. Jerry Falwell and Elmer Towns, *Capturing A Town for Christ* (Grand Rapids, MI: Fleming H. Revell/Baker Book house, 1973), 13-14.
2. "S. Parks Cadman," Wikipedia. Online: http://en.wikipedia.org/wiki/S._Parkes_Cadman (accessed on January 21, 2013).
3. John Franklin Norris, Texas State Historical Association. Online: http://www.tshaonline.org/handbook/online/articles/fno07 (accessed on January 21, 2013).
4. "Charles Coughlin," Wikipedia. Online: http://en.wikipedia.org/wiki/Charles_Coughlin (accessed on January 21, 2013).
5. "Old Fashioned Revival Hour Broadcast." Online: http://www.oldfashionedrevivalhour.com/ (accessed on January 21, 2013).
6. "Rex Humbard," Wikipedia. Online: http://en.wikipedia.org/wiki/Rex_Humbard (accessed on January 21, 2013).
7. Some of the leading agencies and/or authorities included Jerry Huntsinger, of Huntsinger and Jeffer (Richmond, Virginia); Jim Laven, of Epsilon; and Jan Gleason. Another indication of the marketing effectiveness at Thomas Road Baptist Church are the individuals who headed up marketing for Thomas Road Baptist Church/Jerry Falwell and left to form their own marketing companies in nearby Forest, Virginia. These included Dan Reber, Jim Soward, Jimmy Thomas, Sam Pate, Randy Scott and Carl Townsend, who began InService America. These companies handle the accounts for some of the largest Christian television/radio ministries in America, including *The Hour of Power* (Crystal Cathedral, Robert Schuller), Focus on the Family (James Dobson), Benny Hinn, Rod Parsley, James Robison and others.
8. In 2013, there were 12,600 resident students in Lynchburg, Virginia, and 80,000 online students from every state and many foreign countries.
9. In 1978, I was doing my annual survey to find the 100 largest Sunday schools in America. I threw in an innocent question motivated by curiosity: "What Christian college or seminary did you attend that motivated you to pastor and build one of the 100 largest churches in America?" Amazingly, 23 out of 100 answered Baptist Bible College in Springfield, Missouri.

10. Jerry Falwell called this "saturation evangelism," and it became the driving motivation to use media.
11. I visited the thirtieth anniversary of this class in 1983 in the home of Max Hawkins. Daryl was there, and so were about 100 people. It was there I got the interviews for this story.
12. Paul E. Roberts and W. Dayton Pretiz, *Like a Mighty Army: R. Kenneth Strachan and the Global March of Evangelism-in-Depth* (Miami Springs, FL: Latin America Mission, 1998).
13. Jerry Falwell and Elmer Towns, *Capturing a Town for Christ* (Grand Rapids: Fleming H. Revell, 1973), 8-9. This is a bestselling book Jerry and I published that explained the strategy of saturation evangelism.
14. Elmer L. Towns and Jerry Falwell, *America's Fastest Growing Churches* (Nashville, TN: Impact Books, 1972), 31-32.
15. These "super" radio stations had a worldwide outreach, including HCJB in Quito, Ecuador and FEGC in Seoul, South Korea. Each directed its radio signal to various parts of the world, and each targeted gospel programs to language groups in their language, thus reaching the whole world.
16. Dialogue between me and Jerry Falwell during a planning meeting to discuss the early beginnings of Liberty University, around 1970.
17. Falwell and Towns, *Capturing a Town for Christ*, 5.
18. Stan Toler and Elmer Towns, *Developing a Giving Church* (Kansas City, MO: Beacon Hill Press, 1999), 101-103.

Chapter 12: The Influence of Positive Thinking and Financial Prosperity on Churches
1. Norman Vincent Peale, *The Power of Positive Thinking* (New York: Ballantine Books, first published 1952).

Chapter 15: An Aggressive Initiative of Servanthood Evangelism
1. Steve Sjogren, *Conspiracy of Kindness* (Ventura, CA: Regal Books, 2008), n.p.

Chapter 16: A Church-Planting Strategy of Evangelism
1. Bob Roberts, Jr., *The Multiplying Church* (Grand Rapids, MI: Zondervan, 2008).
2. Ed Stetzer and Warren Bird, *Viral Churches: Helping Church Planters Become Movement Makers* (San Francisco, CA: Jossey-Bass, 2010), 162.

Afterthought: What Can We Learn from These Churches?
1. Elmer L. Towns and Jerry Falwell, *America's Fastest Growing Churches* (Nashville, TN: Impact Books, 1972), 10.
2. Ibid., n.p.
3. God blesses those who put themselves in a place where He can bless them.
4. My historical phrase, "enculturated," has become the modern term "contextualization." As Christian leaders become more effective in planting new churches, they have adapted the term "contextualization." However, the aim is not "context" but "culture." The following is a response by Dennis Hesselbarth, April 12, 2010, to comments made by David Watson on his blog page Touchpoint: http://www.davidlwatson.org/2010/04/10/opinion-%E2%80%93-contextualization-personal-evangelism-and-disciple-making/.
5. Andrew Walls, in his book *The Missionary Movement in Christian History,* suggests there are two impulses as the message of the gospel penetrates a culture: the Indigenous Principle and the Pilgrim Principle (Mary Knoll, NY: Orbis Books, 2001, 7-9). The gospel can and must become indigenous in every culture, finding a home in the culture. That's the indigenous impulse, and it is inevitable. We all interpret the Bible in terms of our existing worldview, but at the same time, the gospel begins to produce a pilgrim mindset. It loosens people from their culture, criticizes and corrects culture, and turns people into pilgrims and aliens and exiles in their own culture. Western culture, individualistic to the extreme, understands conversion and discipleship as an individual process, relatively independent of family or friends. Other more collective cultures can't conceive of conversion or discipleship apart from their group. See David Watson's blog,

"Opinion—Contextualization, Personal Evangelism and Disciple Making," Touchpoint, April 10, 2010 [Cited June 17, 2013]. Online: http://www.davidlwatson.org/2010/04/10/opinion-%E2%80%93-contextualization-personal-evangelism-and-disciple-making/.

6. Ernst Troeltsch, *The Social Teaching of the Christian Churches,* trans. Olive Wyan (London: George Allen and Unwin, 1931). This is an outstanding analysis of the factors that cause deterioration in churches.

7. Harvey Cox, *The Secular City* (New York: The MacMillan Co., 1965), 1-13.

8. There is one quality of methods: they change when culture changes. Because a leader attempts to reach his or her generation with the gospel with a unique method, when the life that surrounds the church changes, the church has to change to meet the new needs from the new culture in which it finds itself. And when a church doesn't change, it loses its influence. There's an old adage that guides this insight: "Methods are many, principles are few; methods may change, but principals never do" (unknown).

9. "Shout to the Lord," lyrics by Darlene Zschech, elyrics.net [Cited April 19, 2013]. Online: http://www.elyrics.net/read/d/darlene-zschech-lyrics/shout-to-the-lord-lyrics.html.

10. "Augustine of Hippo Quotes," Goodreads [Cited June 17, 2013]. Online: http://www.goodreads.com/quotes/332507-in-essentials-unity-in-non-essentials-liberty-in-all-things-charity.

Appendix A: Research Techniques to Find the 10 Churches of Greatest Influence

1. The list of the 100 largest Sunday schools (1967–1976) and the fastest growing Sunday Schools (1977–1985) were released yearly in the October issues of *Christian Life* magazine, published in Wheaton, Illinois. I was the Sunday school editor and was responsible for compiling the list.

2. Elmer L. Towns, *The 10 Largest Sunday Schools and What Makes Them Grow* (Grand Rapids, MI: Baker Book House, 1969).

3. Elmer L. Towns and Douglas Porter, *The Ten Greatest Revivals* (Ann Arbor, MI: Servant Publications, 2000).

4. The 19 members of the panel who ranked *The 10 Greatest Revivals* are (in alphabetical order): Bill Bright, founder of Campus Crusade for Christ, Orlando, Florida (Interdenominational); Gerald Brooks, pastor of Grace Outreach Center, Plano, Texas (Pentecostal/Charismatic); David Yonggi Cho, pastor of The Full Gospel Church, Seoul, South Korea (Pentecostal/Charismatic); Robert Coleman, director of the Billy Graham Center Institute of Evangelism, Wheaton, Illinois (Methodist); James O. Davis, national evangelism director for the Assemblies of God, Springfield, Missouri (Pentecostal); Lewis Drummond, president of the Southeastern Baptist Theological Seminary, Wake Forest, North Carolina (Baptist); Dale Galloway, director of the doctor of ministry program, Asbury Theological Seminary, Wilmore, Kentucky (Methodist); Eddie Gibbs, professor at Fuller Theological Seminary, Pasadena, California (Church of England/Anglican); Jack Hayford, pastor of The Church on the Way, Van Nuys, California (Pentecostal/Charismatic); Charles Kelly, president of the New Orleans Baptist Theological Seminary, New Orleans, Louisiana (Baptist); D. James Kennedy, pastor of Coral Ridge Presbyterian Church, Fort Lauderdale, Florida (Presbyterian); Ron Phillips, pastor of Central Baptist Church, Hixson, Tennessee (Charismatic/Baptist); Alvin Reid, professor at Southeastern Baptist Theological Seminary, Wake Forest, North Carolina (Baptist); Chuck Smith, pastor of Calvary Chapel of Costa Mesa, Santa Ana, California (Pentecostal/Charismatic); Tommy Tenney, evangelist, Pineville, Louisiana (Pentecostal/Charismatic); C. Peter Wagner, professor at Fuller Theological Seminary and director of the World Prayer Center, Colorado Springs, Colorado (Pentecostal/Charismatic); Steve Wingfield, evangelist, Harrisonburg, Virginia (Wesleyan).

5. Elmer Towns and Warren Bird, *Into the Future* (Grand Rapids, MI: Fleming H. Revell, 1999).

6. Elmer Towns, Ed Stetzer and Warren Bird, *11 Innovations in the Local Church* (Ventura, CA: Regal Books, 2007).

7. Elmer L. Towns and Ed Stetzer, *Perimeters of Light* (Chicago, IL: Moody Publishers, 2004).

ALSO BY ELMER L. TOWNS

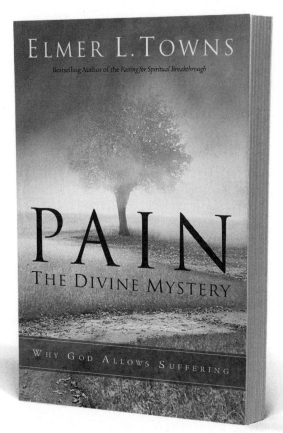

DISCOVER THE
DIVINE PURPOSE
FOR YOUR
PAIN

Pain—The Divine Mystery:
Why God Allow Suffering

10 digit ISBN: 0-7684-0513-0
13 digit ISBN: 978-0-7684-0513-2
Ebook ISBN: 978-0-7684-0514-9

Pain is an enigma—a haunting reality—we all face. Whether the pain you are experiencing is chronic or the result of a new injury or illness, you have no doubt asked the Lord, *Why? Why must I suffer? Why must the pain be so intense or so never-ending?*

Pain: The Divine Mystery will help you look at your own suffering through the eyes of the Master Sculptor—He who has the highest purpose in place for your life. You will be challenged to examine your deepest fears, to discover God's part in your healing, and to pursue better overall health in the process.

You will find that pain can be endured when you have a purpose to live through it. As you seek to understand the "why" behind your own suffering, **God will reveal much more than you can imagine: He will reveal Himself.**

WWW.DESTINYIMAGE.COM
"Promoting Inspired Lives."